Everyday Success

Preschool

American Education Publishing™
An imprint of Carson-Dellosa Publishing LLC
Greensboro, North Carolina

Cover was printed by Lehigh Phoenix (Hagerstown, MD) on Transilwrap's Azuna™ 3D.

Interiors printed and bound by Globus Printing Company (Minster, OH).

American Education Publishing™
An imprint of Carson-Dellosa Publishing LLC
P.O. Box 35665
Greensboro, NC 27425 USA

ISBN 978-1-60996-291-3

03-255117784

Table of Contents

INTRODUCTION

INTRODUCTION

Welcome to the *Everyday Success* series!

Building a strong foundation is an essential part of your child's everyday success. This series features a variety of activity pages that make learning fun, keeping your child engaged and entertained at the same time. These colorful workbooks will help children meet important proficiency standards with activities that strengthen their basic skills, math, and reading.

With the *Everyday Success* series, learning isn't just contained to the pages of the workbook. Each activity offers "One Step Further," a suggestion for children to continue the learning activity on their own. This encourages children to take what they've learned and apply it to everyday situations, reinforcing their comprehension of the activity while exploring the world around them, preparing them with the skills needed to succeed in the 21st century.

These books provide an outstanding educational experience and important learning tools to prepare your child for the future. The *Everyday Success* series offers hours of educational entertainment that will make your child want to come back for more!

Basic Skills

Circle

Directions: Trace the **circles**.

Directions: Trace the word.

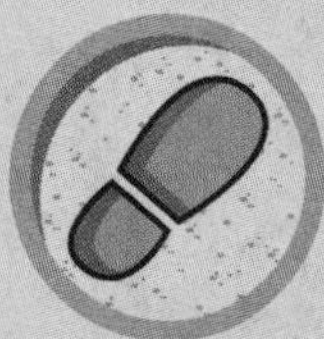

One Step Further

Draw a silly face using circles.
What else can you draw using circles?

Circle

Directions: This picture has **circles** in it. Trace the circles.

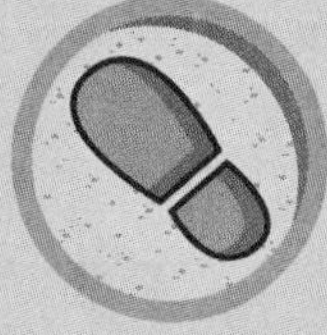

One Step Further

What is your favorite thing to do when it snows? Tell a story about it.

Square

Directions: Trace the **squares**.

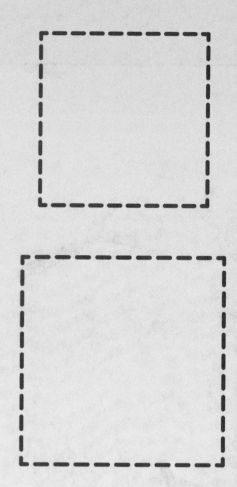

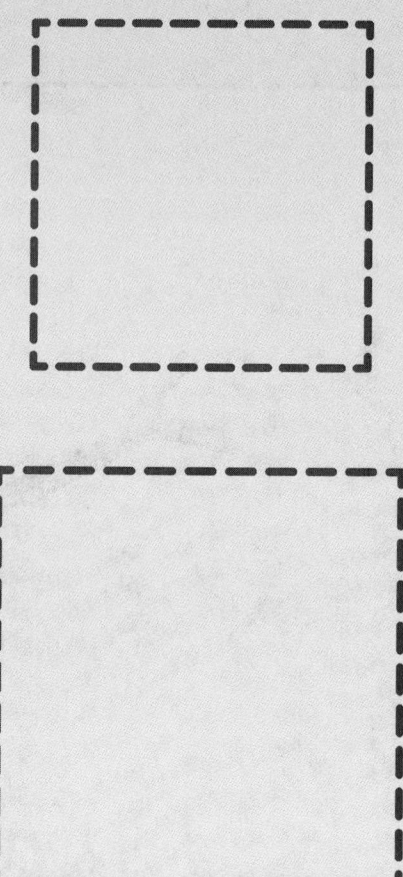

Directions: Trace the word.

square

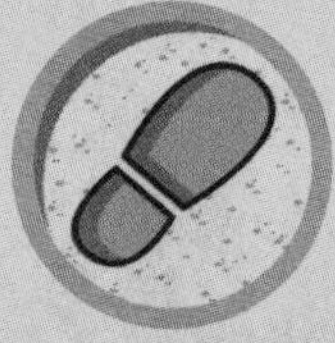

One Step Further
Pretend the squares on this page are boxes.
Draw a picture inside each box.

Square

Directions: This picture has **squares** in it. Trace the squares.

A

B

C

One Step Further

Look around you for objects that are squares. What did you find?

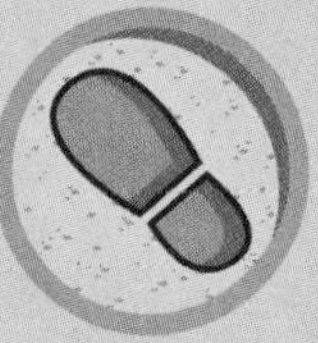

Triangle

Directions: Trace the **triangles**.

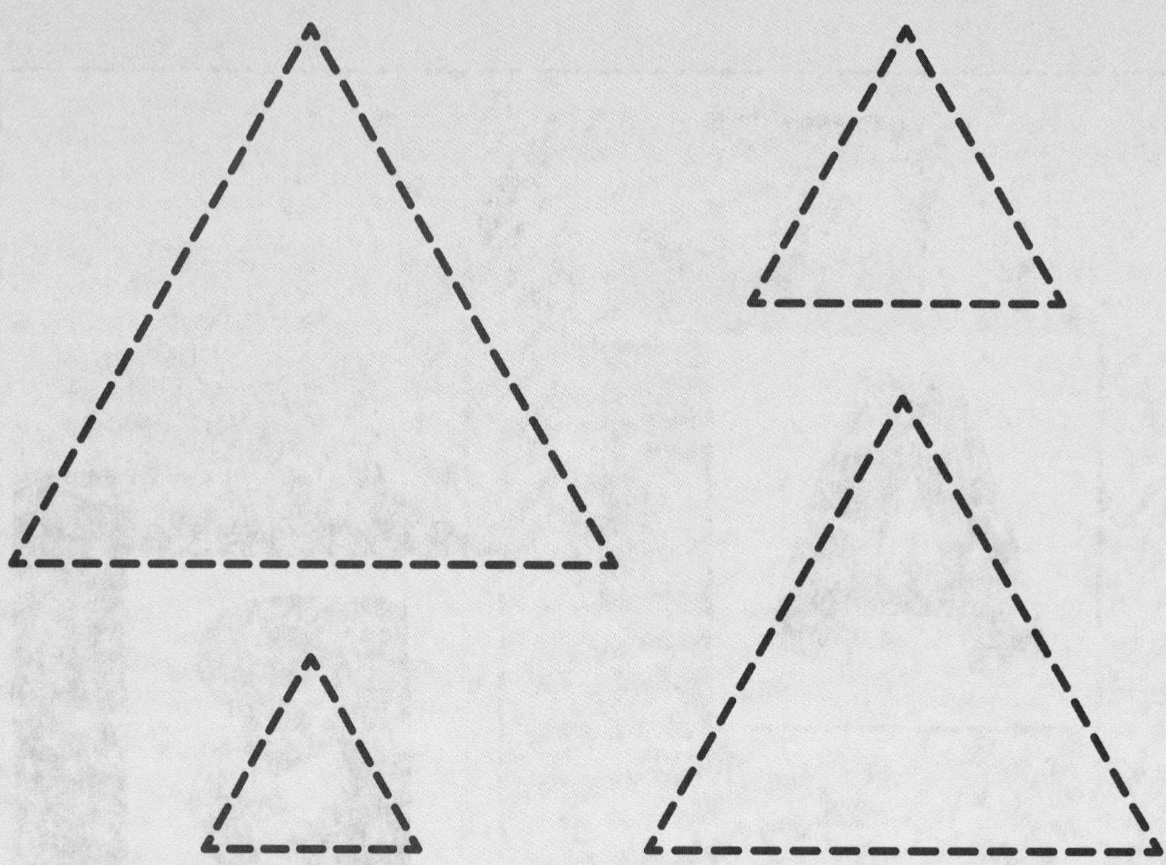

Directions: Trace the word.

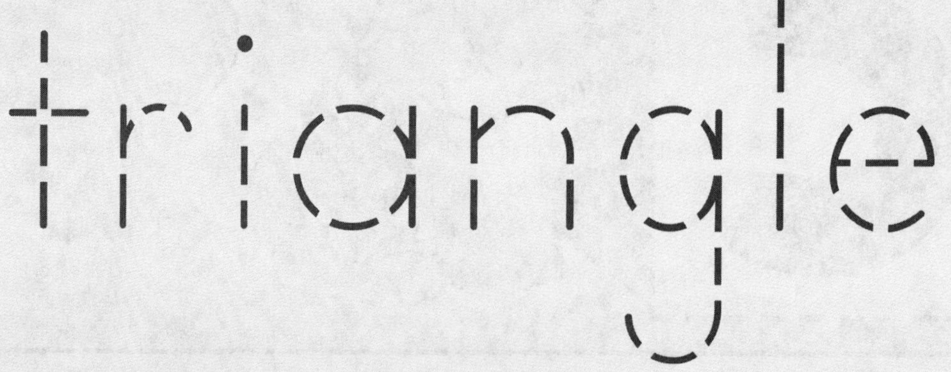

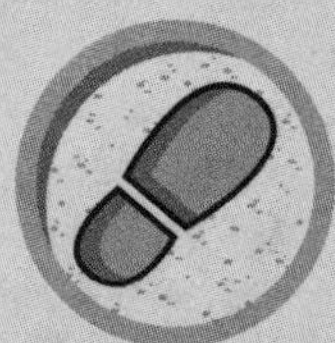

One Step Further
Draw a house using squares and triangles. What other shapes could you use?

Triangle

Directions: This picture has **triangles** in it. Trace the triangles.

SPIKE

SPOT

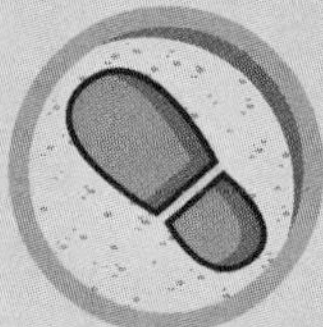

One Step Further

What is happening in the picture? Tell a story about it.

Rectangle

Directions: Trace the **rectangles**.

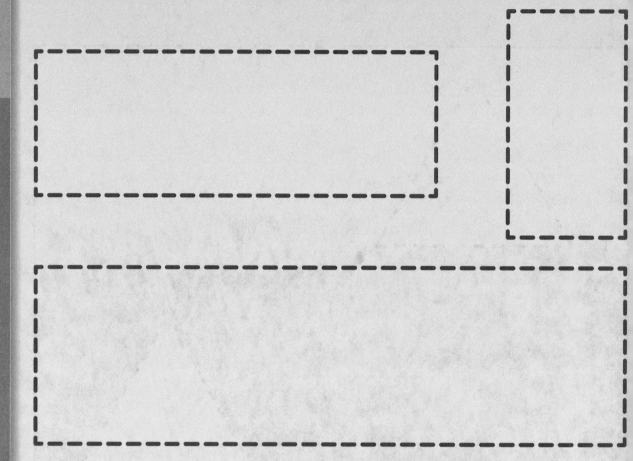

Directions: Trace the word.

rectangle

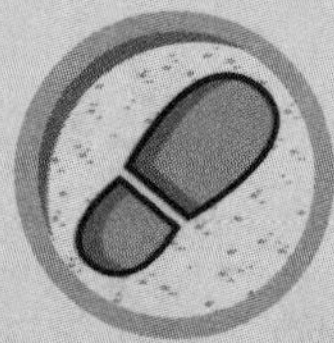

One Step Further
Draw a picture using the shapes you have learned so far. What did you draw?

Rectangle

Directions: This picture has **rectangles** in it. Trace the rectangles.

One Step Further

What is happening in the picture?
Where do you think the train is going?

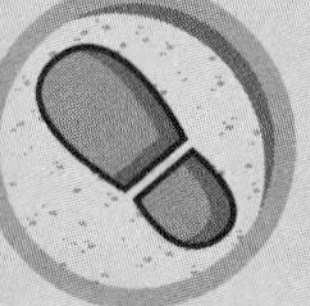

Oval

Directions: Trace the **ovals**.

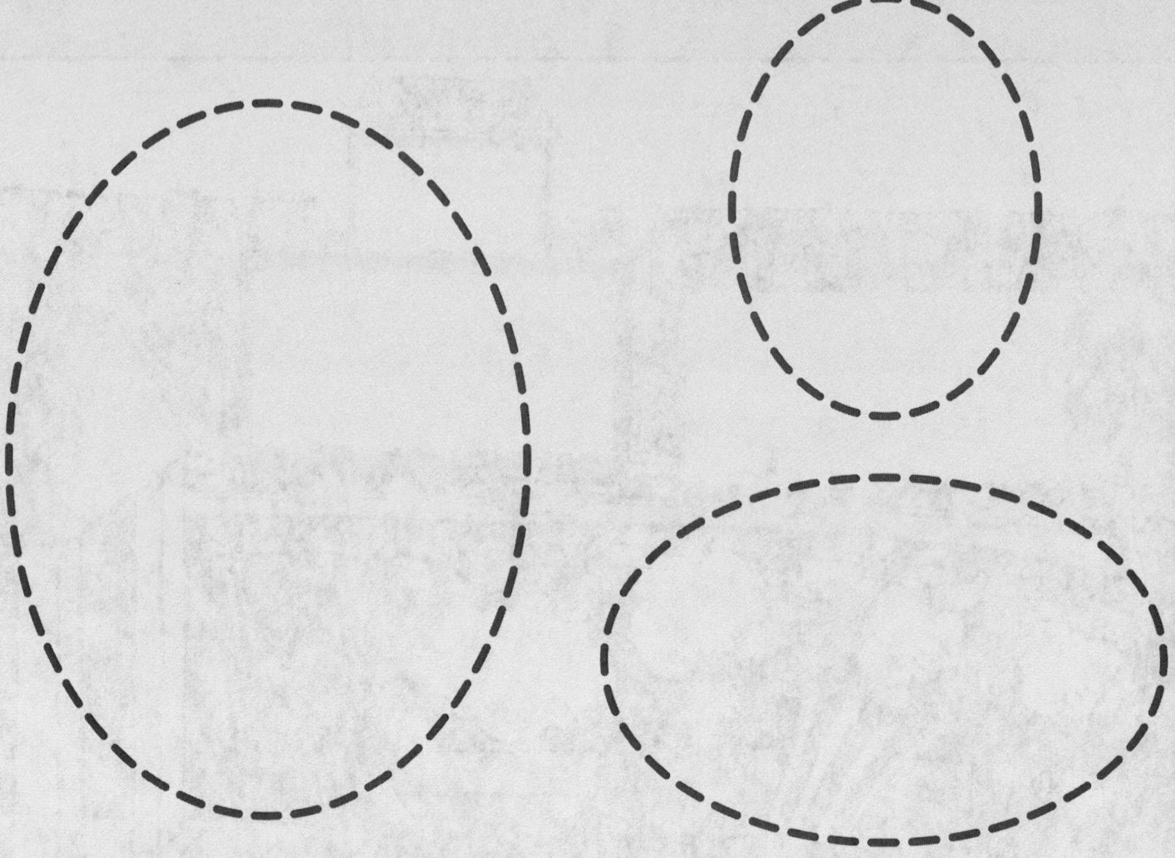

Directions: Trace the word.

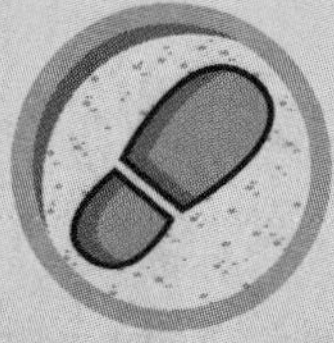

One Step Further

How are ovals different from circles?
Can you find an object that is an oval?

Oval

Directions: This picture has **ovals** in it. Trace the ovals.

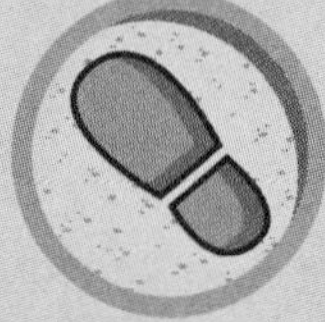

One Step Further

What color are your eyes? Find a friend.
Are your eyes the same color?

Rhombus

Directions: Trace the **rhombuses**.

Directions: Trace the word.

rhombus

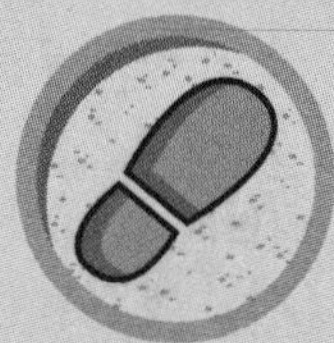

One Step Further

Draw a rhombus. Ask a friend to name the shape.

Rhombus

Directions: This picture has a **rhombus** in it. Trace the rhombus.

One Step Further

What is your favorite sport to play? What do you like about playing that sport?

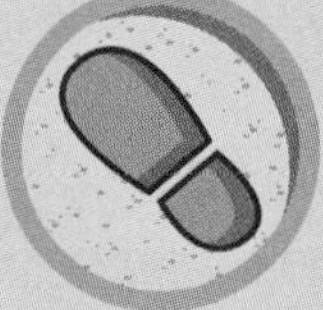

Same Size

Directions: Circle the shape in each row that is the **same size** as the first shape.

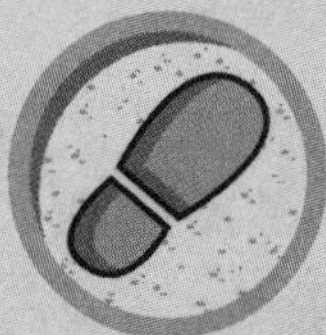

One Step Further

Find two crayons. Are they the same size?
Find two objects that are the same size.

Big and Small

Directions: Draw a line to match the shapes that are the same. Then, color each **big** shape **red** and each **small** shape **green**.

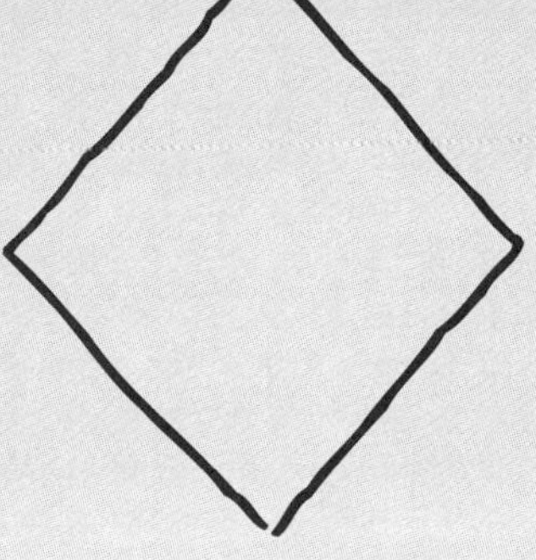

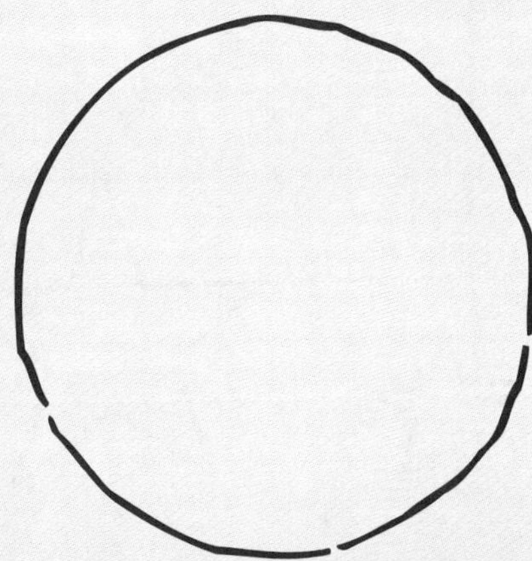

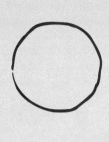

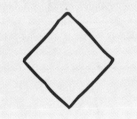

One Step Further

Find two books. What shape are they? Which one is bigger?

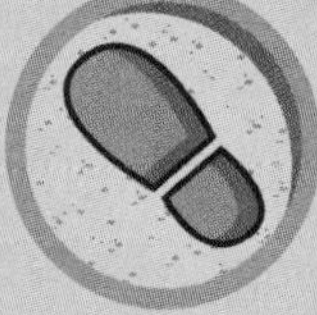

Biggest

Directions: Find the **biggest** shape in each row. Color it **orange**.

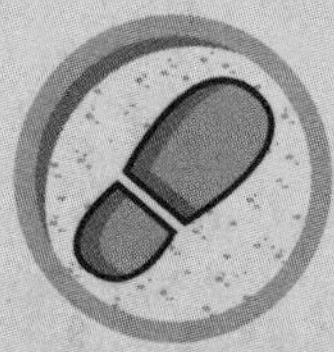

One Step Further
Look around for objects shaped as circles. What is the biggest one you can find?

Smallest

Directions: Find the **smallest** shape in each row. Color it **purple**.

One Step Further

Look outside for objects shaped as squares. What is the smallest one you can find?

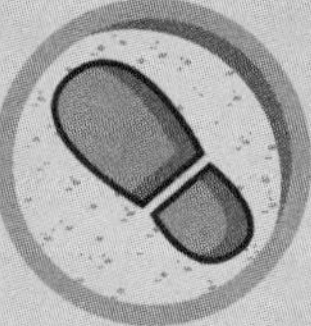

Short and Tall

Directions: Circle each **short** person below. Draw a line under each **tall** person.

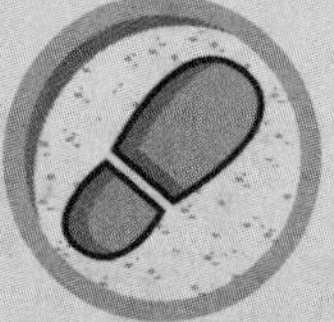

One Step Further

Ask two friends to stand next to each other. Which one is shorter? Which one is taller?

Shorter

Directions: Look at the flagpole and flag below. Draw another flagpole and flag beside it. Make your flagpole **shorter** than the first one.

One Step Further

Stand next to a friend. Who is shorter? How much shorter?

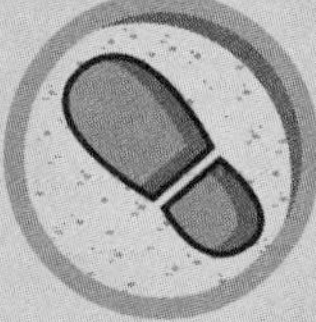

Taller

Directions: Look at the table below. Draw another table beside it. Make your table **taller** than the first one.

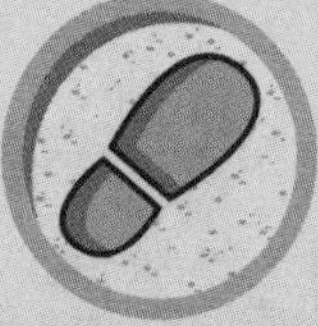

One Step Further

Find something in your home that is taller than you. What is it?

Long and Short

Directions: Circle each **long** thing. Then, draw a line under each **short** thing.

One Step Further

Find a pencil. Find a crayon.
Which is longer? Which is shorter?

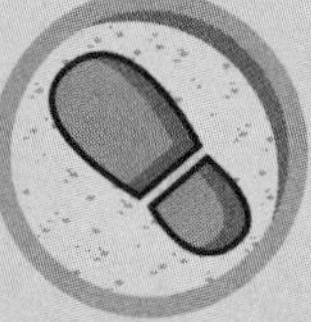

Longer

Directions: Look at the snake. Draw a **longer** snake below it.

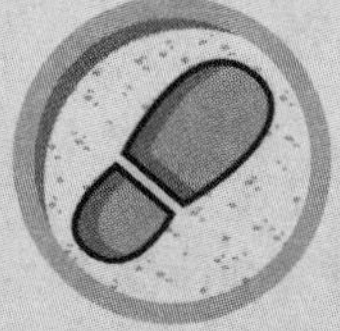

One Step Further

Ask a friend to draw a ruler.
Then, draw a longer ruler next to it.

Shorter

Directions: Look at the top cat. Draw a **shorter** tail on the bottom cat.

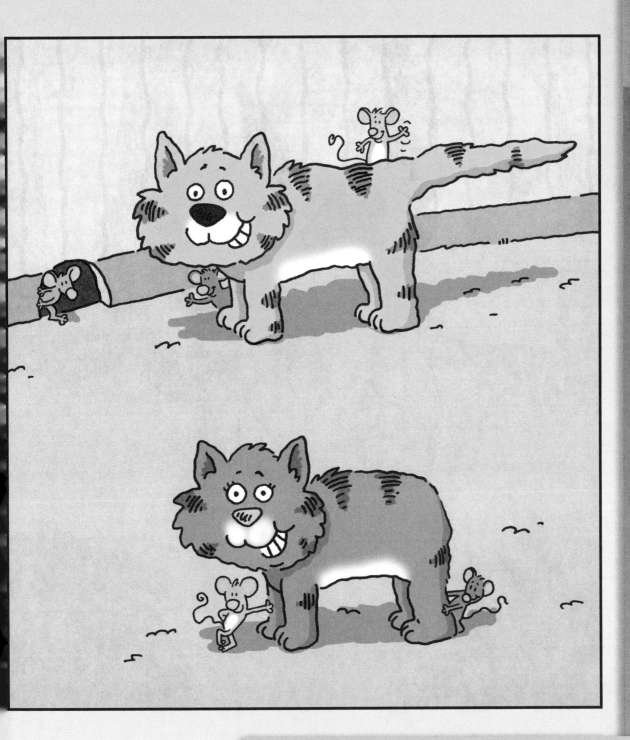

One Step Further

What is happening in the picture? Tell a story about it.

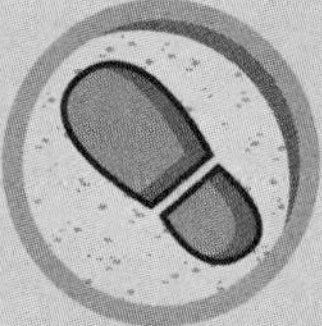

Big

Directions: Look at the picture. Trace the word.

big

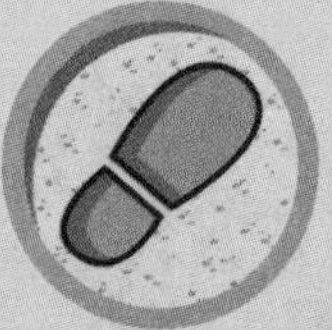

One Step Further
Look around your room for a big object.
What did you find?

Little

Directions: Look at the picture. Trace the word.

little

One Step Further
Look around your room for a little object. What did you find?

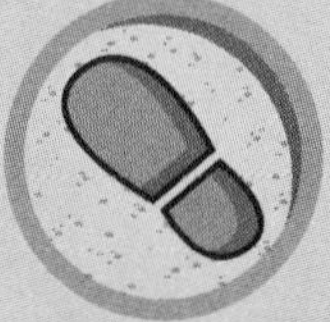

Slow

Directions: Look at the picture. Trace the word.

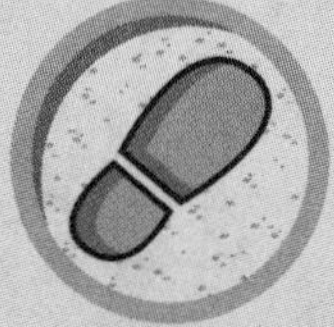

One Step Further

Turtles walk slow. Walk slowly around a table or desk.

Fast

Directions: Look at the picture. Trace the word.

fast

One Step Further

Bunnies hop fast. Hop like a bunny five times.
What else can you do that is fast?

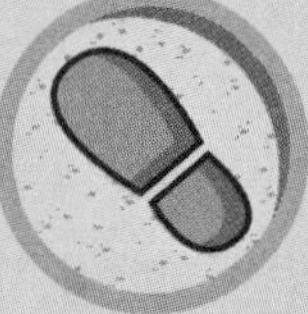

Hard

Directions: Look at the picture. Trace the word.

hard

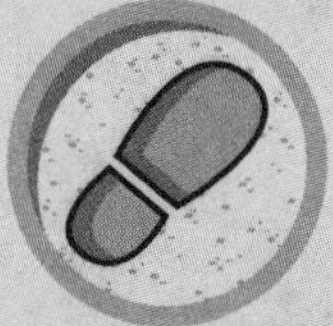

One Step Further

Go outside and find a rock or pebble.
Is it hard? Is it big or little?

Soft

Directions: Look at the picture. Trace the word.

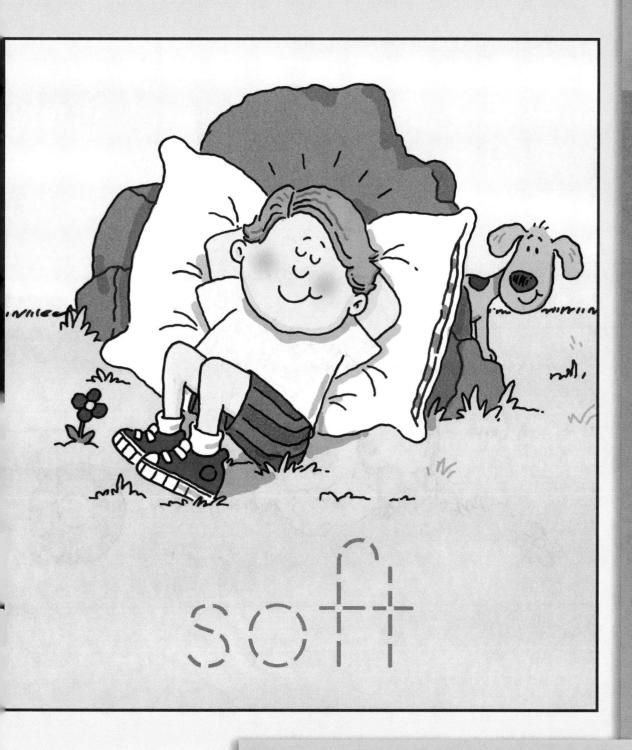

soft

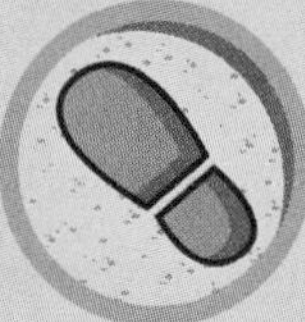

One Step Further

Find your favorite stuffed animal.
Does it feel soft?

In

Directions: Look at the picture. Trace the word.

in

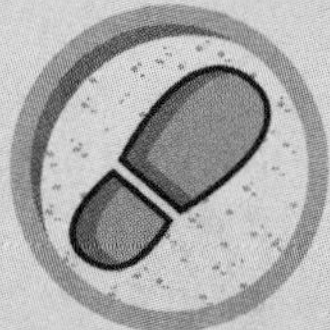

One Step Further

What is your favorite game to play inside? Ask a friend to play it with you.

Out

Directions: Look at the picture. Trace the word.

out

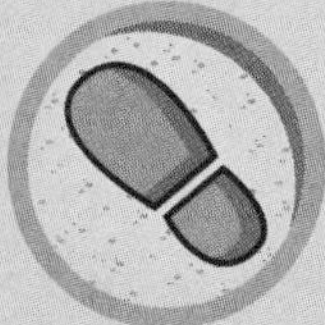

One Step Further

What is your favorite game to play outside?
What do you like about it?

Top

Directions: Look at the picture. Trace the word.

top

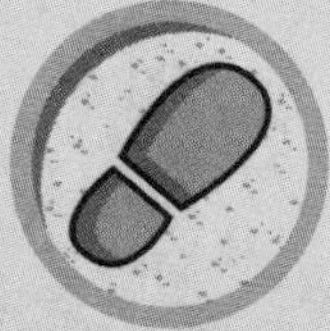

One Step Further

What is happening in the picture?
What do you think will happen next?

Bottom

Directions: Look at the picture. Trace the word.

bottom

One Step Further

What is your favorite thing to do on the playground? What do you like about it?

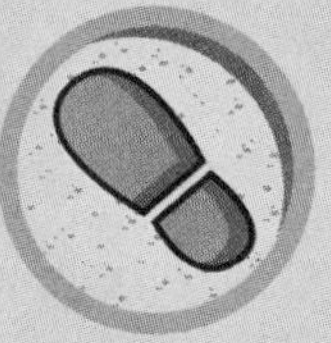

Full

Directions: Look at the picture. Trace the word.

full

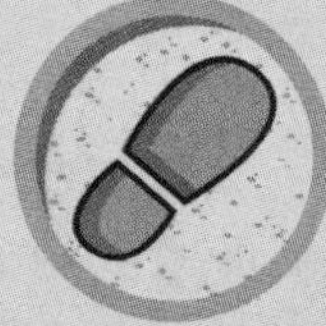

One Step Further

Ask an adult to give you a cup of water.
Is the cup full?

Empty

Directions: Look at the picture. Trace the word.

empty

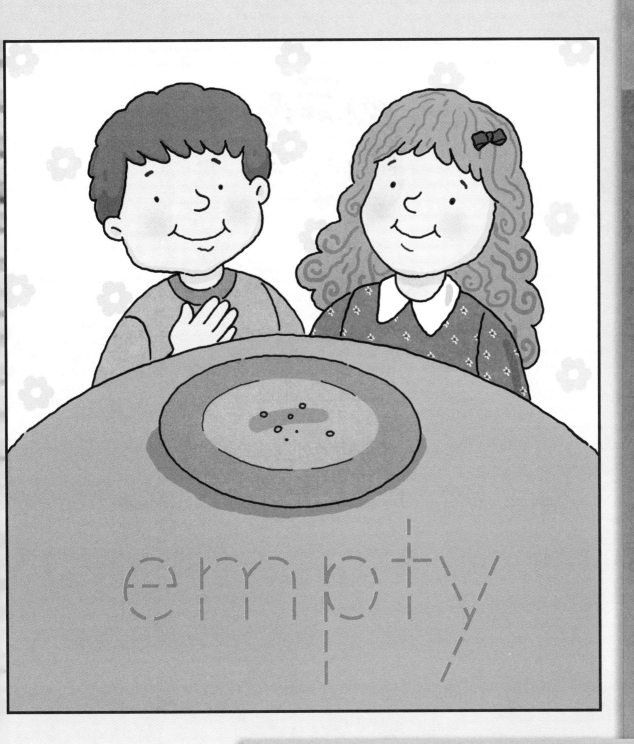

One Step Further
Drink some water from the cup.
Is the cup empty?

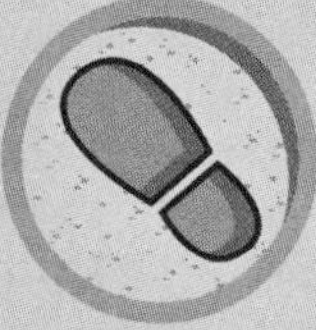

Happy

Directions: Look at the picture. Trace the word.

happy

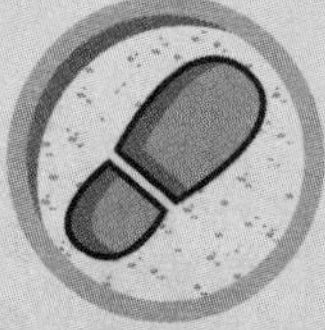

One Step Further

What treat makes you happy?
What do you like about it?

Sad

Directions: Look at the picture. Trace the word.

sad

One Step Further
What is happening in the picture?
Tell a story about it.

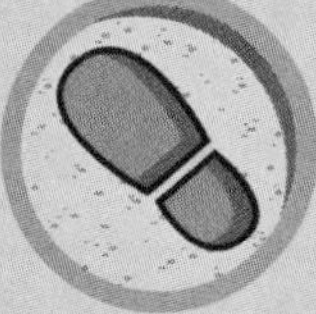

Up

Directions: Look at the picture. Trace the word.

up

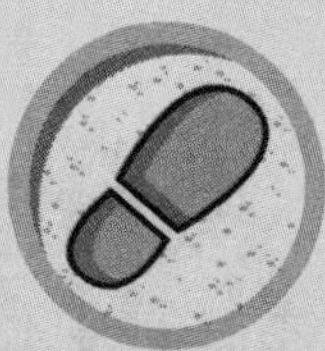

One Step Further

Go outside and look up.
What do you see?

Down

Directions: Look at the picture. Trace the word.

down

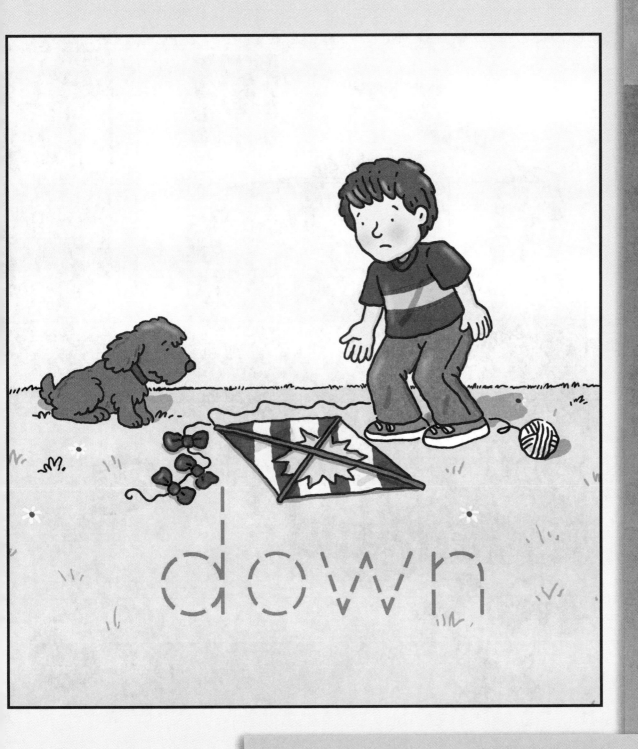

One Step Further

Go inside and look down at the floor.
What do you see?

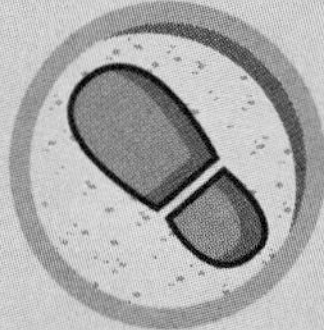

On

Directions: Look at the picture. Trace the word.

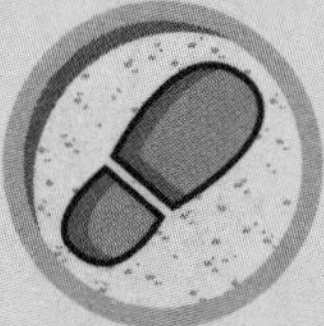

One Step Further

Look around your bedroom.
What is hanging on the walls?

Off

Directions: Look at the picture. Trace the word.

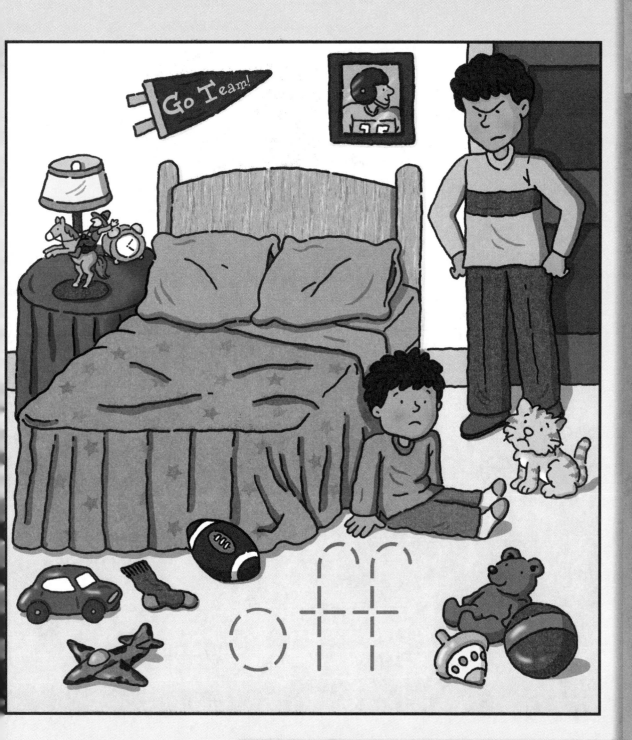

One Step Further

What is happening in the picture?
Tell a story about it.

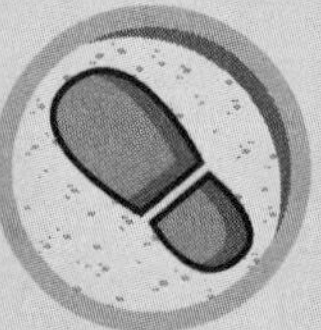

Opposites

BASIC SKILLS

Over

Directions: Look at the picture. Trace the word.

over

One Step Further

Draw a square over a circle. Ask a friend to tell you which one is over the other.

Under

Directions: Look at the picture. Trace the word.

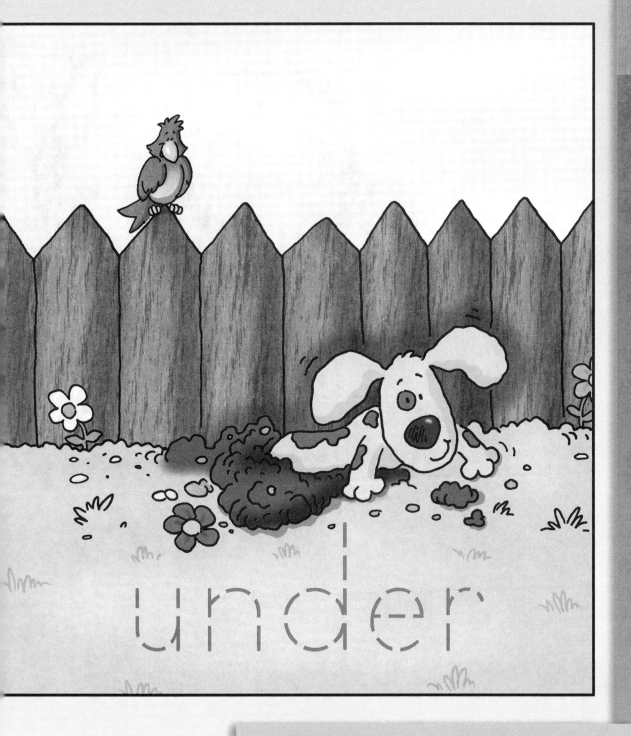

under

One Step Further

What objects can you go under?
Can you crawl under your bed?

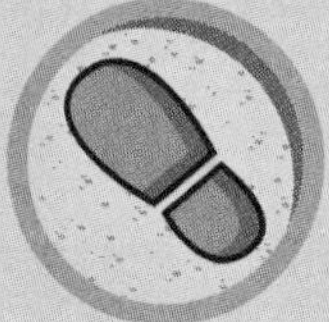

Old

Directions: Look at the picture. Trace the word.

old

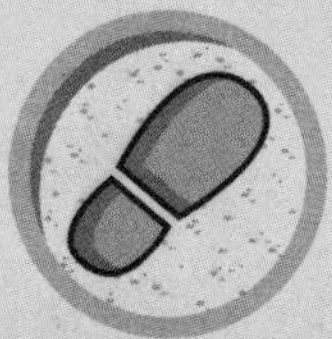

One Step Further

Find something in your home that is old.
Do you know how old it is?

New

Directions: Look at the picture. Trace the word.

new

One Step Further

Look at the shirt you are wearing right now.
Is it old or new?

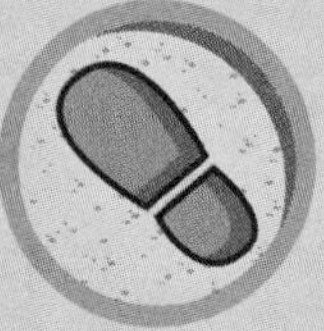

Wet

Directions: Look at the picture. Trace the word.

Wet

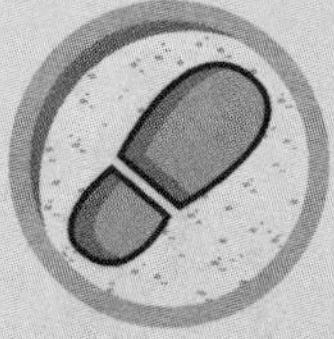

One Step Further

What is your favorite thing to do when it's raining outside?

Dry

Directions: Look at the picture. Trace the word.

dry

One Step Further

Look outside. Is the weather wet or dry?
Which type of weather is your favorite?

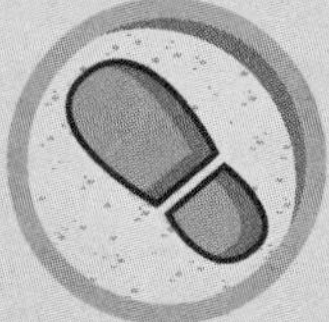

Hot

Directions: Look at the picture. Trace the word.

hot

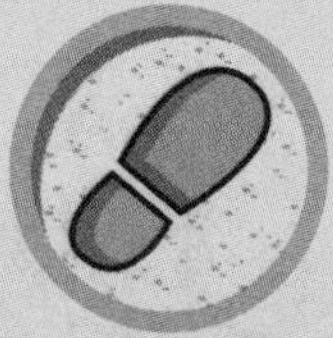

One Step Further

What is happening in the picture?
What do you think will happen next?

Cold

Directions: Look at the picture. Trace the word.

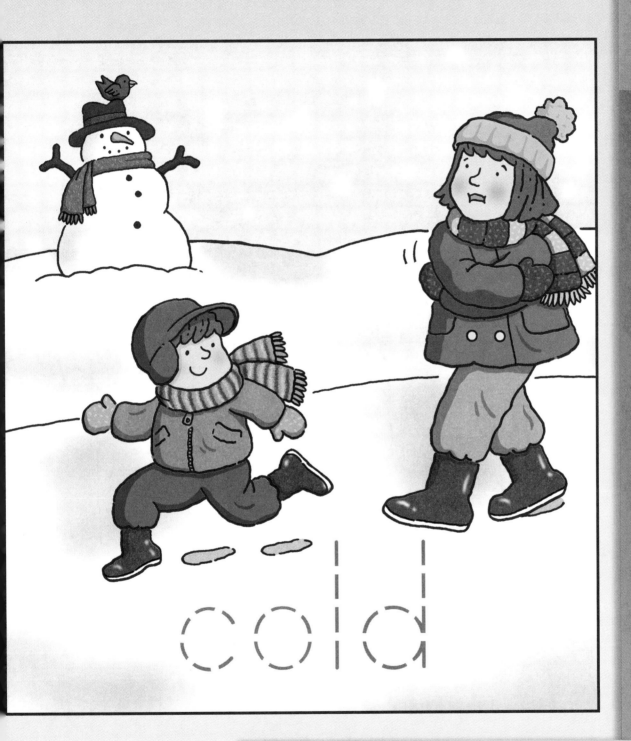

cold

One Step Further

Look outside. Is the weather hot or cold?
How can you tell?

Long

Directions: Look at the picture. Trace the word.

long

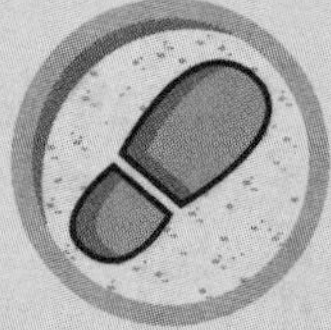

One Step Further
Go outside and find a long stick on the ground.

Short

Directions: Look at the picture. Trace the word.

short

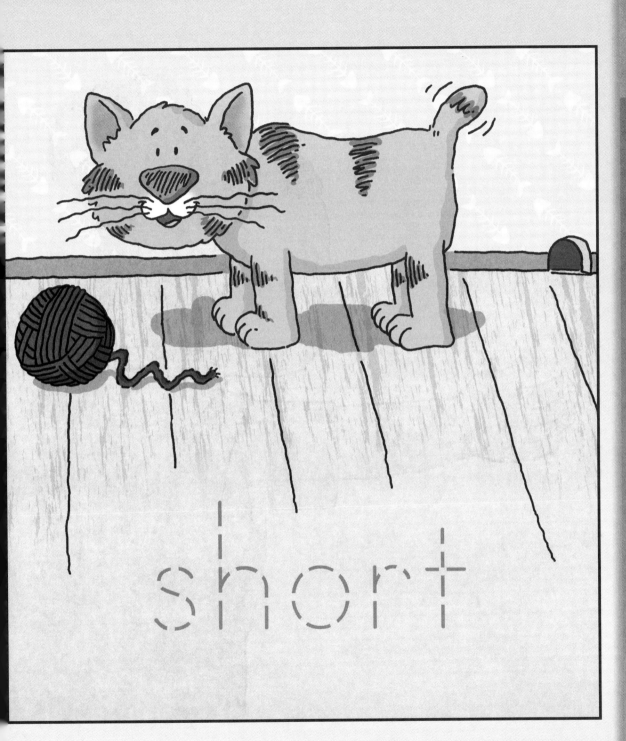

One Step Further
Look in the mirror. Is your hair long or short?
What else can you see that is short?

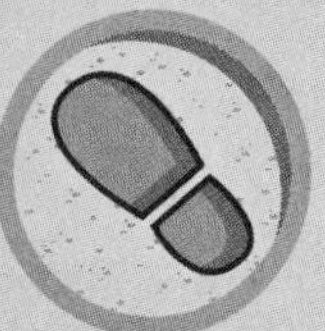

Left

Directions: Look at the picture. Trace the word.

left

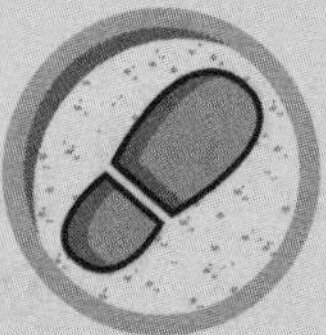

One Step Further

Look to your left. What do you see?
Name things that are nearby and far away.

Right

Directions: Look at the picture. Trace the word.

right

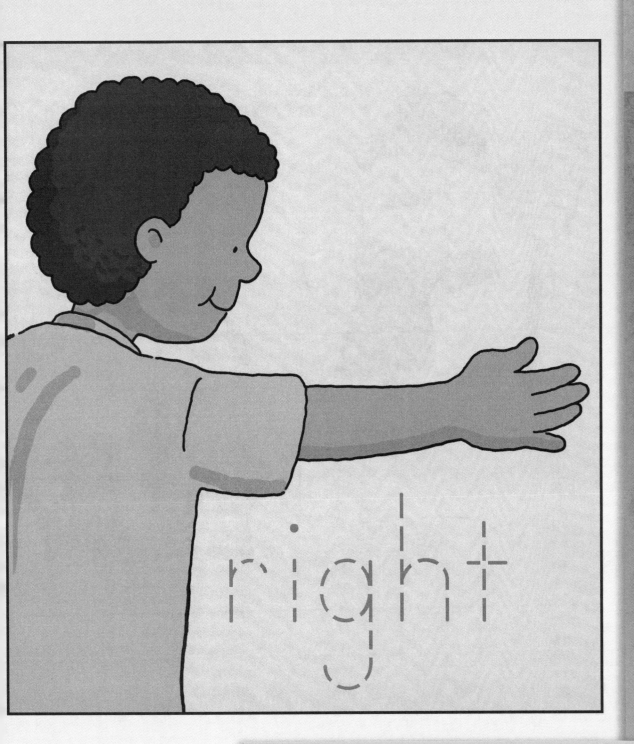

One Step Further

Look to your right. What do you see? Is it different from what you saw on your left?

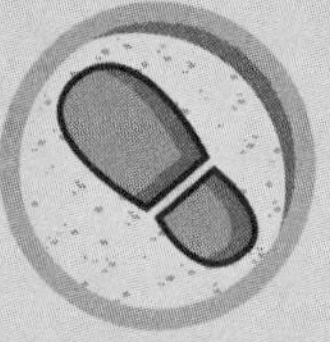

Front

Directions: Look at the picture. Trace the word.

front

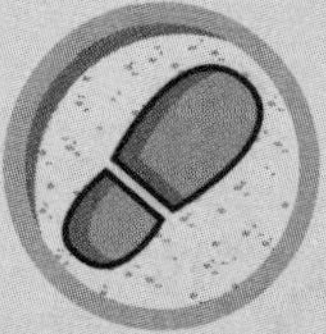

One Step Further
Find a book. Look at the front of it.
Describe what you see.

Back

Directions: Look at the picture. Trace the word.

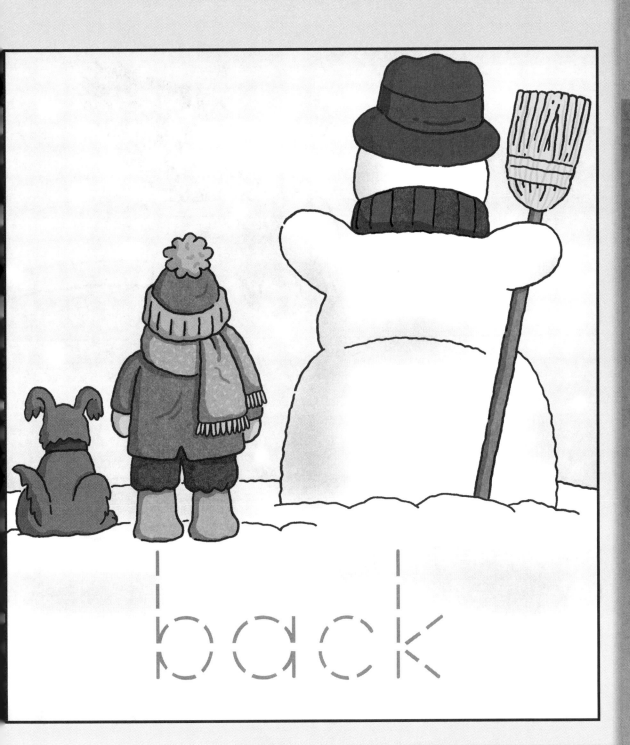

back

One Step Further

Find a book. Look at the back of it.
Describe what you see.

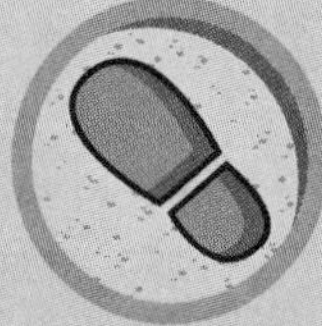

Above

Directions: Look at the picture. Trace the word.

above

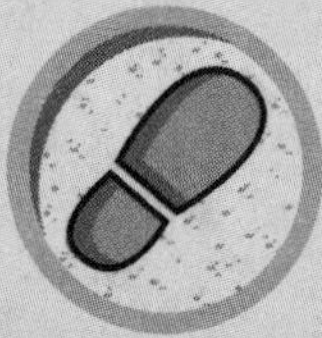

One Step Further

Raise your hands above your head.
Clap 10 times.

Below

Directions: Look at the picture. Trace the word.

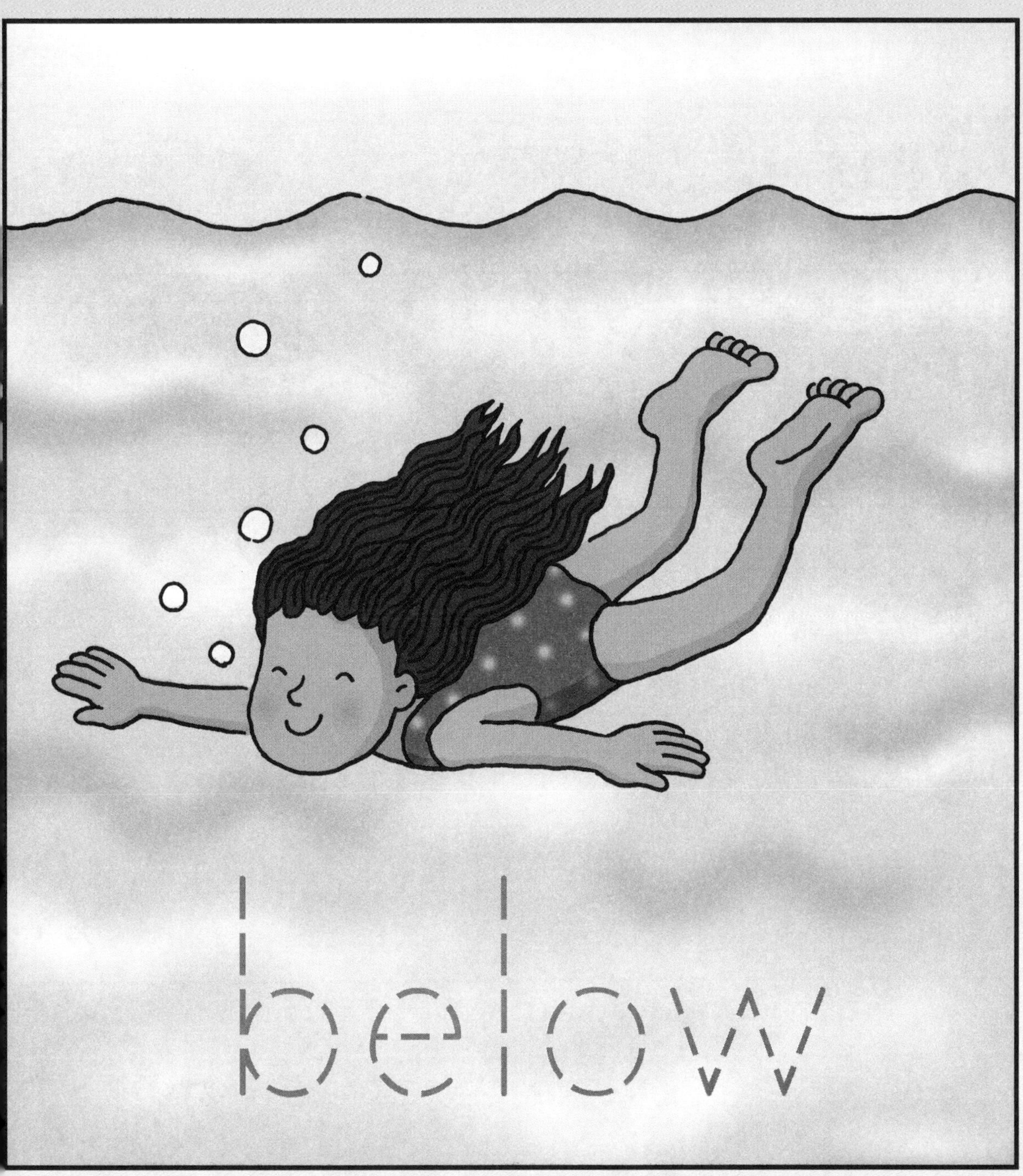

below

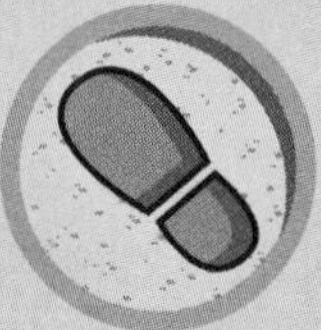

One Step Further

Ask a friend to hold his or her arm straight out. Walk or crawl below your friend's arm.

Far

Directions: Look at the picture. Trace the word.

far

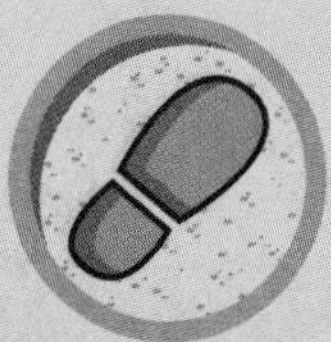

One Step Further
Go outside. What can you see that is far away?

Near

Directions: Look at the picture. Trace the word.

near

One Step Further

Look around you. What can you see that is near?

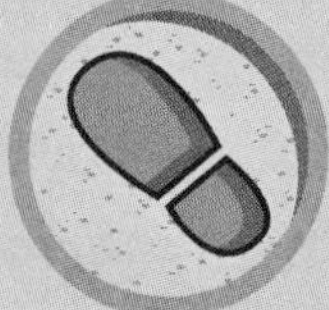

Go-Togethers

Directions: Look at the pictures in each row. Circle the picture that goes together with the first picture

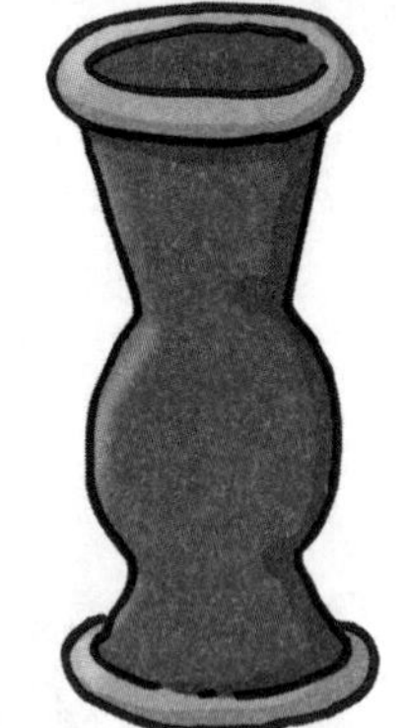

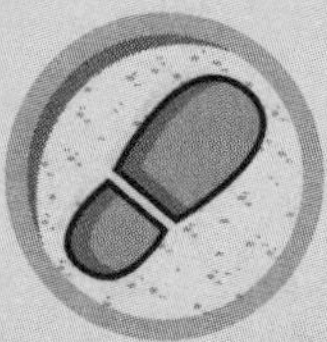

One Step Further

Choose one object on this page.
What goes together with that object?

Go-Togethers

Directions: Look at the pictures in each row. Circle the picture that goes together with the first picture.

One Step Further

Find two objects in your room that go together. Why do they go together?

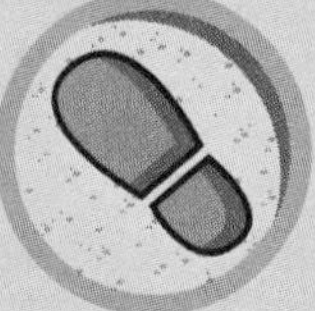

Same

Directions: Look at the pictures in each row. Circle the picture that is the **same** as the first picture in each row.

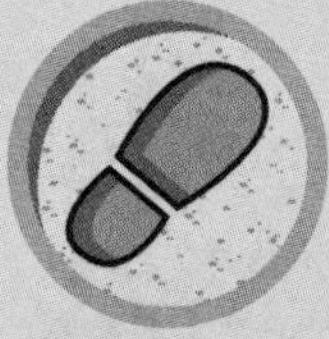

One Step Further

Find three pencils.
Are any of them the same?

Different

Directions: Look at the pictures in each row. Circle the picture that is **different** in each row.

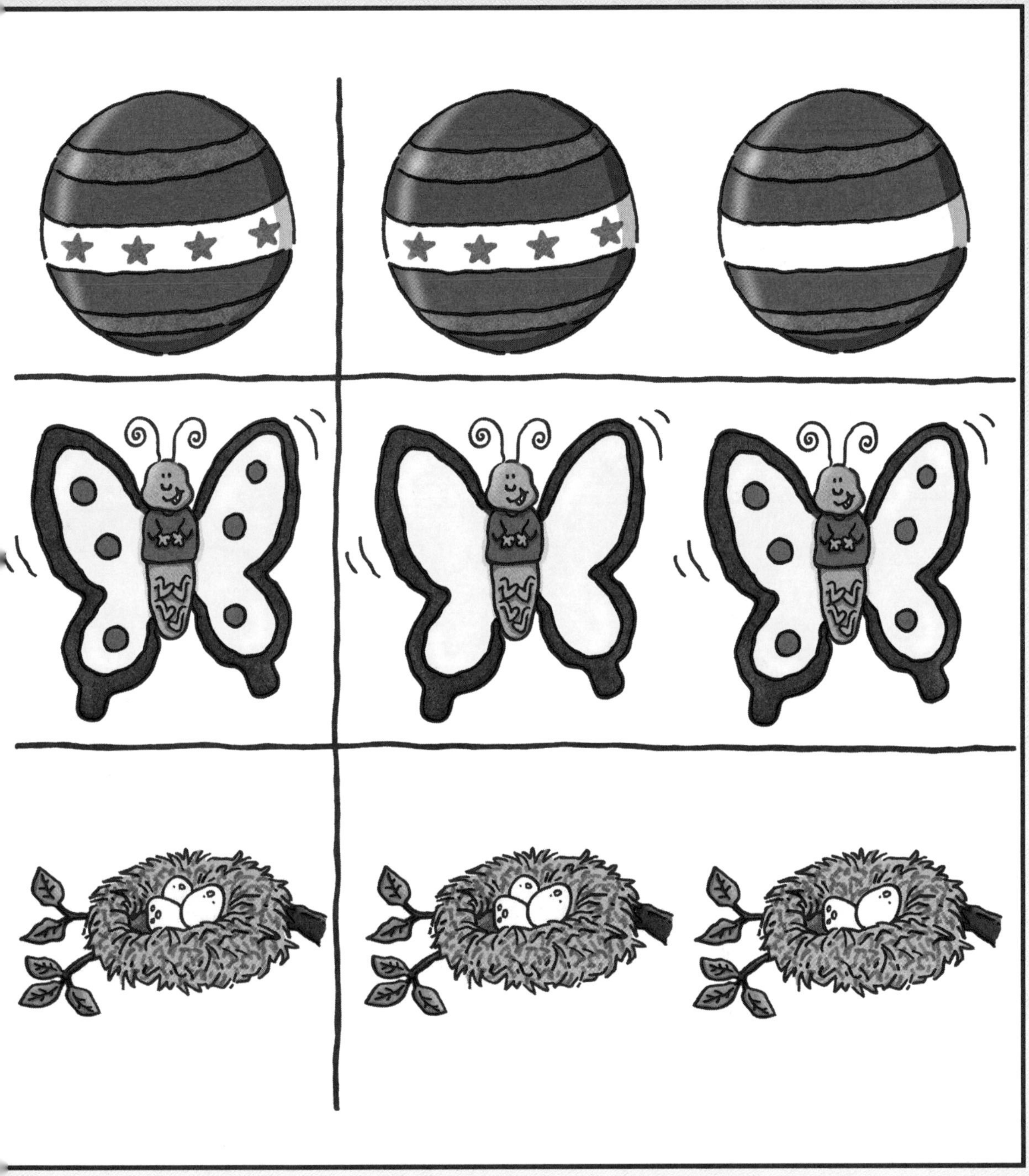

One Step Further

Find two of your favorite books. What makes them different?

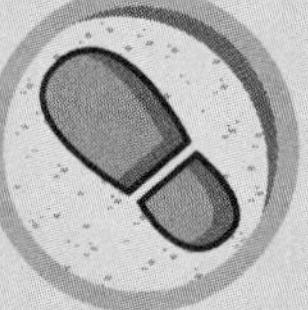

Same

Directions: Look at the shapes in each row. Color the shape that is the **same** as the first shape in each row.

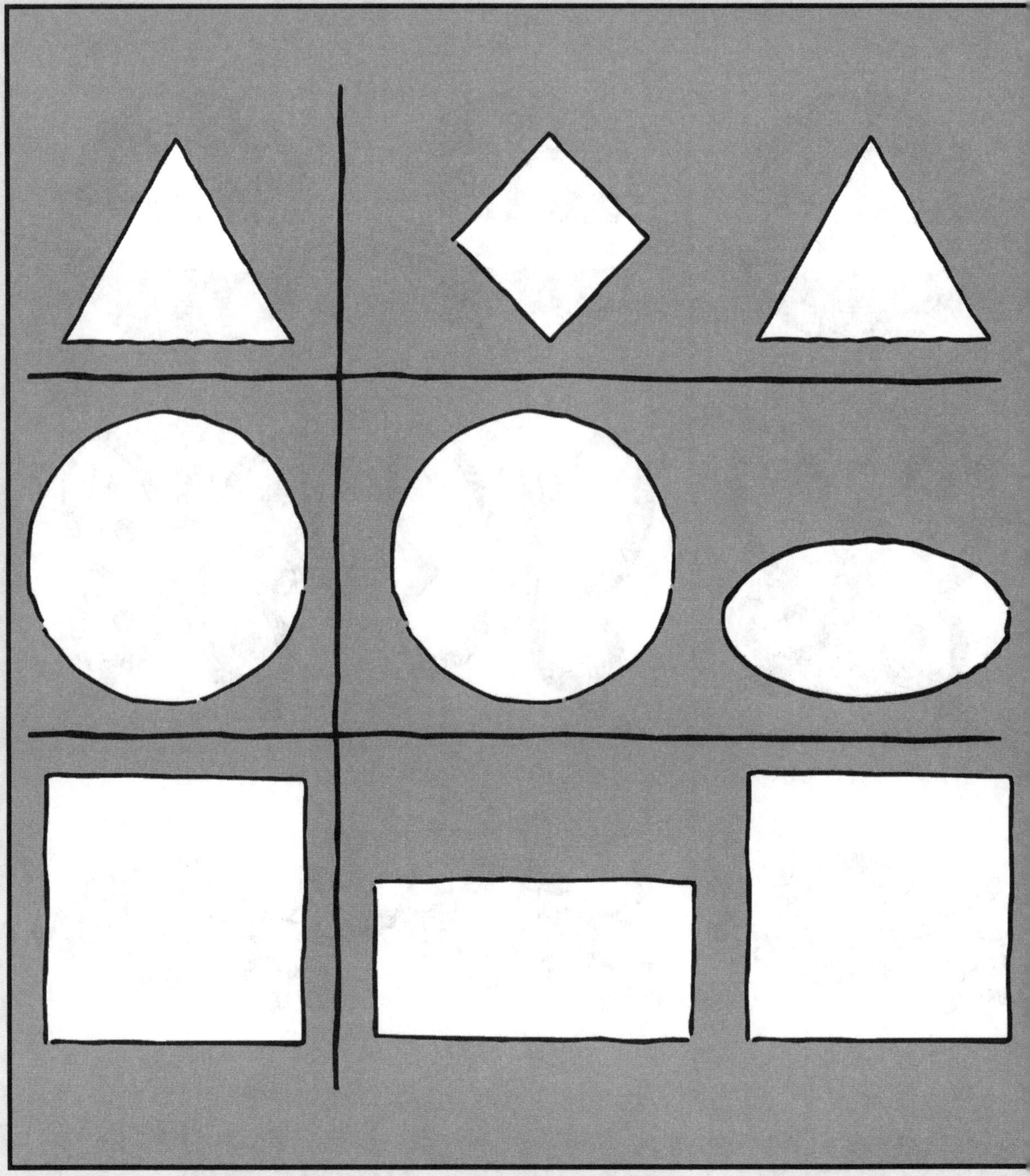

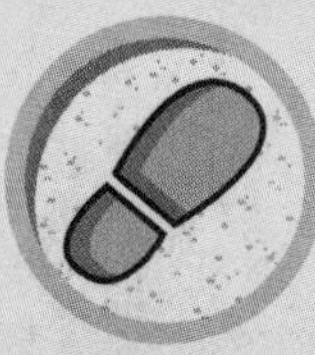

One Step Further

Draw two rhombuses and one square. Ask a friend to tell you which two are the same.

Different

Directions: Color the shape in each row that is **different**.

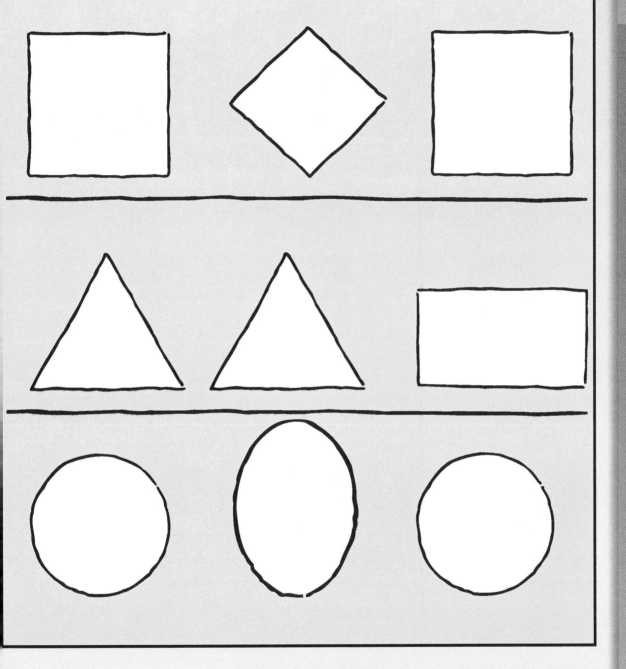

One Step Further

Draw two different objects.
What makes these objects different?

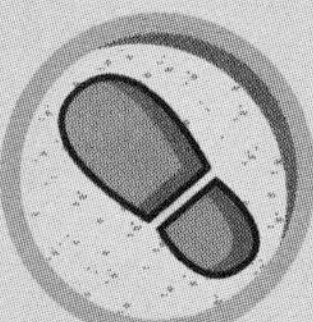

Same

Directions: Look at the letters in each row. Circle the letter that is the **same** as the first letter in each row.

E	F	E
R	B	R
M	M	N

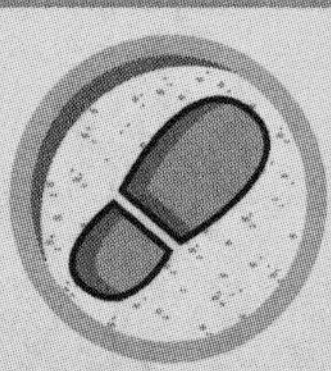

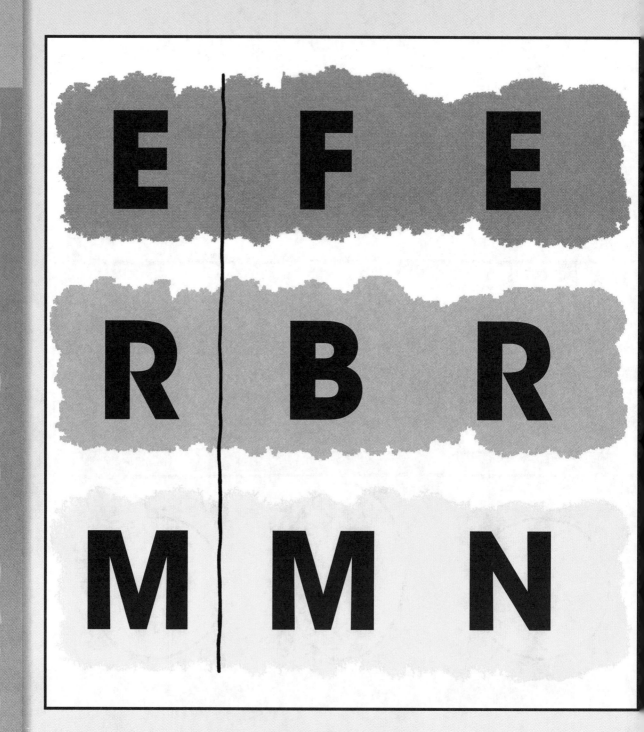

One Step Further

Pick a letter on this page. Can you think of a word that starts with that letter?

Left to Right

Directions: Help the cat get to the milk. Follow the arrow to trace a path to the milk.

Directions: Help the rabbit get to the carrot. Follow the arrow to trace a path to the carrot.

One Step Further

Give these animals a name.
Tell a story about them.

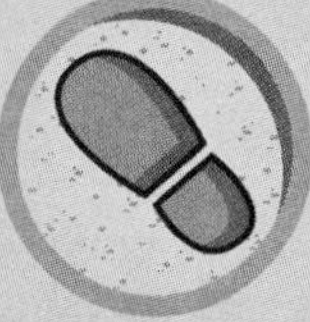

Left to Right

Directions: Help the bear get to the honey. Follow the arrow to trace a path to the honey.

Directions: Help the cow get to the grass. Follow the arrow to trace a path to the grass.

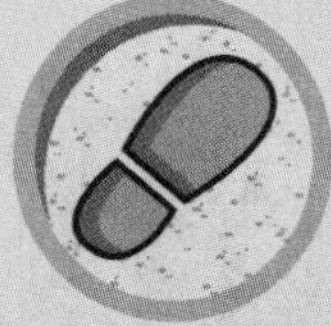

One Step Further

What do you think the bear will do when he gets to the honey?

Left to Right

Directions: Trace the lines from left to right to help each mother find her baby.

→

→

→

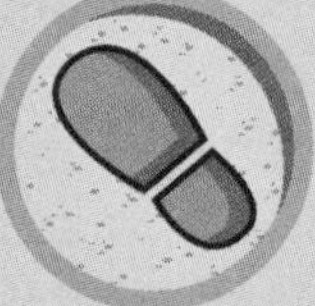

One Step Further

Look outside. Do any of these animals live near you?

Top to Bottom

Directions: Help the children hold onto their balloons. Trace the balloon strings from top to bottom.

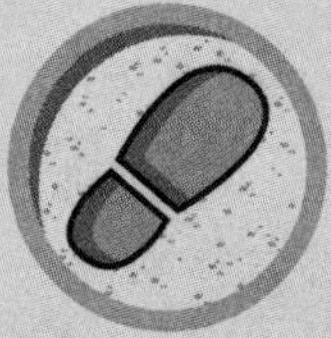

One Step Further

Tell a story about this picture.
Where do you think the kids are going?

Top to Bottom

Directions: Help the spiders make their web. Trace the lines from top to bottom.

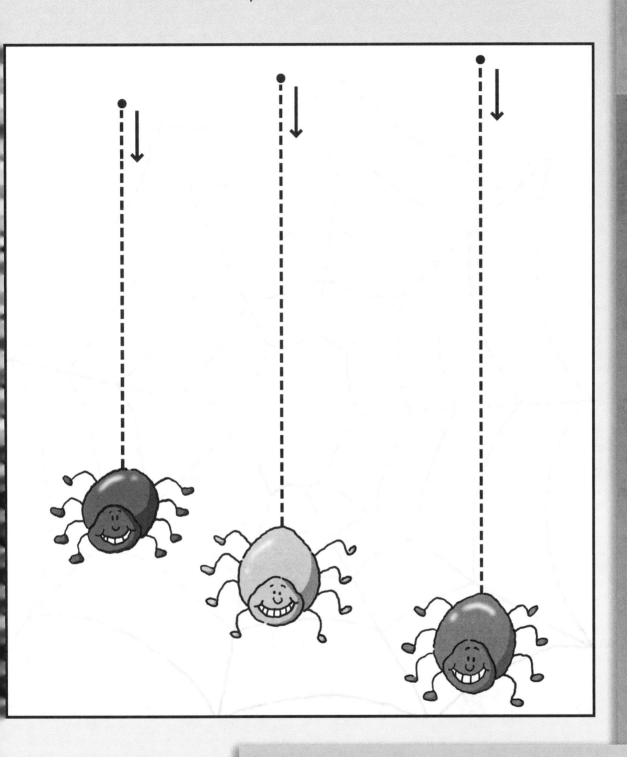

One Step Further

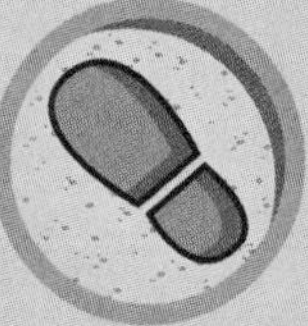

A spider has eight legs.
Find eight objects near you.

Top to Bottom

Directions: Trace the lines from top to bottom to make stems on the flowers.

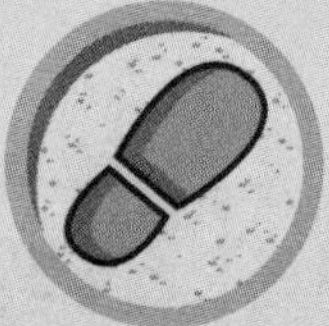

One Step Further

What is your favorite flower?
What do you like about it?

Slanted Lines

Directions: Help the children slide down the hill. Trace the lines from top to bottom.

One Step Further

Pretend it's snowing outside.
Play your favorite indoor game.

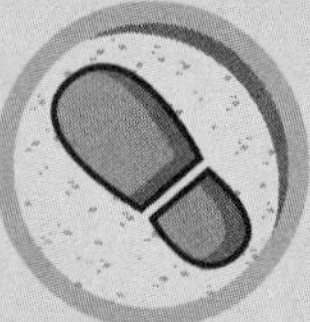

Slanted Lines

Directions: Help the children go down the slides. Trace the lines from top to bottom.

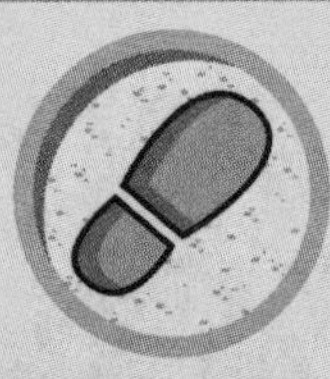

One Step Further
What is your favorite thing to do when it's hot outside?

Curved Lines

Directions: Trace each ball's bounces from left to right.

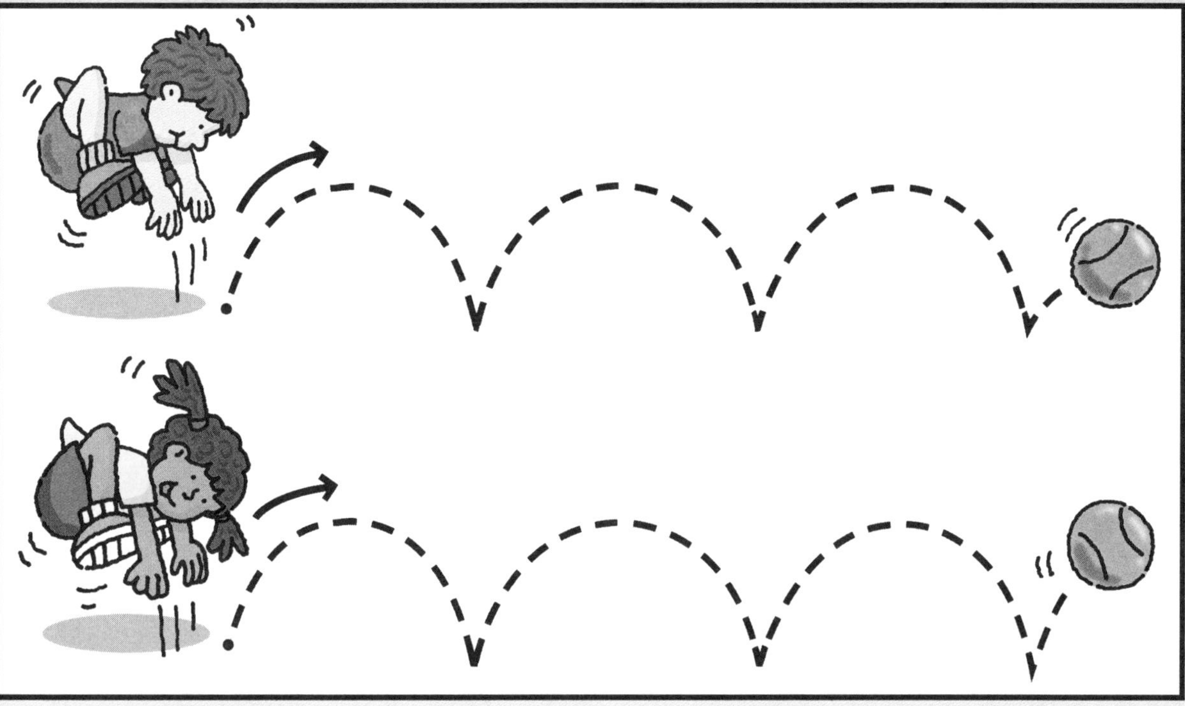

Directions: Draw the ball's bounces from left to right.

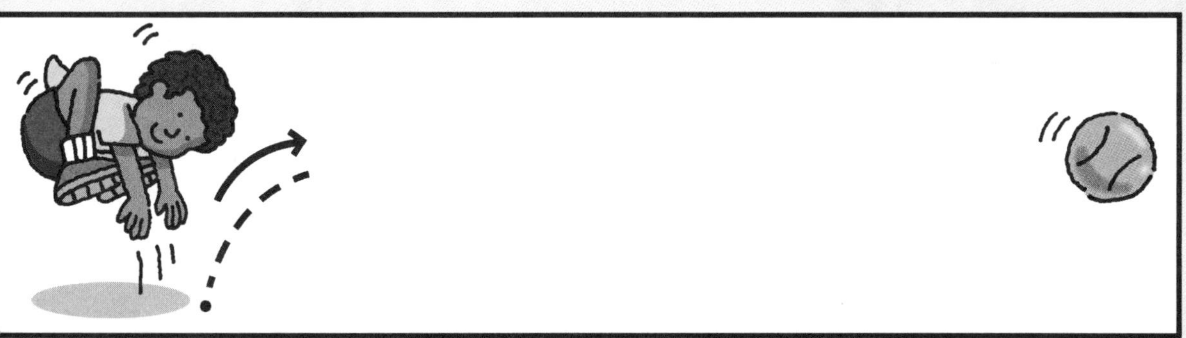

One Step Further
Bounce from left to right four times.
How far can you bounce?

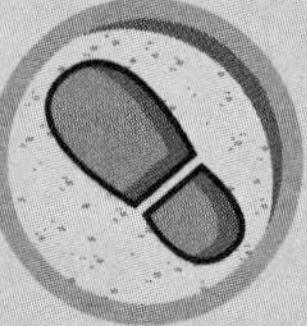

Forward Circles

Directions: Follow the arrows to trace the circles on each scoop of ice cream.

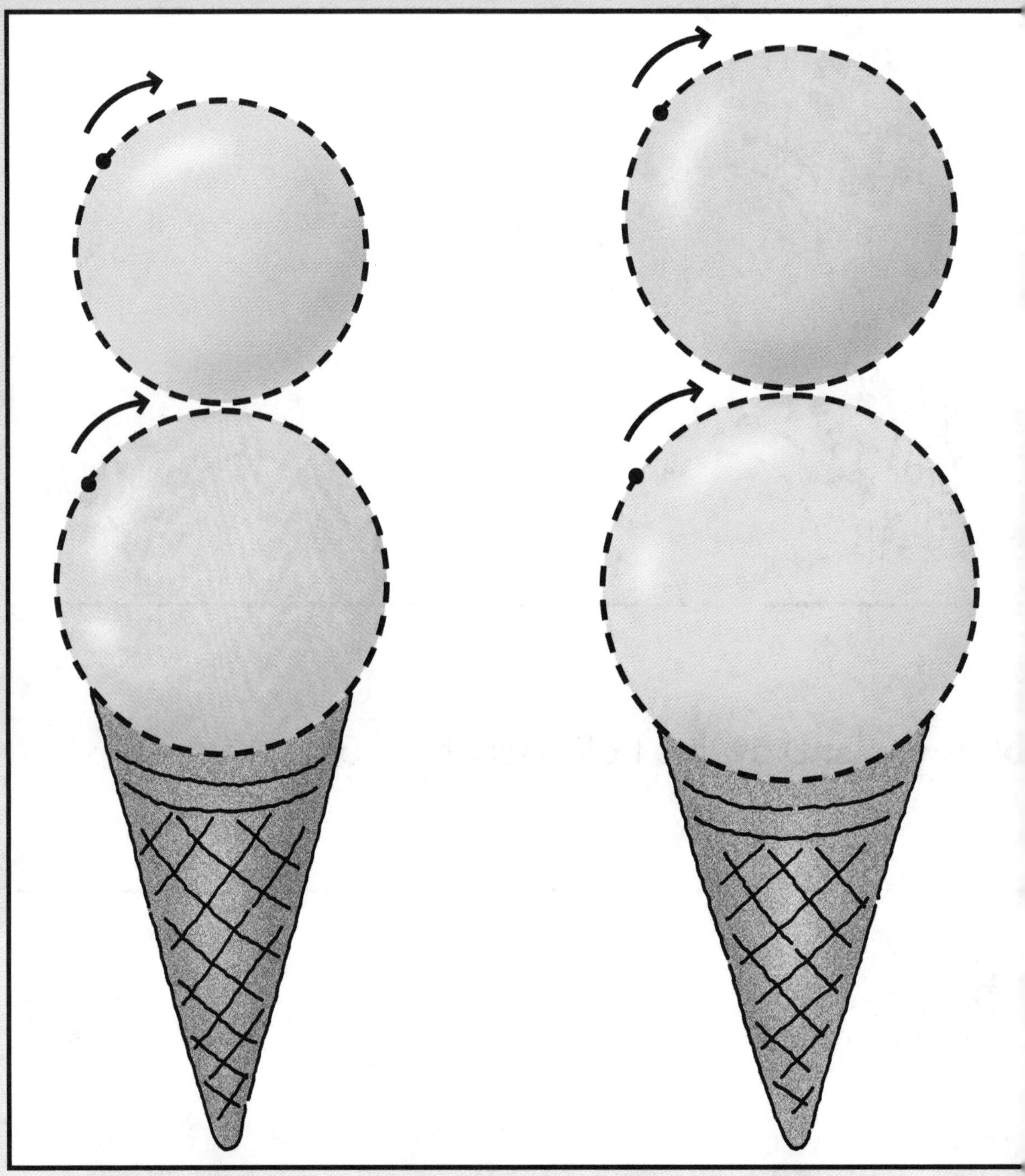

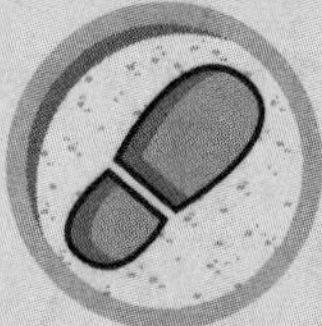

One Step Further
Ice cream is a yummy summer treat.
What other treats do you like to eat?

Backward Circles

Directions: Follow the arrows to trace the plates on the picnic table.

One Step Further

Pretend you and a friend are having a picnic. What will you bring with you?

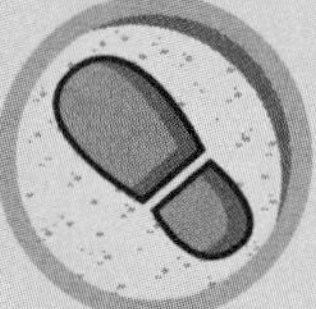

Top-to-bottom Lines

Directions: Start at the top. Follow the arrows to trace the dotted lines.

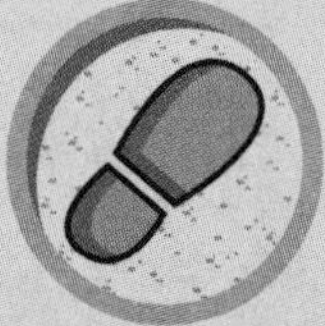

One Step Further

Toss a small object straight up. Watch the line it makes as it falls straight down.

Slanted Lines

Directions: Start at the top. Follow the arrows to trace the dotted lines.

One Step Further

Lay in the grass and look up at the clouds. What shapes do you see?

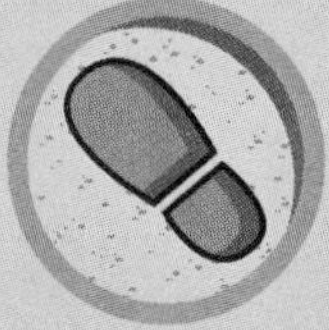

Writing

BASIC SKILLS

Curved Lines

Directions: Start at the dots on the left. Follow the arrows to trace the dotted lines.

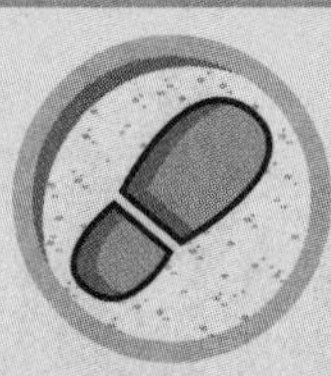

One Step Further

Go outside and take one big hop as far as you can.

Circles

Directions: Start at the dots. Follow the arrows to trace the dotted lines.

One Step Further
Stand up and spin in circles.
Be careful not to get dizzy!

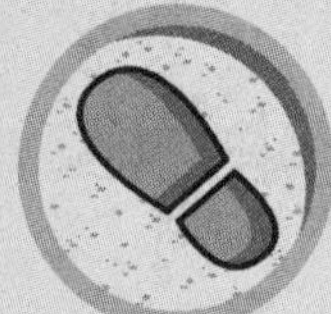

MATH

Math

Zero 0

Directions: Color the **0**.

Directions: Circle the box that shows **0**.

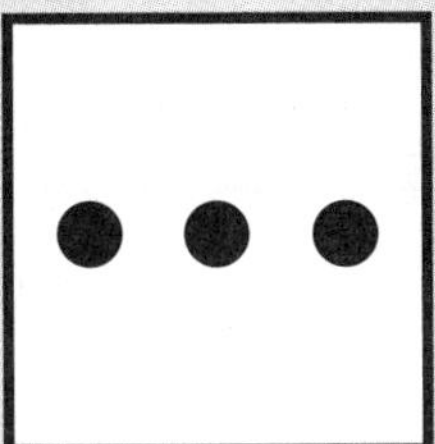

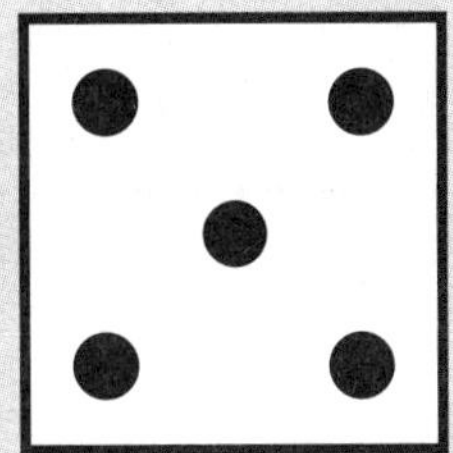

One Step Further

Name an object that looks like a zero.
Describe the object to a friend.

Trace and Write 0

Directions: Trace the number. Trace the word.

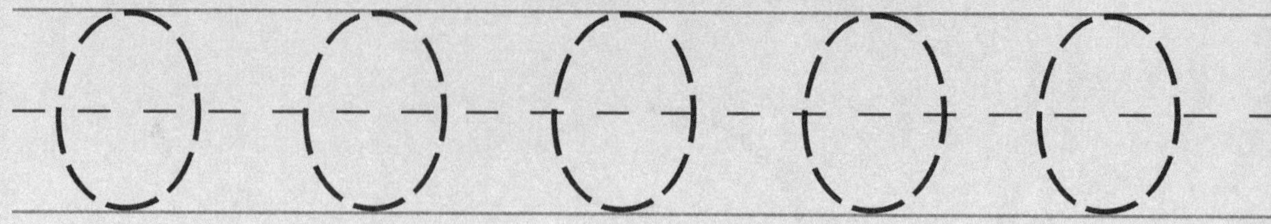

Directions: Now practice writing the number and the word by yourself on the lines below.

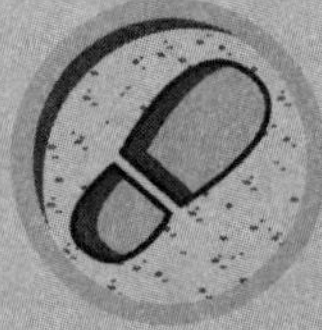

One Step Further
Count the number of elephants that are on this page. How many do you see?

Number 0

Directions: Color the fish with **0** spots **orange**.

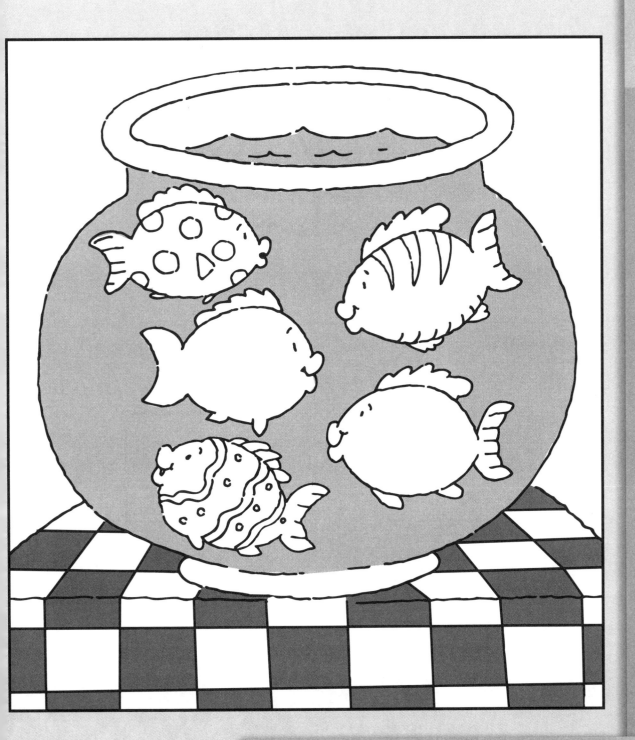

One Step Further

Color the rest of the fish blue.
How many of these fish are green?

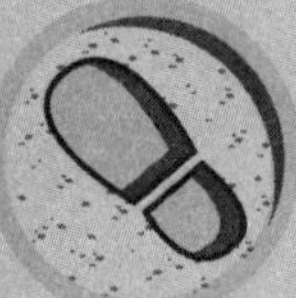

One 1

Directions: Color the number **1** as well as the one duck.

Directions: Circle the box that shows **1**.

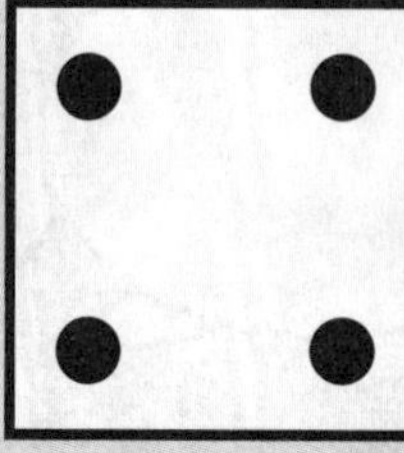

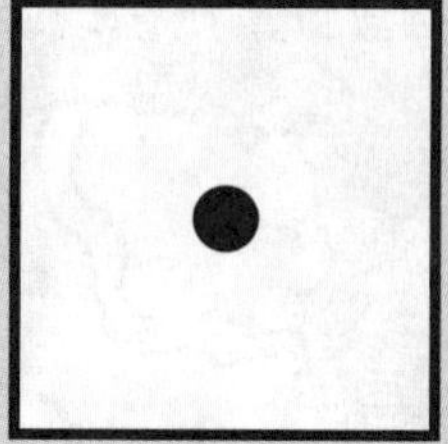

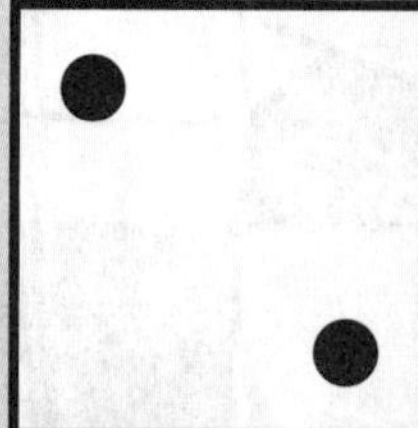

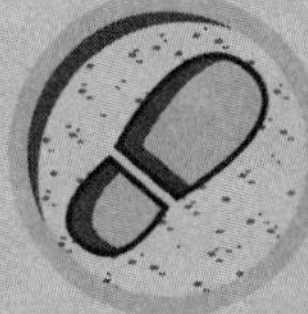

One Step Further

Point to your nose. How many noses do you have?

Trace and Write 1

Directions: Trace the number. Trace the word.

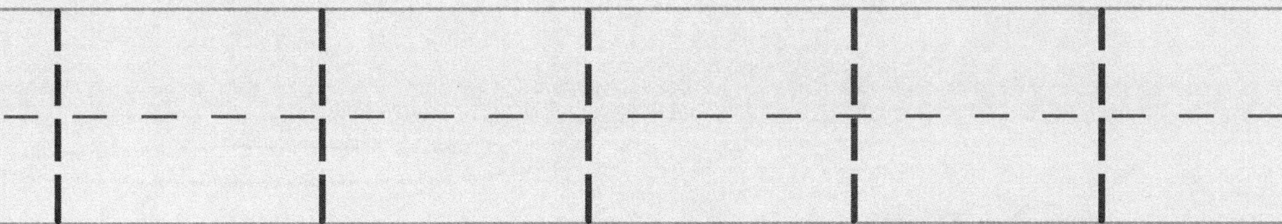

one one

Directions: Now practice writing the number and the word by yourself on the lines below.

One Step Further

Name an object that you own one of. What do you like about that object?

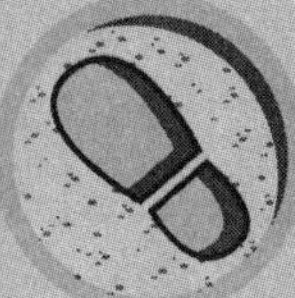

Number 1

Directions: Color **1** glass of juice **purple**, **1** glass of juice **orange**, and **1** glass of juice **red**.

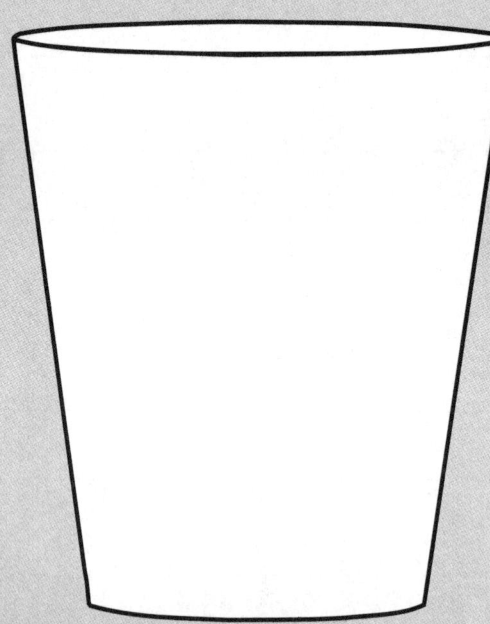

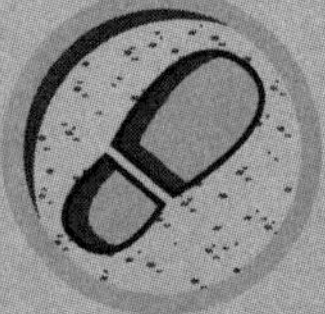

One Step Further

What is your favorite kind of juice?
What color is it?

Two 2

Directions: Color the number **2** as well as the two cats.

Directions: Circle the box that shows **2**.

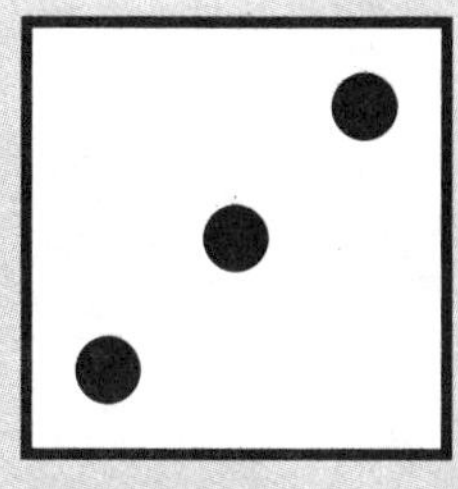

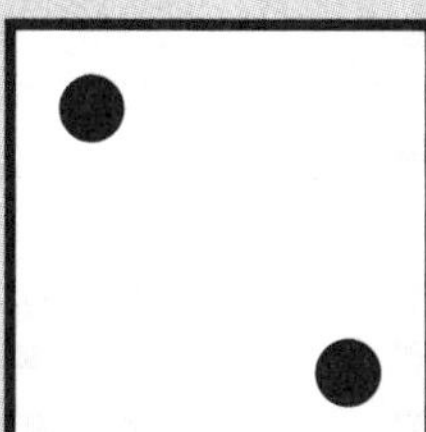

One Step Further

Draw a cat. Then, draw another cat.
How many cats are there?

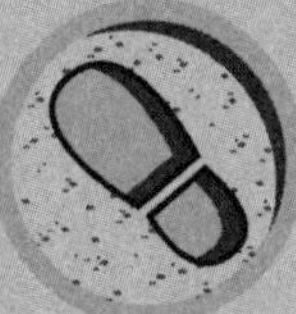

Trace and Write 2

Directions: Trace the number. Trace the word.

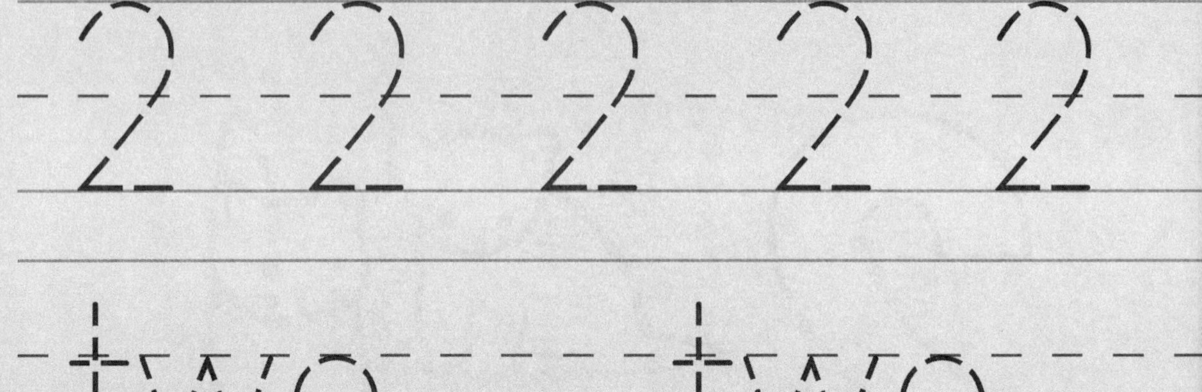

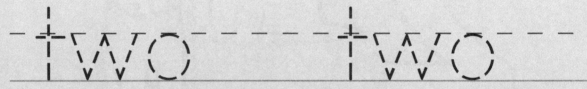

Directions: Now practice writing the number and the word by yourself on the lines below.

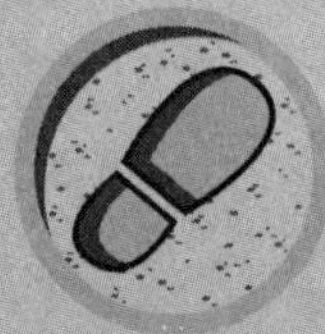

One Step Further

Find two leaves. What color are the leaves? Are they the same color?

Number 2

Directions: Color the spaces: 2 = **black**, two = **blue**, 1 = **white**, and ●● = **orange**.

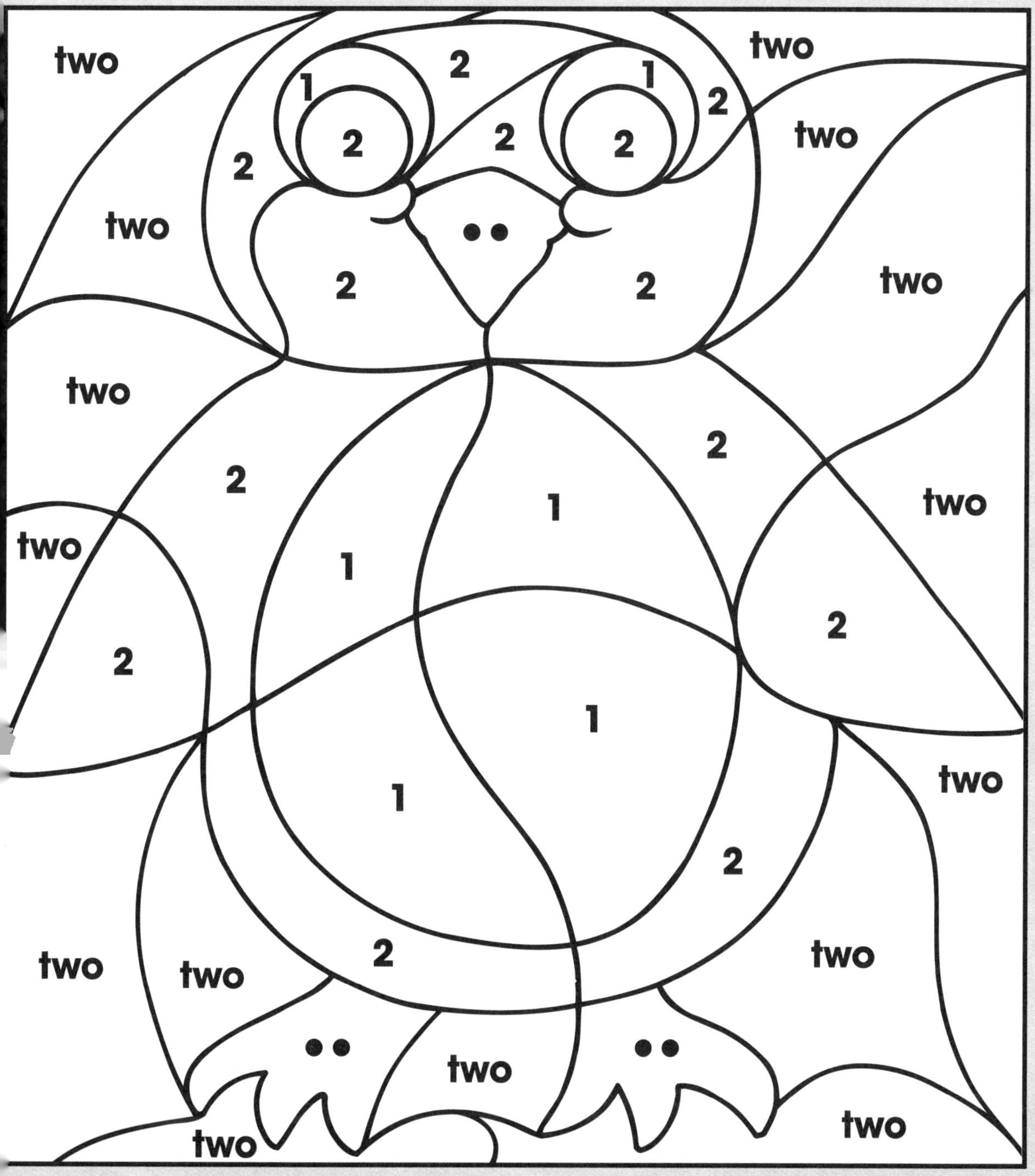

One Step Further

After you finish coloring this picture, count the feet. How many do you see?

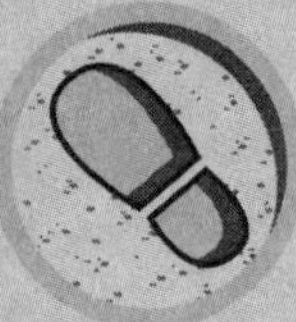

Three 3

Directions: Color the number **3** as well as the three dogs.

Directions: Circle the box that shows **3**.

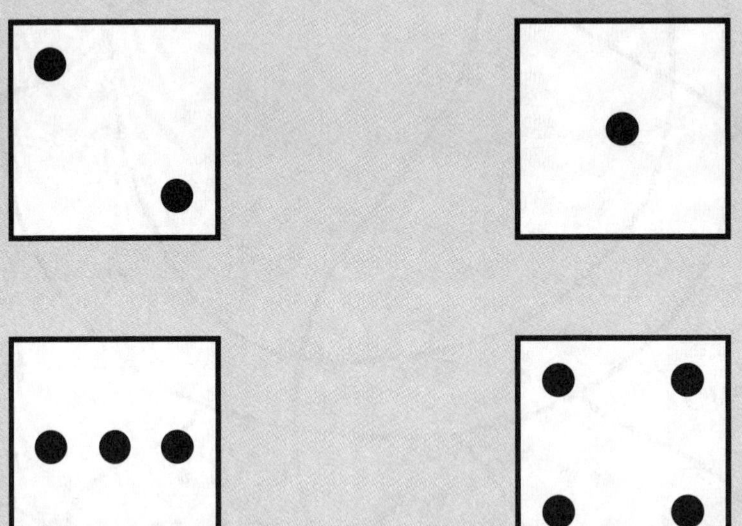

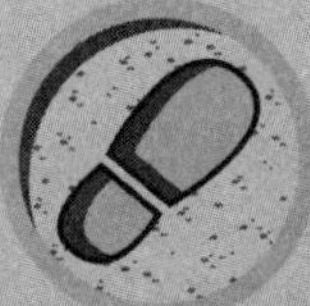

One Step Further

Make three greeting cards.
Give them to three friends.

Trace and Write 3

Directions: Trace the number. Trace the word.

3 3 3 3 3

three three

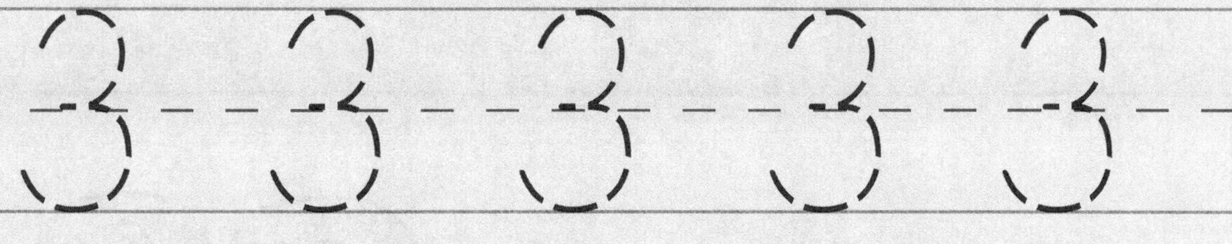

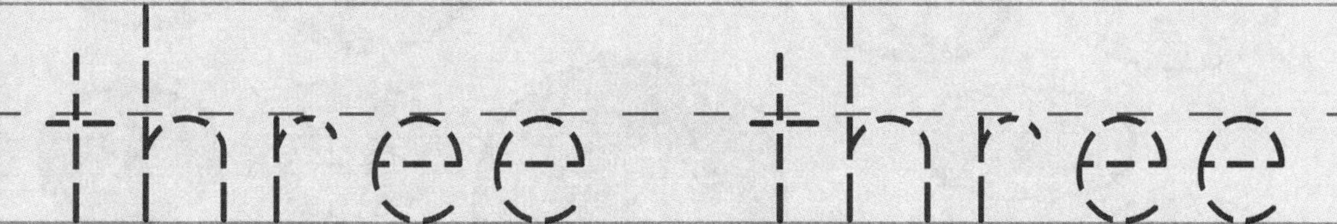

Directions: Now practice writing the number and the word by yourself on the lines below.

One Step Further
Look around your neighborhood.
Count three mailboxes.

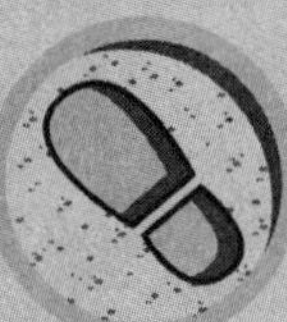

Number 3

Directions: Circle **3** of each kind of cookie to go in the cookie jar.

COOKIES

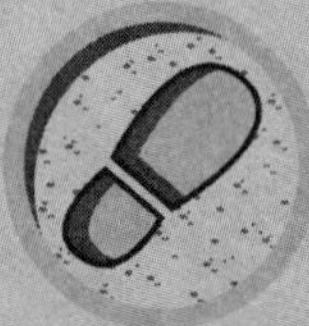

One Step Further

What is your favorite kind of cookie? Ask an adult to help you bake some.

Four 4

Directions: Color the number **4** as well as the four animals.

Directions: Circle the boxes that show **4**.

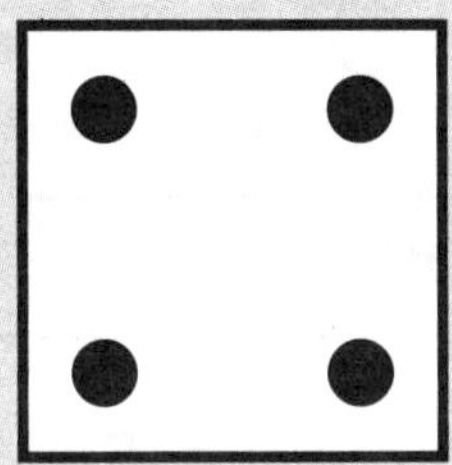

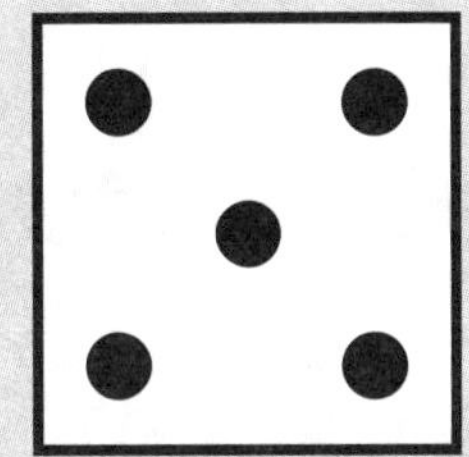

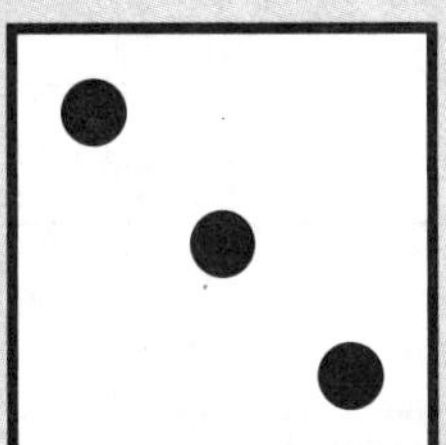

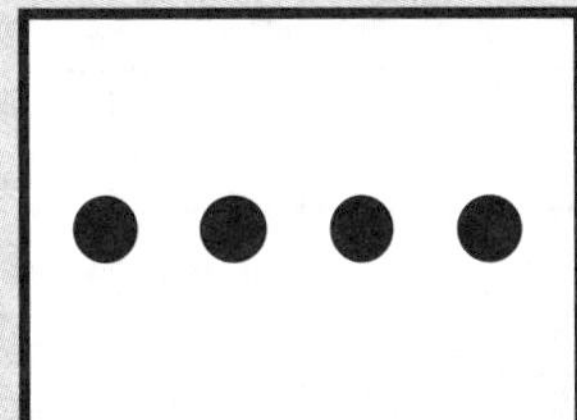

One Step Further

Name four different animals.
Which is your favorite? Why?

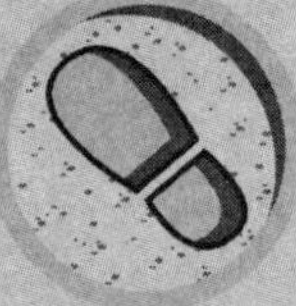

Trace and Write 4

Directions: Trace the number. Trace the word.

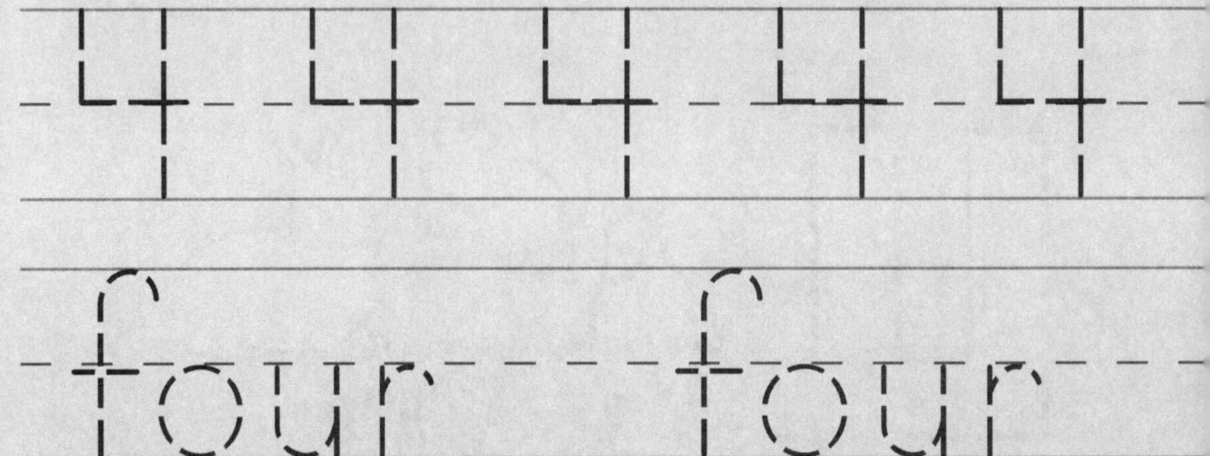

Directions: Now practice writing the number and the word by yourself on the lines below.

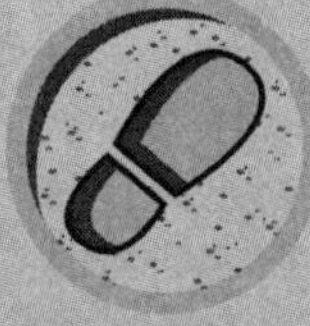

One Step Further

Draw a square. How many sides does the square have?

Number 4

Directions: Draw **4** flowers in the vase.

One Step Further

Count the petals on the flowers you drew. How many are there?

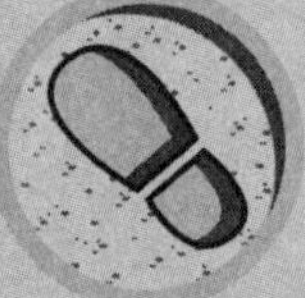

Five 5

Directions: Color the number **5** as well as the five chicks.

Directions: Circle the boxes that show **5**.

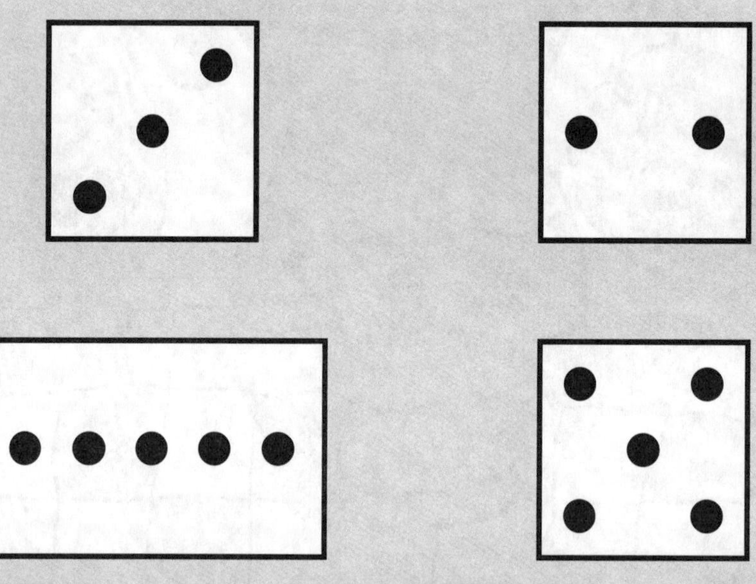

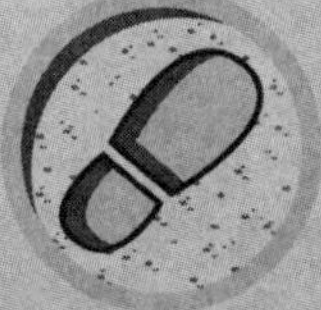

One Step Further
Name five different kinds of fruit.
Which is your favorite?

Trace and Write 5

Directions: Trace the number. Trace the word.

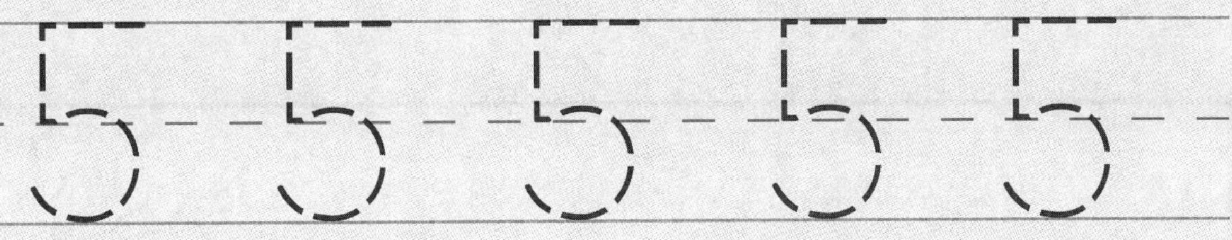

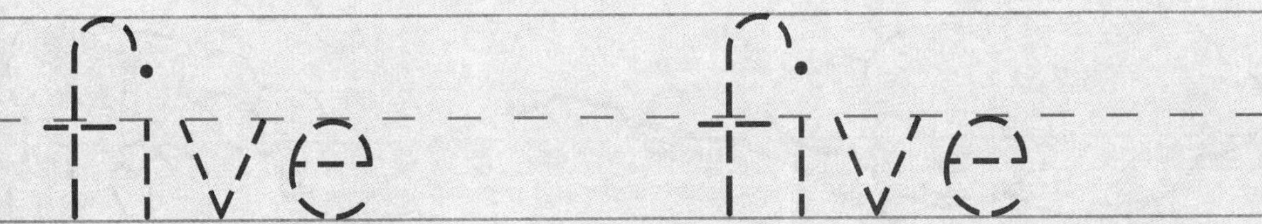

Directions: Now practice writing the number and the word by yourself on the lines below.

One Step Further

Count your fingers on one hand.
Then, count your toes on one foot.

Number 5

Directions: Draw **5** ☆s on the ⛰. Color the ☆s.

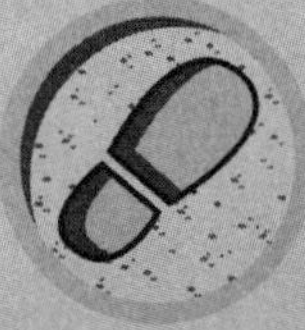

One Step Further

Draw a star. Count the points on the star.
How many are there?

Numbers 0–5

Directions: Count the dots. Color the spaces: 1 = **red**, 2 = **yellow**, 3 = **green**, 4 = **blue**, and 5 = **orange**.

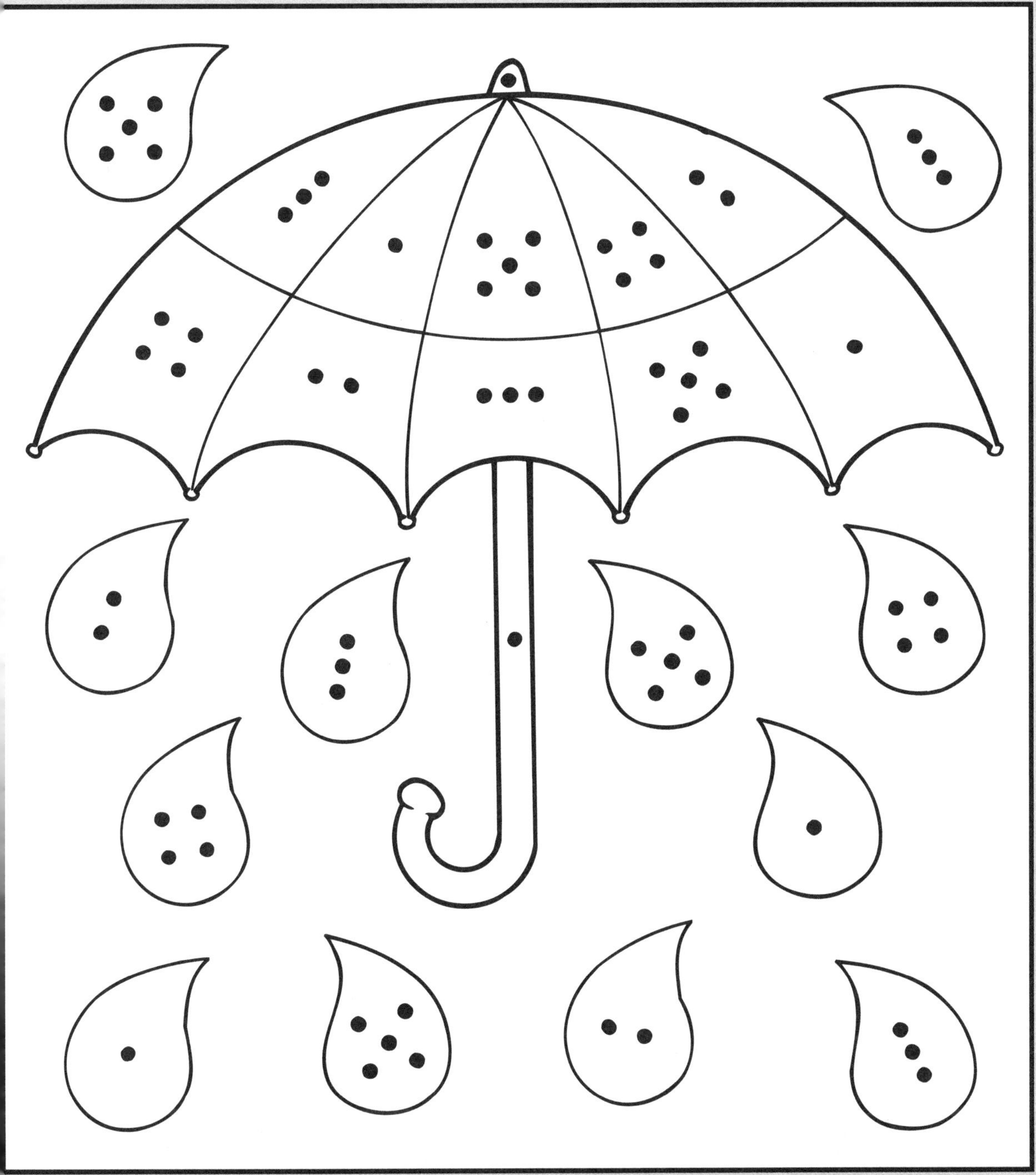

One Step Further

Pretend it's raining! Snuggle under a blanket and read a book.

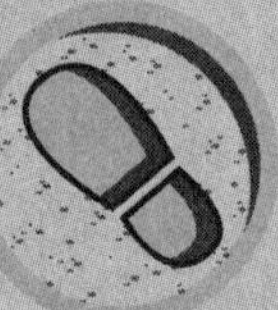

Numbers 0–5

Directions: Count each group of vegetables. Write the number in the box. Color the vegetables.

1 2 3 4 5

How many?

How many?

How many?

How many?

How many?

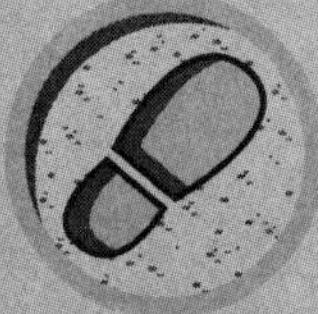

One Step Further

How many more vegetables can you name? Which is your favorite?

Six 6

Directions: Color the number **6** as well as the six turtles.

Directions: Circle the boxes that show **6**.

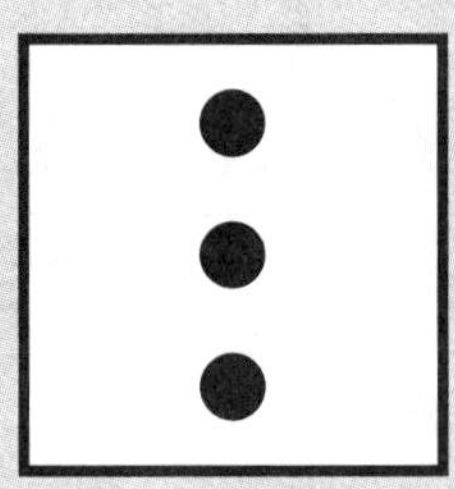

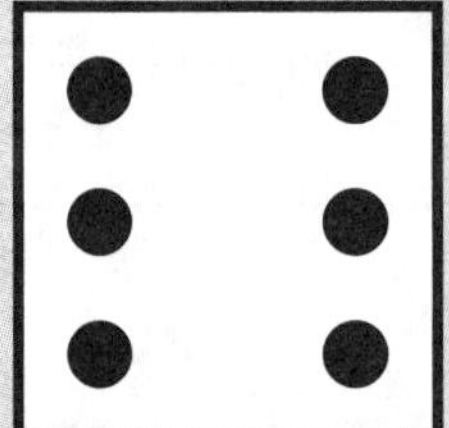

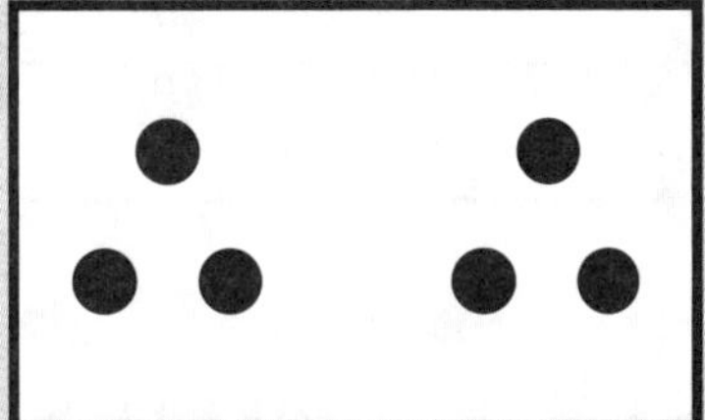

One Step Further

Roll two dice. What numbers come up?
Roll until you get a six.

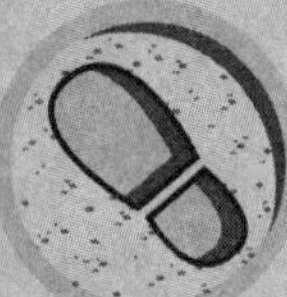

Trace and Write 6

Directions: Trace the number. Trace the word.

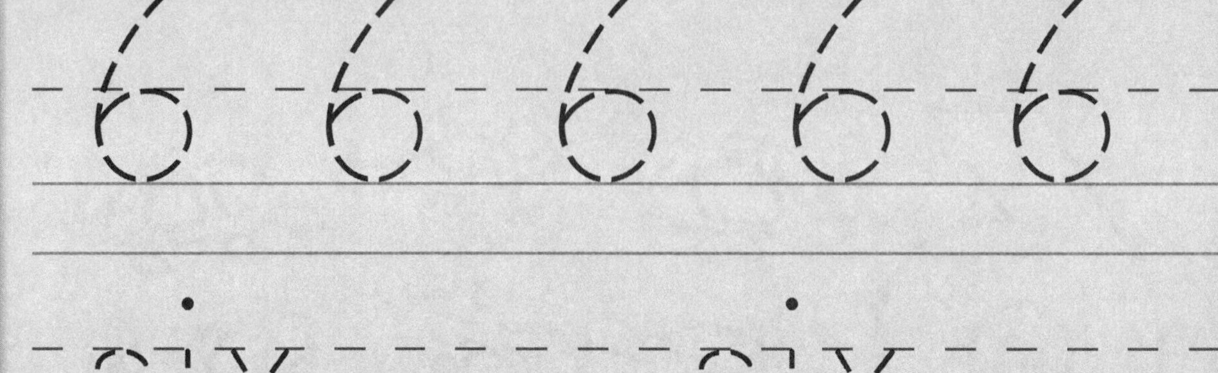

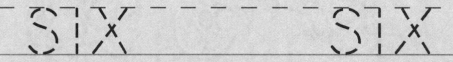

Directions: Now practice writing the number and the word by yourself on the lines below.

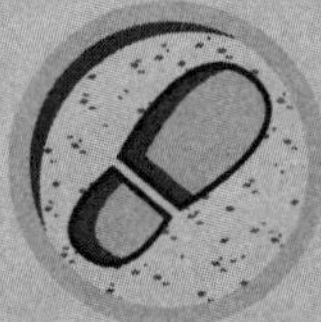

One Step Further
Look around the room and find six things that are red. What did you find?

Number 6

Directions: Circle **6** things in each box. Write the number **6** on each line.

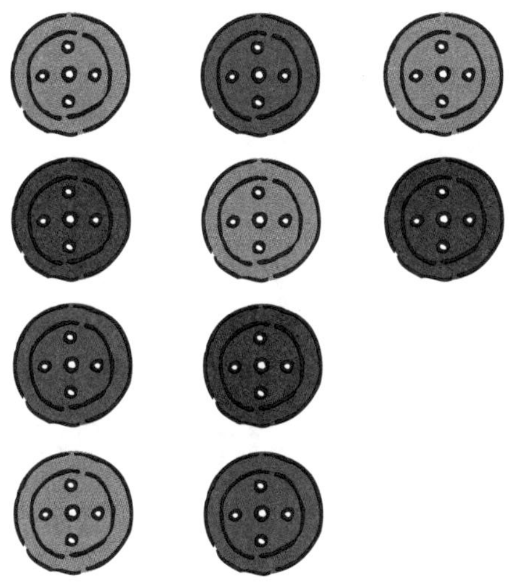

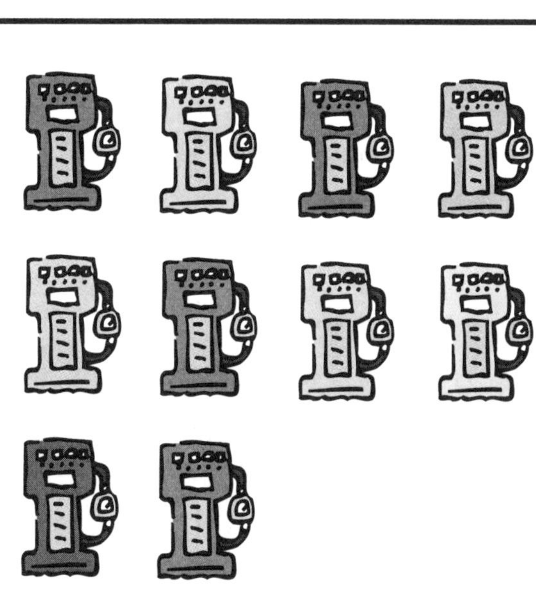

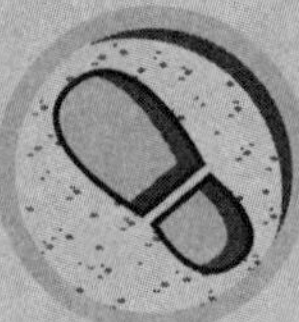

One Step Further
Look outside. Count the first six cars you see. What color are those cars?

Seven 7

Directions: Color the number **7** as well as the seven butterflies.

Directions: Circle the boxes that show **7**.

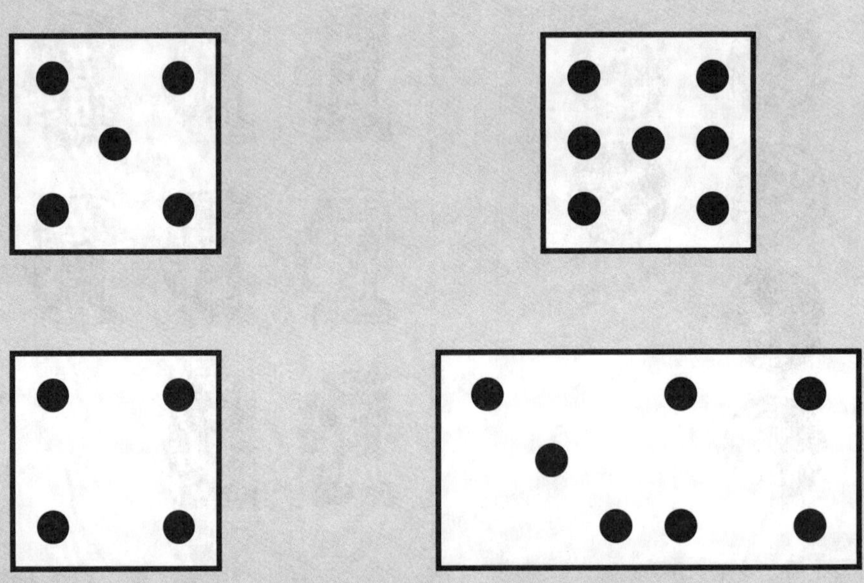

One Step Further

Draw seven flowers for the butterflies to land on. Color them your favorite color.

Trace and Write 7

Directions: Trace the number. Trace the word.

7 7 7 7 7

seven seven

Directions: Now practice writing the number and the word by yourself on the lines below.

One Step Further

Look through this book. Can you find seven pictures of dogs or any other animals?

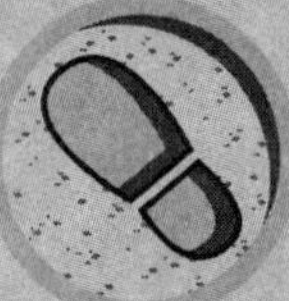

Number 7

Directions: Circle **7** things on each shelf.

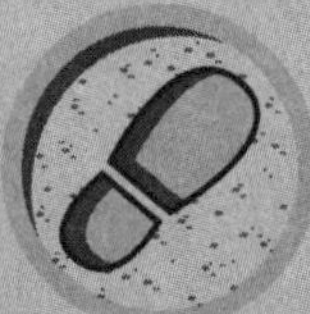

One Step Further

What are seven things you might buy at a grocery store?

Eight 8

Directions: Color the number **8** as well as the eight bees.

Directions: Circle the boxes that show **8**.

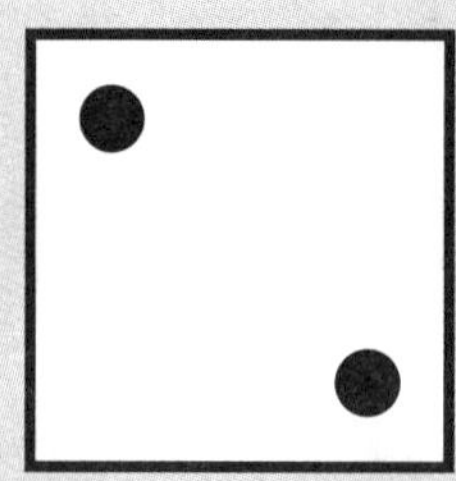

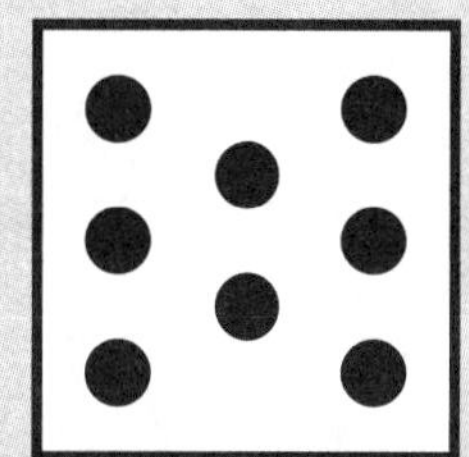

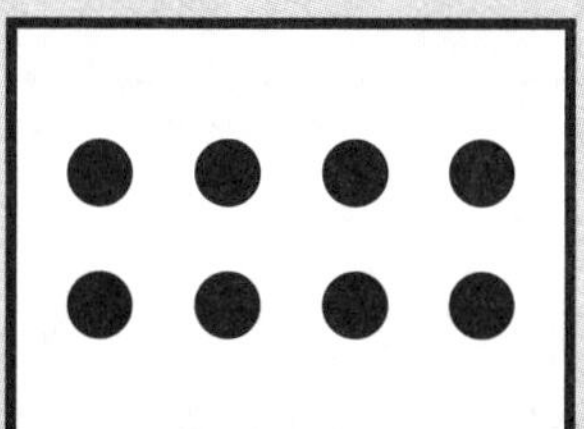

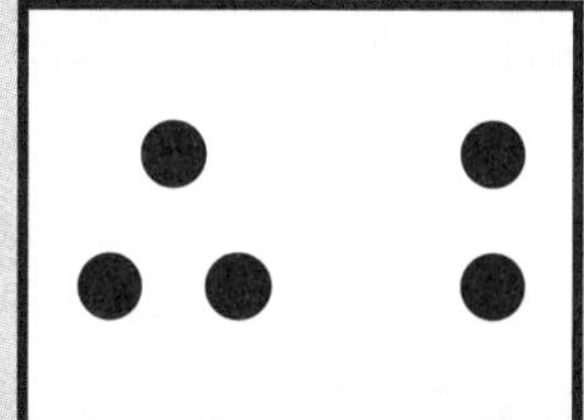

One Step Further

Name an animal that has eight legs.
How many legs do you have?

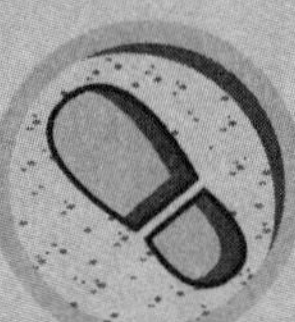

Trace and Write 8

Directions: Trace the number. Trace the word.

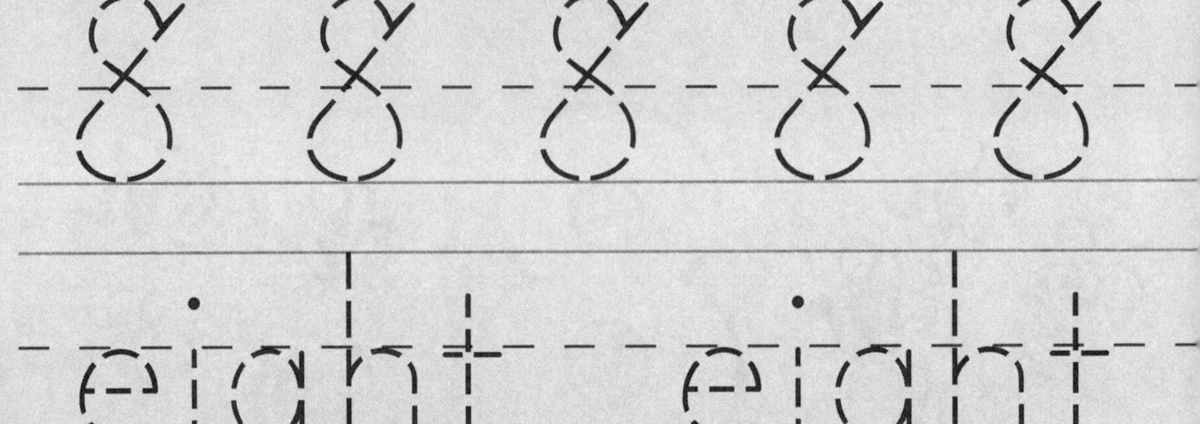

Directions: Now practice writing the number and the word by yourself on the lines below.

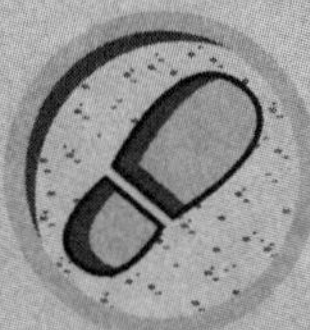

One Step Further

Draw eight circles. Color each circle a different color.

Number 8

Directions: Put these **8** shoes into pairs. Draw a line to match each shoe on the left with a shoe that is the same on the right.

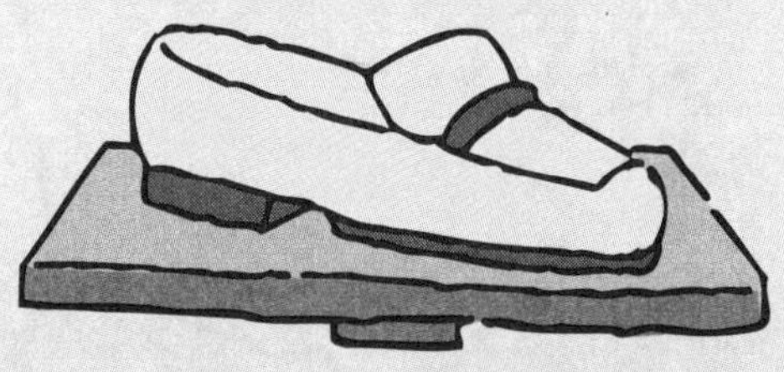
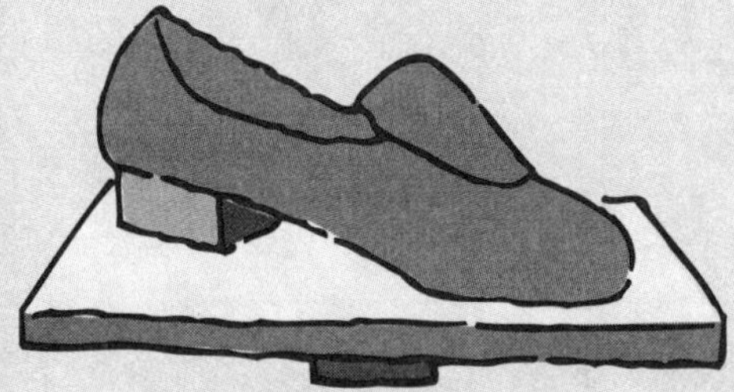

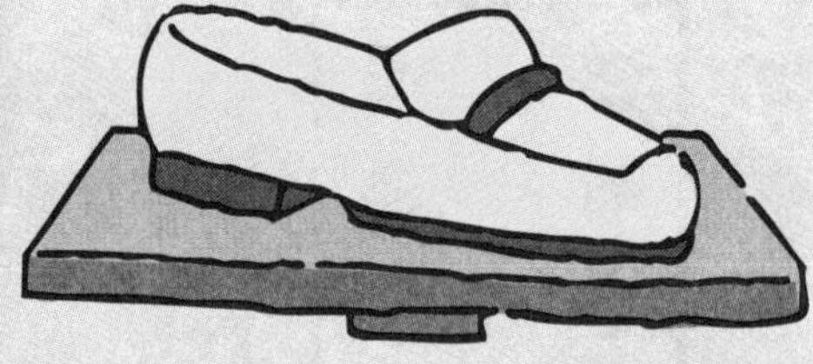

One Step Further

Find your favorite pair of shoes. Put them on and walk eight steps.

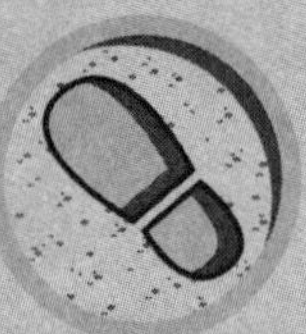

Nine 9

Directions: Color the number **9** as well as the nine birds.

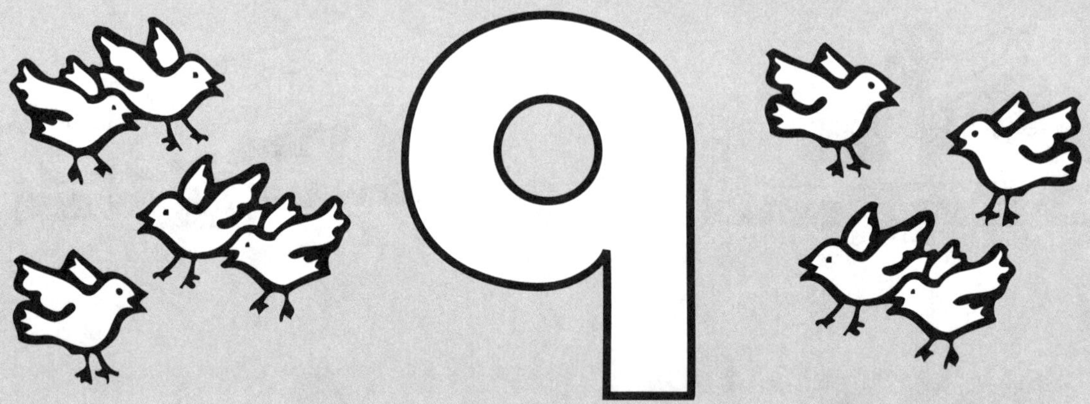

Directions: Circle the boxes that show **9**.

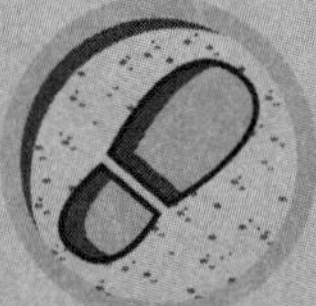

One Step Further

Name nine things you do every day.
What is your favorite thing to do?

Trace and Write 9

Directions: Trace the number. Trace the word.

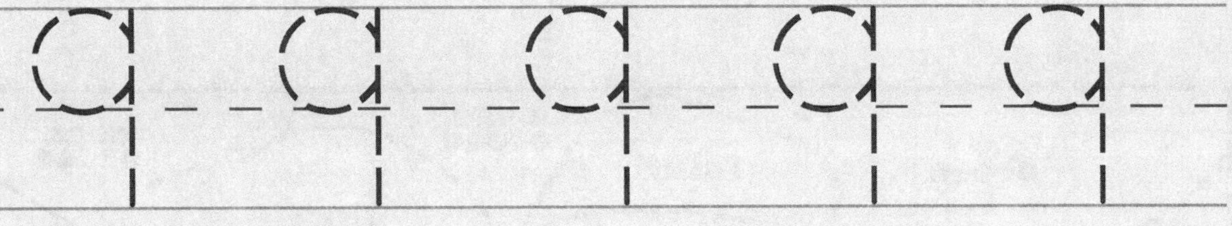

Directions: Now practice writing the number and the word by yourself on the lines below.

One Step Further

Look outside for nine things that are green. What did you find?

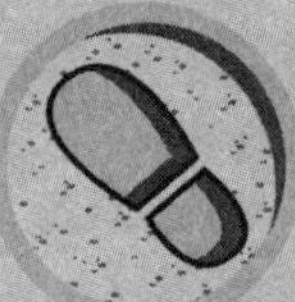

Number 9

Directions: Color the spaces: 9 = **white**, ●●●●●●●●● = **blue**, and nine = **red**.

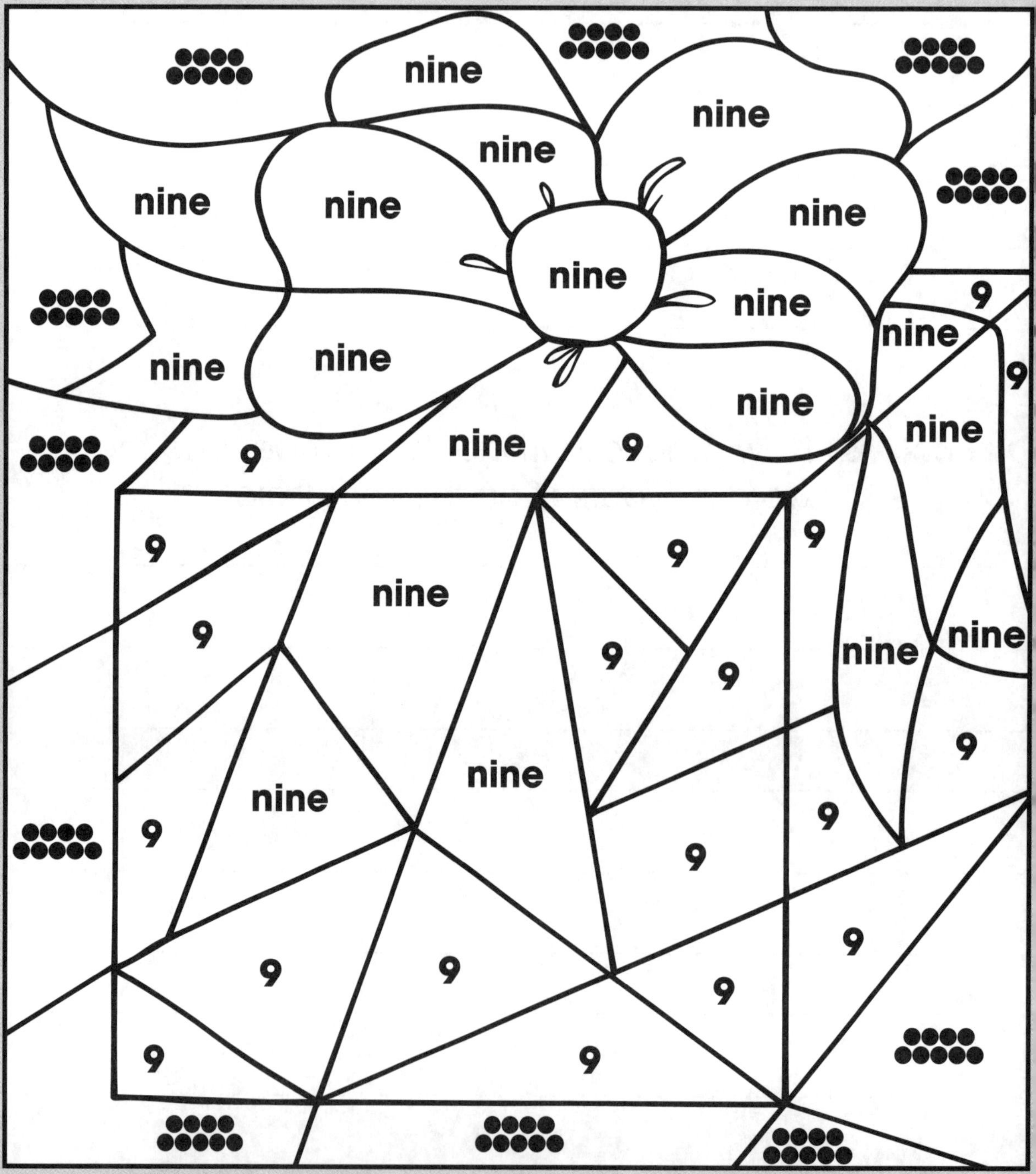

One Step Further

Create a gift and give it to a friend. What did your friend say about the gift?

Ten 10

Directions: Color the number **10** as well as the ten chipmunks.

Directions: Circle the boxes that show **10**.

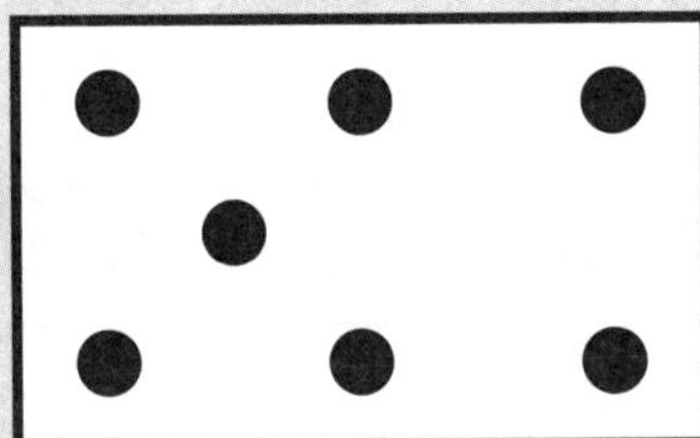

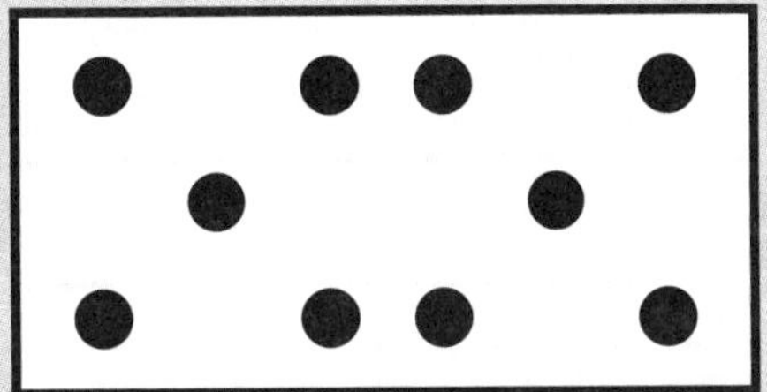

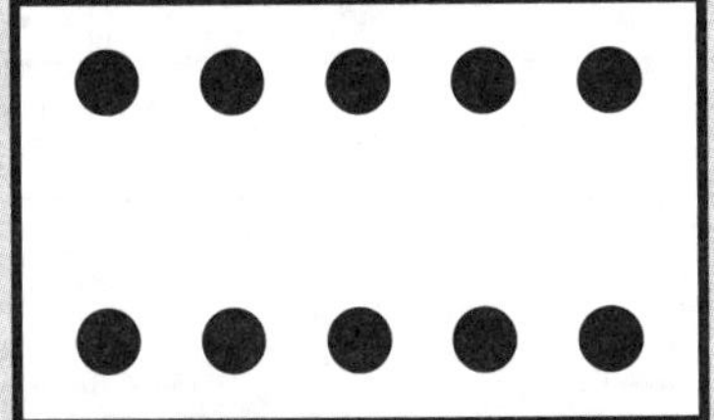

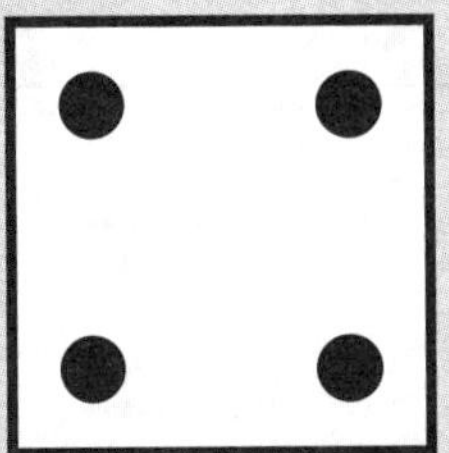

One Step Further

Count to 10. Can you count backward? Walk backward for 10 steps.

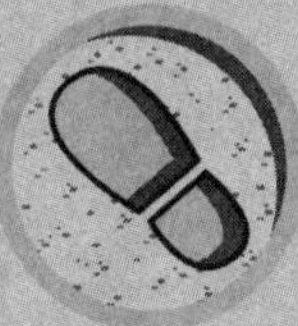

Trace and Write 10

Directions: Trace the number. Trace the word.

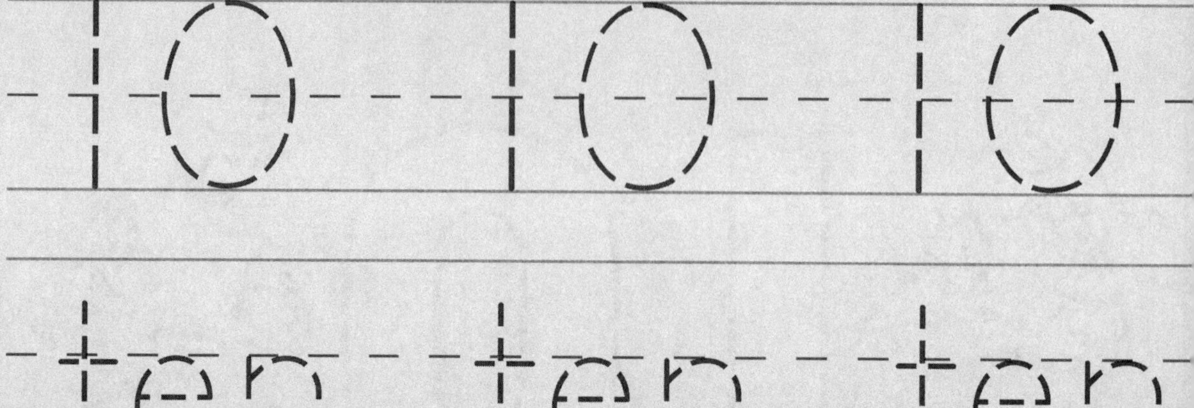

Directions: Now practice writing the number and the word by yourself on the lines below.

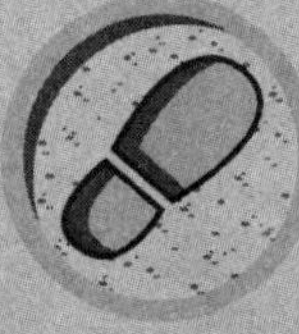

One Step Further

Find your favorite book.
Read the first 10 words.

Number 10

Directions: Draw **10** leaves on the branches for the caterpillar to eat.

One Step Further

Go outside and find 10 leaves.
Were they on a tree or on the ground?

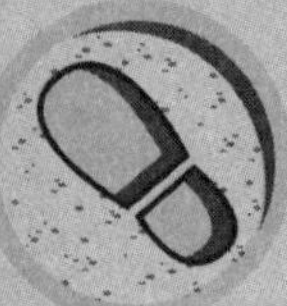

Numbers 0–10

Review

Directions: Color the correct number of marbles in each bag.

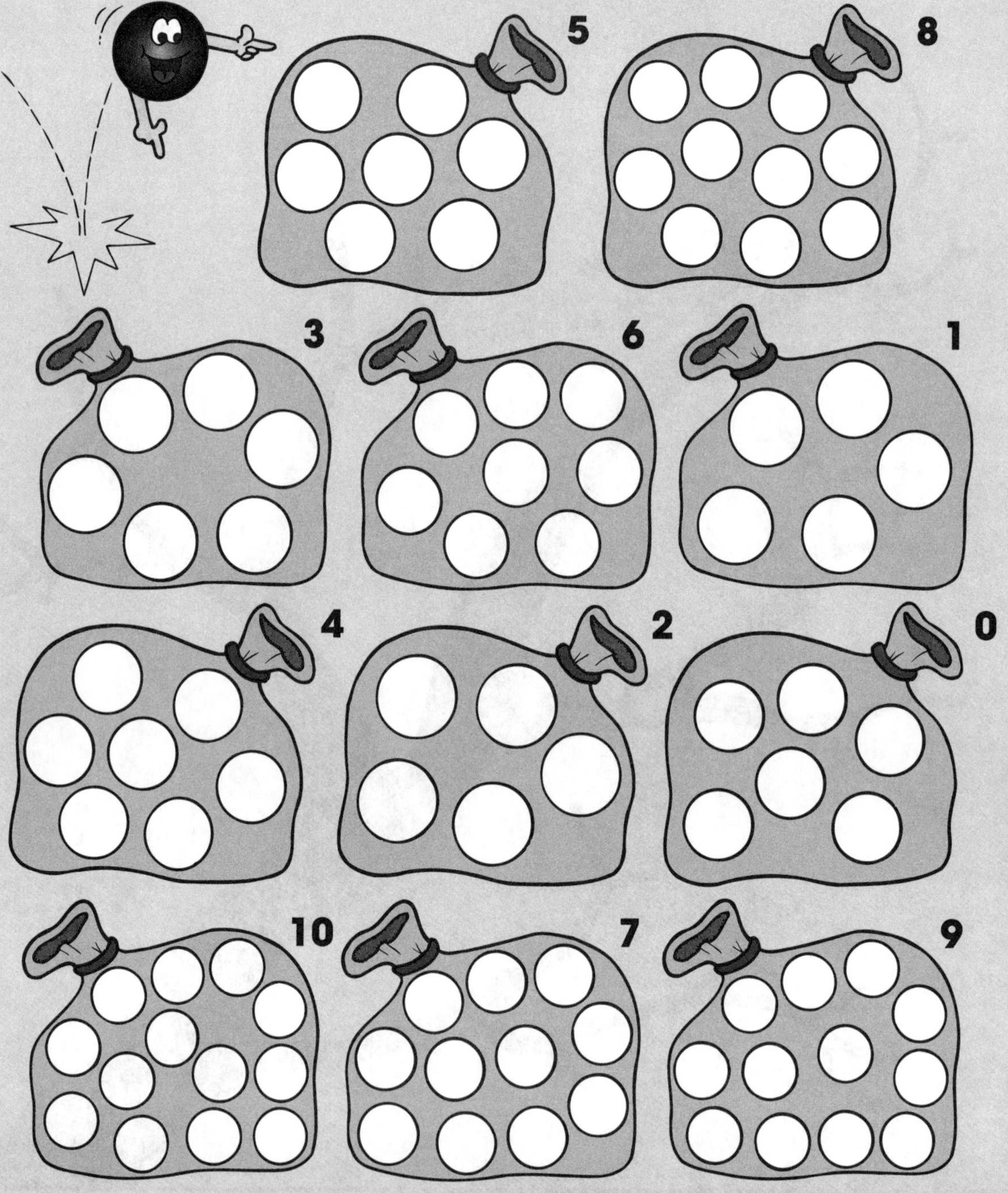

5

8

3

6

1

4

2

0

10

7

9

MATH

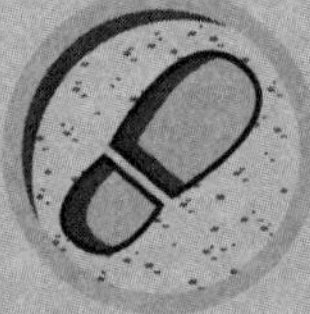

One Step Further

Fill a bag with 10 small objects. Ask a friend to guess how many objects are in the bag.

Numbers 0–10

Directions: Count each picture. Write the number on each line.

______

______

______

______

______

______

______

______

______

______

One Step Further

Find 10 plastic cups. Stack them in a pyramid as high as you can.

Numbers 0–10

Directions: Draw an **X** on the extra things in each row.

2

5

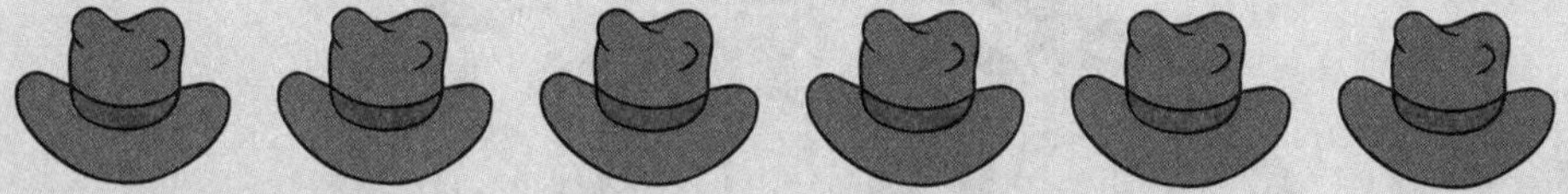

10

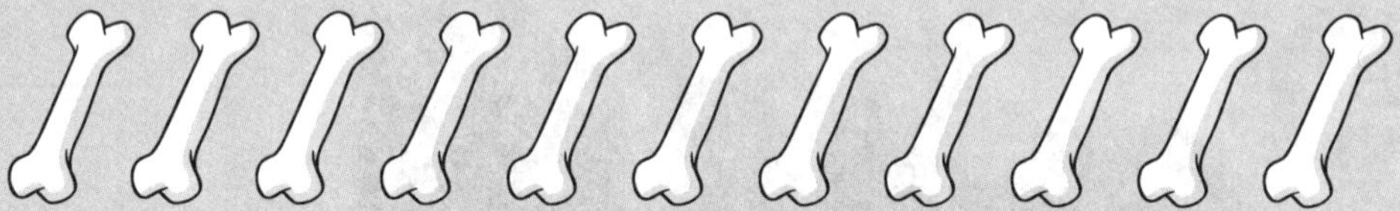

6

1

7

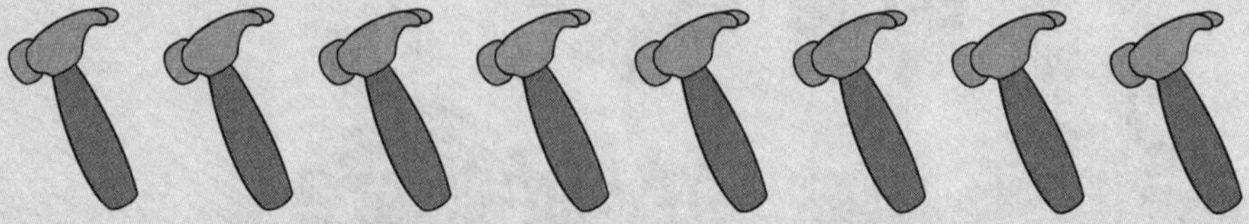

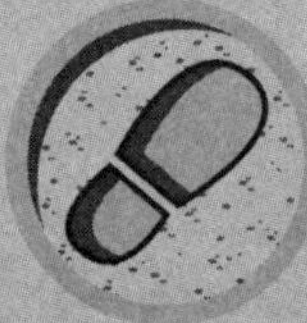

One Step Further

Choose an object on this page.
Can you find it in your home?

Ordinal Numbers

Directions: Circle the **third** person in line. Draw a line under the **second** person.

Directions: Draw an **X** on the **first** person on the bench. Draw a hat on the **fifth** person.

One Step Further

Line up with your friends in a row. Who is the fourth person in line?

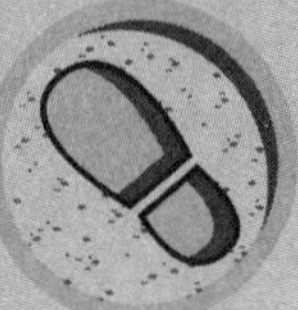

Ordinal Numbers

Directions: Draw an **X** on the **fifth** tree. Draw a box around the third tree.

Directions: Draw a line under the **second** tree. Circle the **first** tree.

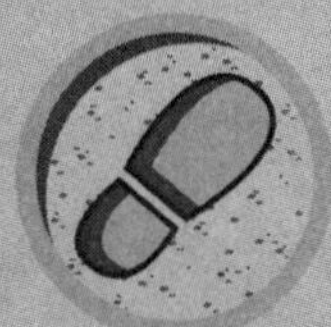

One Step Further

Look around your neighborhood.
What color is the fourth car you see?

Ordinal Numbers

Directions: Circle the **second** box. Draw a **green** line under the **fifth** box.

Directions: Draw **red** dots on the **third** box. Draw a **blue** bow on the **fourth** box.

One Step Further

What do you think is inside the boxes? Tell a story about the picture.

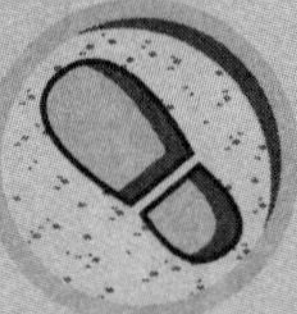

Ordinal Numbers

Directions: Look at the pictures. What happened **first**? What happened **second**? What happened **third**? Draw a line from the correct word to the picture.

first

second

third

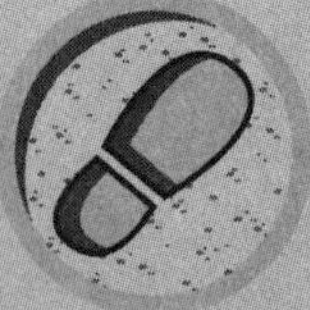

One Step Further

What is the first thing you did today?
What is the first thing you will do tomorrow?

Ordinal Numbers

Directions: Write **1**, **2**, and **3** in the boxes to show what happens **first**, **second**, and **third**.

One Step Further

It's time for dinner! What is the first thing you do? What is the second?

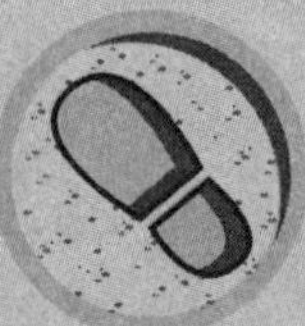

More

Directions: Circle the group that has **more**.

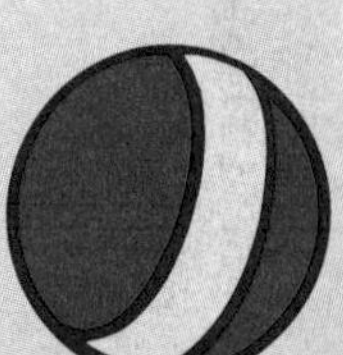

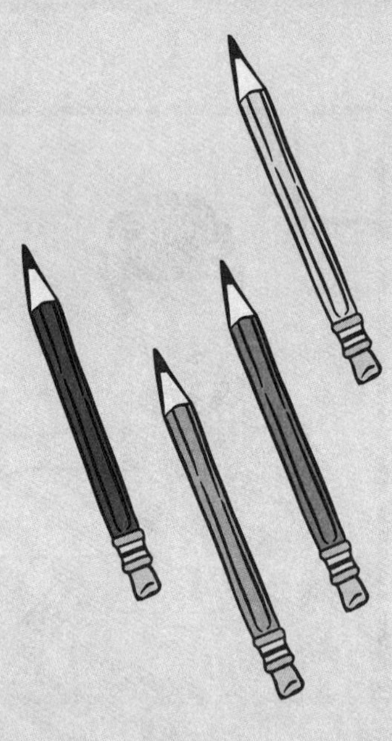

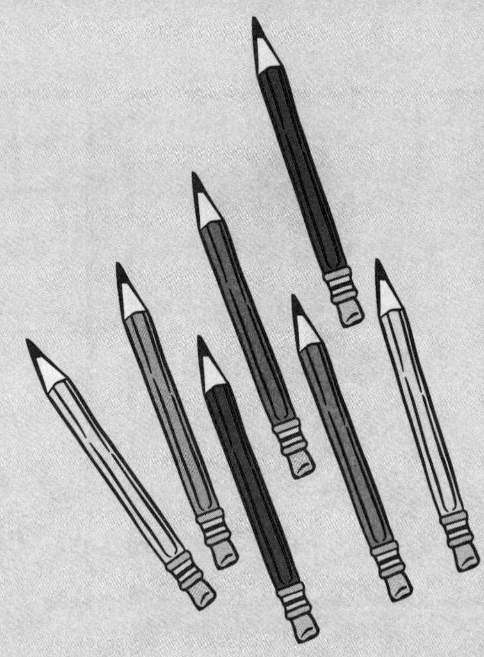

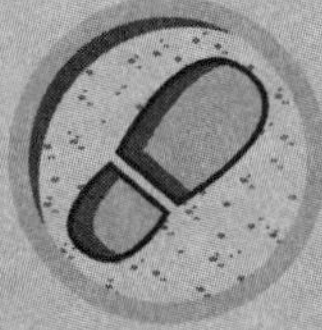

One Step Further

Put a group of crayons in two piles.
Which pile has more crayons?

Fewer

Directions: Color the group that has **fewer**.

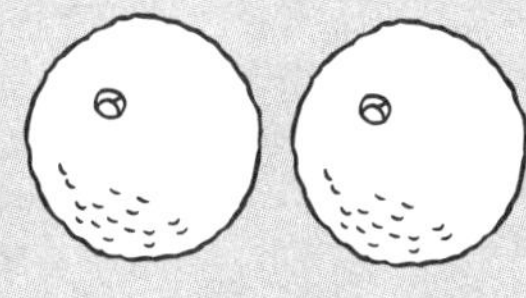
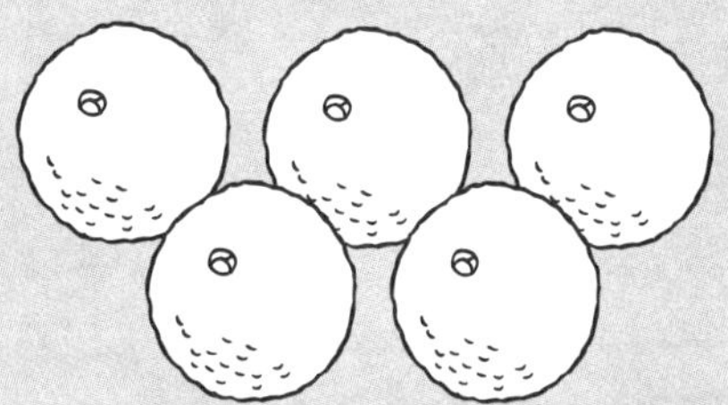

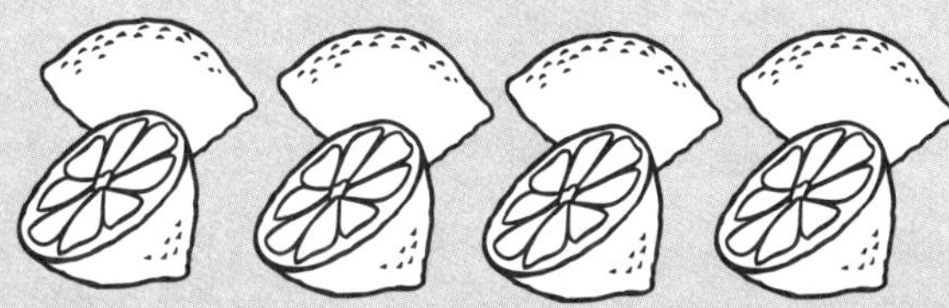
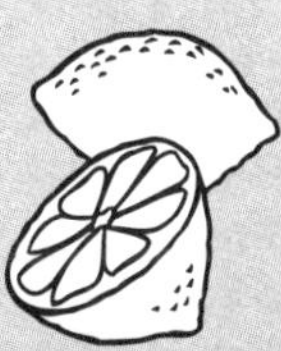

One Step Further

Find two objects in your kitchen.
Which do you see fewer of?

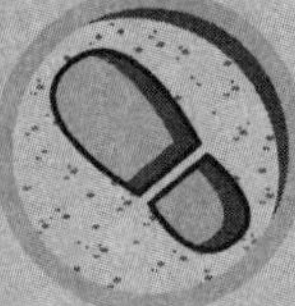

More

Directions: Count the blocks each child is playing with. Circle the child who has **more** blocks.

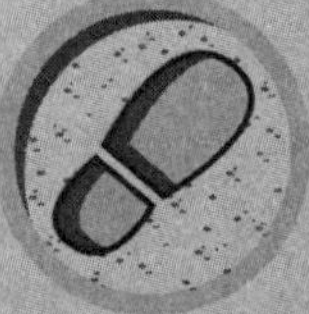

One Step Further

Count the blocks you own. Do you have more than the children on this page?

Fewer

Directions: Count the cars each child is playing with. Circle the child who has **fewer** cars.

One Step Further

What game do you like to play with toy cars?
How many toy cars do you own?

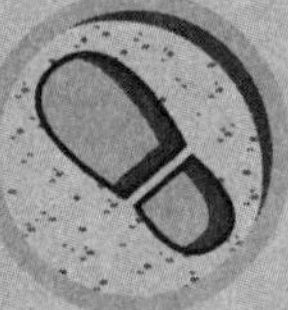

More

Directions: Count the blocks in the first group. Then, draw a group of blocks that has **more**.

A

B

C

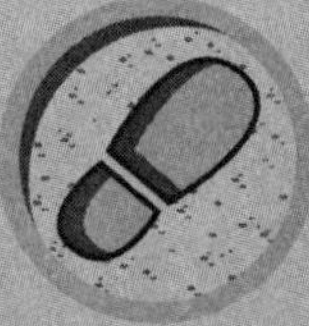

One Step Further

Look around you. How many windows do you see? Draw a group of more windows.

Patterns

Directions: Complete the shape patterns. At the end of the row, draw the shape that comes next. Then, color the shape.

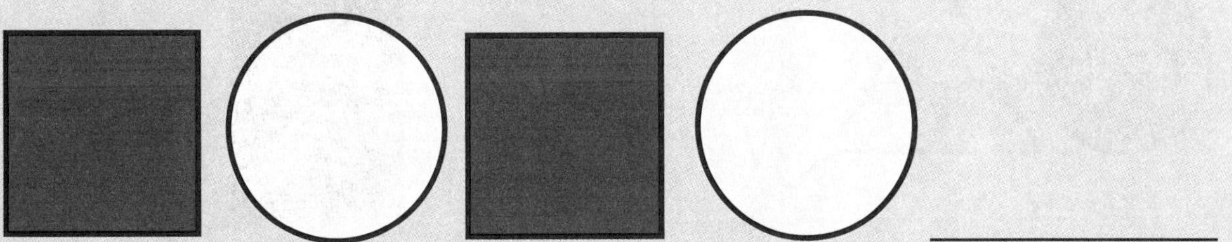

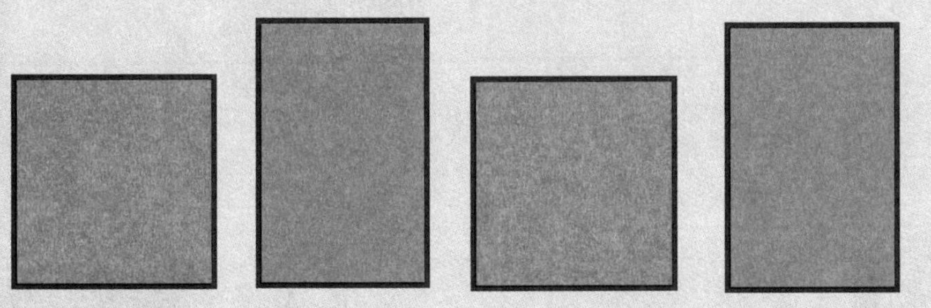

MATH

One Step Further
Create your own pattern of shapes. Ask a friend to draw what comes next.

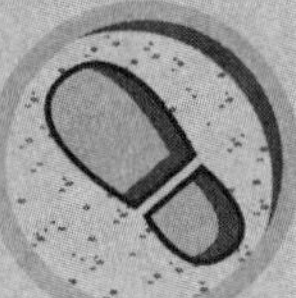

Patterns

Directions: Draw a line to match the shape patterns on the left with the shape patterns on the right.

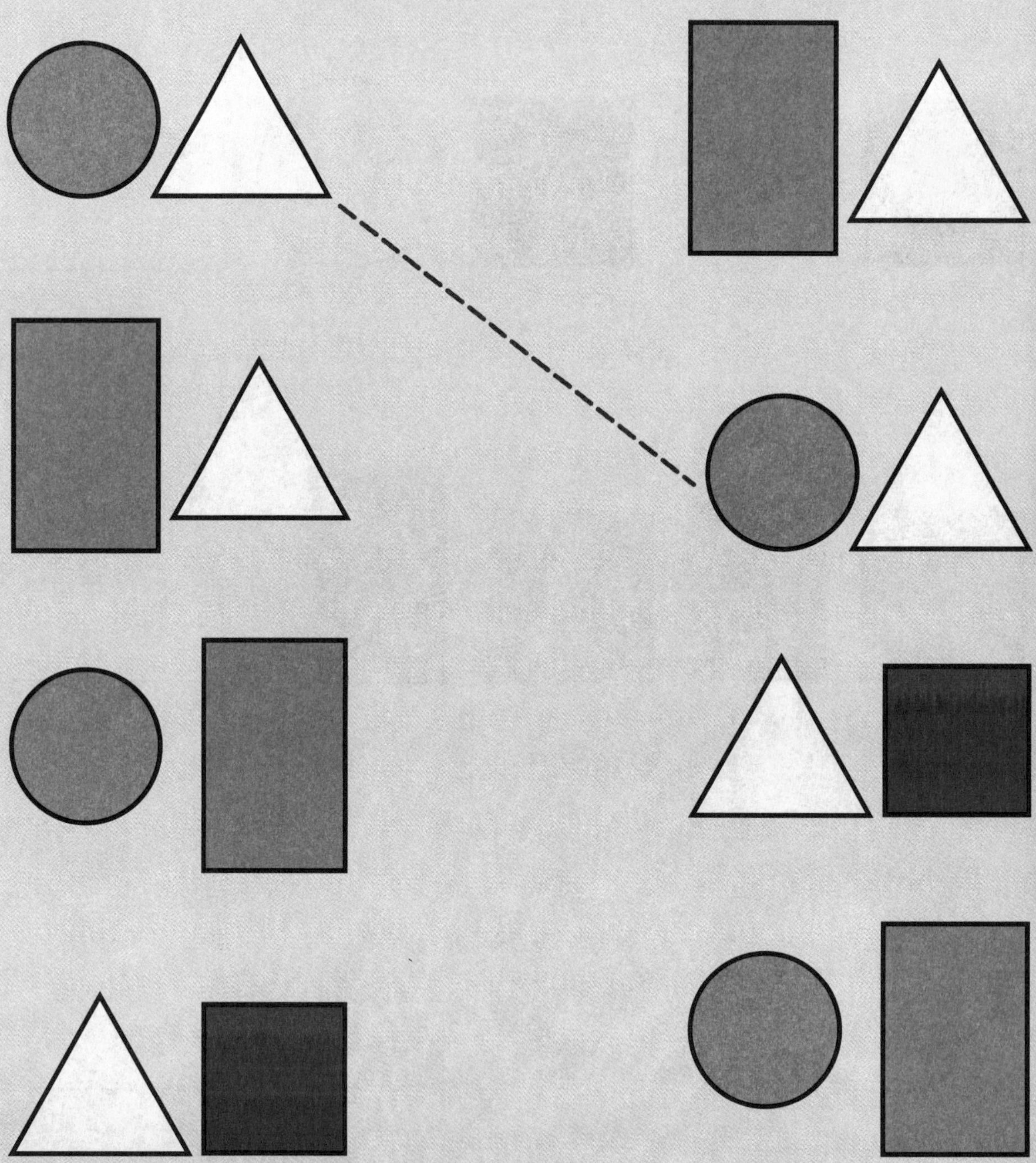

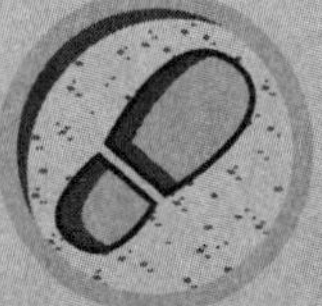

One Step Further

Look around your home or classroom.
Do you see any patterns?

Patterns

Directions: What comes next? Draw the picture that comes next in each row.

    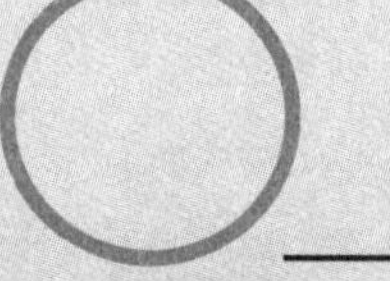

 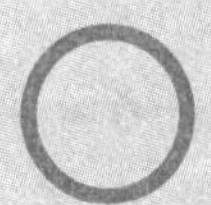   

One Step Further

Play a game of tic-tac-toe with a friend. What patterns do you see on the grid?

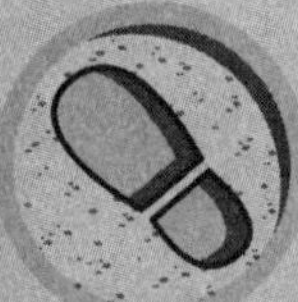

Patterns

Directions: Look at the beads in each row. Color the shape that comes next in the pattern.

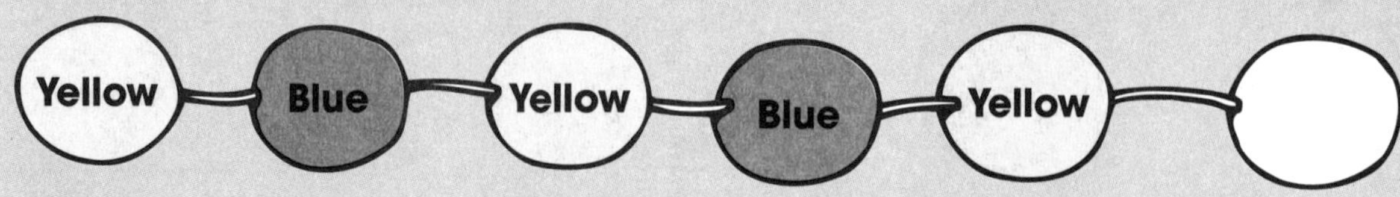

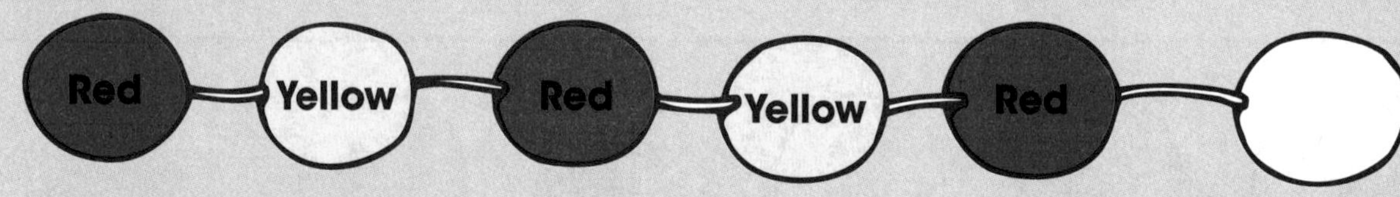

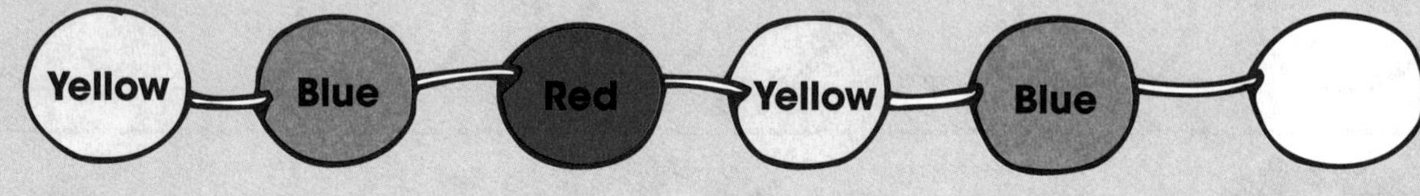

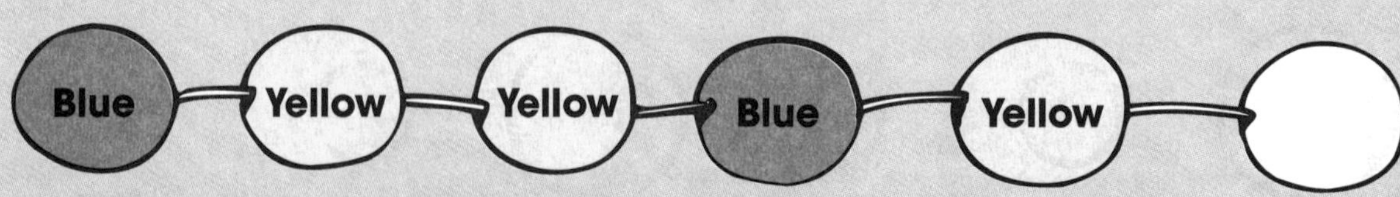

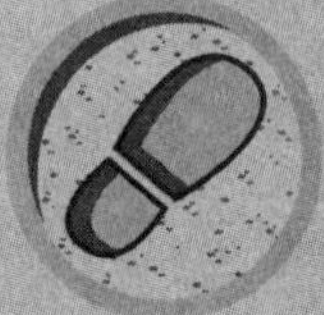

One Step Further

Find several objects, like coins or cotton balls. How many patterns can you make?

Patterns

Directions: Complete the number patterns. At the end of the row, write the number that comes next.

1 2 1 2 1 ____

3 4 4 3 4 ____

8 7 8 7 8 ____

One Step Further

Create your own number pattern. Ask a friend to guess what number comes next.

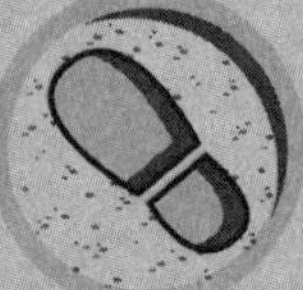

MATH

One Half

Directions: Color one half of each shape. The first one has been done for you.

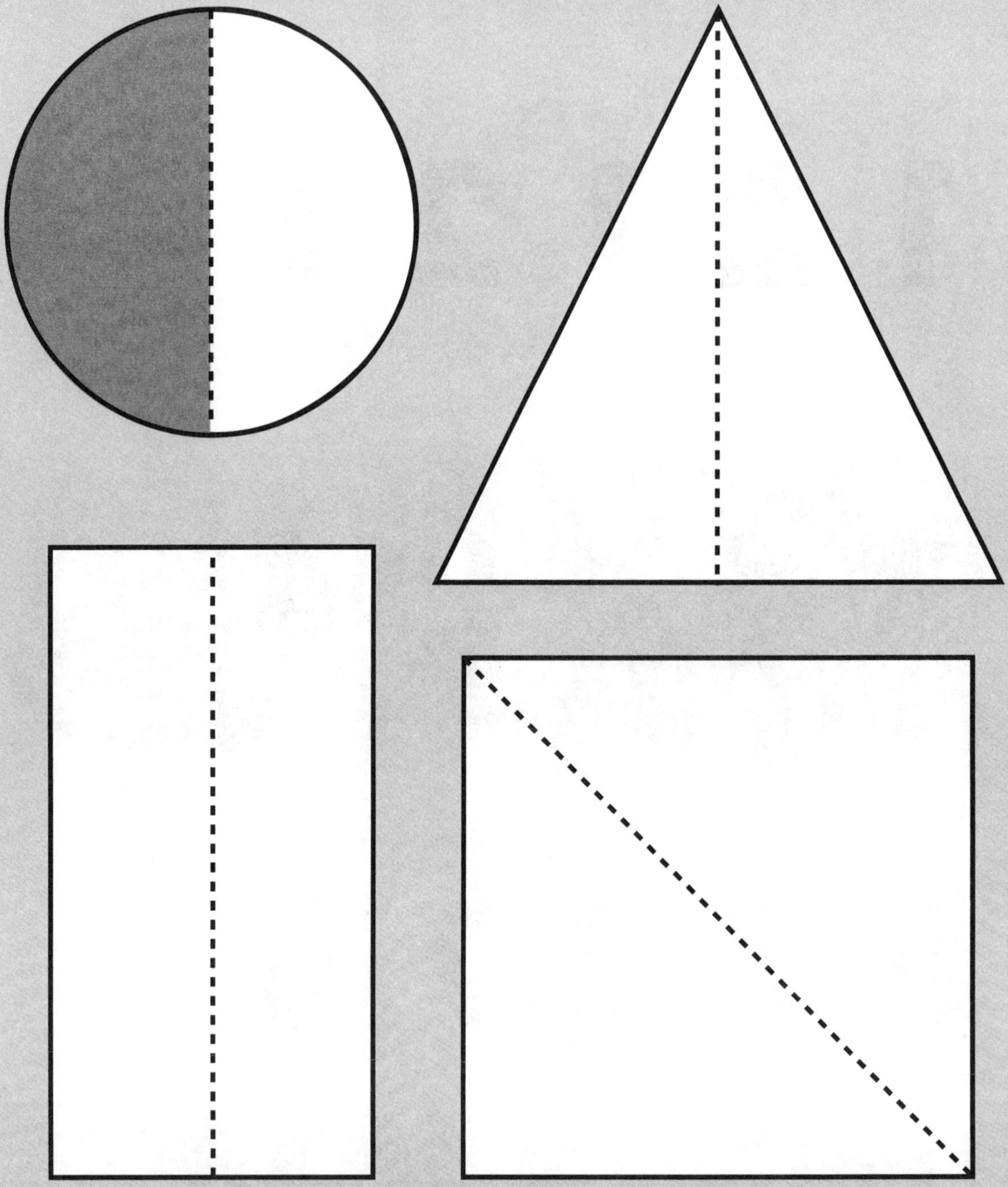

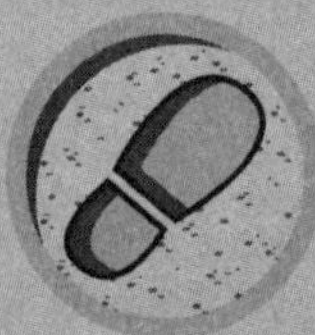

One Step Further

Find a piece of blank paper. Fold it in half. Color each half a different color.

Half

Directions: These things have been cut in half! Draw the halves that are missing. Then, color the pictures.

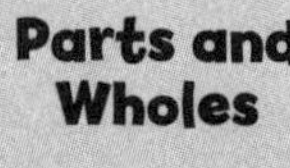

One Step Further
Pour a cup of water. Dump half of the water in the sink. How much is left?

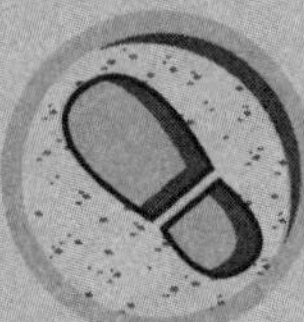

Half

Directions: Draw the other half of this clown. Then, color the picture.

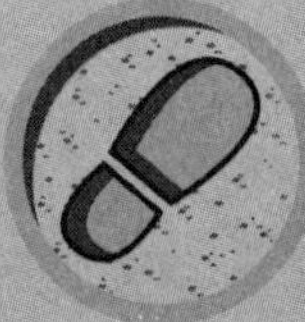

One Step Further

Draw half of a house. Then, draw the other half to complete the picture.

Half and Half

Directions: How many circles are there?

Circle your answer. **1 2 3 4 5 6 7 8**

Color half of each circle a different color.
How many different colors did you use?

Circle your answer. **1 2 3 4 5 6 7 8**

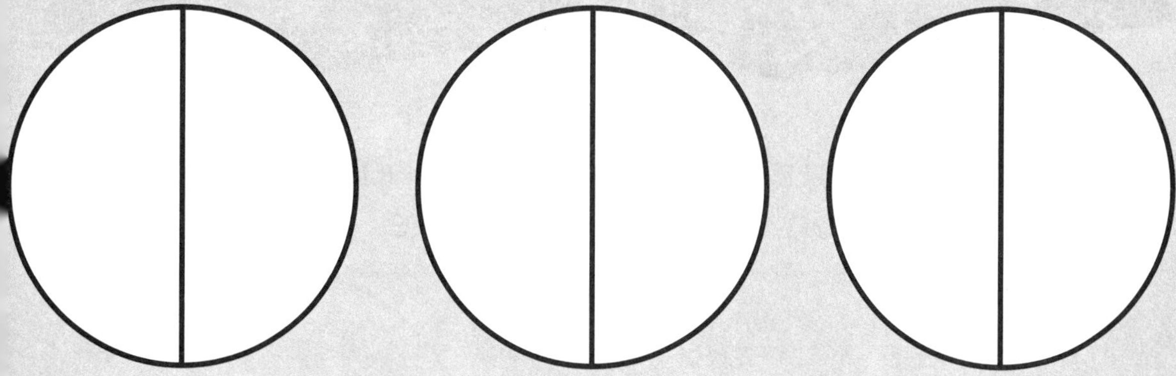

Directions: Draw three circles. Color half of each one a different color.

One Step Further

Find several cotton balls. Put half the cotton balls in one pile and half in another.

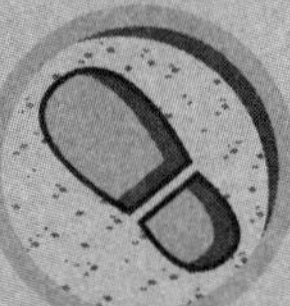

Parts and Wholes

Which one would you rather have: **1** piece of a candy bar cut into **3** pieces or **1** piece of the same-sized candy bar cut into **9** pieces?

Directions: Circle your answer.

1 piece of 3 **1 piece of 9**

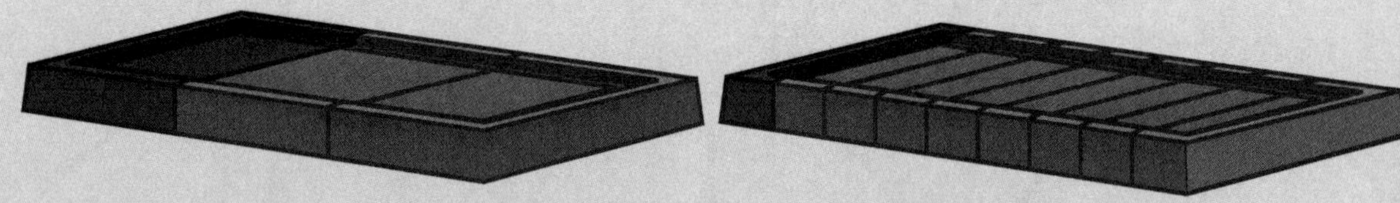

Directions: Color half of each shape below. Use a different color for each one.

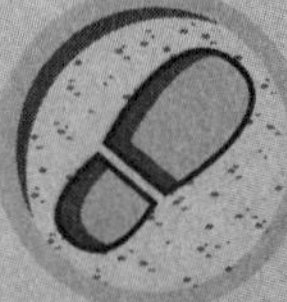

One Step Further

Ask an adult to cut one piece of fruit into three pieces, and another into six pieces.

Parts and Wholes

Mom cut a pie into eight pieces. Her children ate half ($\frac{1}{2}$) of the pie for dessert. How many pieces were left?

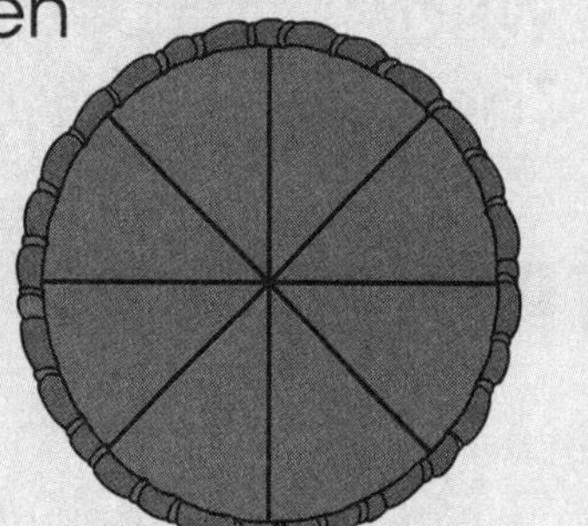

Directions: Circle your answer.

0 1 2 3 4 5 6 7 8

Directions: Color only half of the circles in each row below. Use a different color for each one.

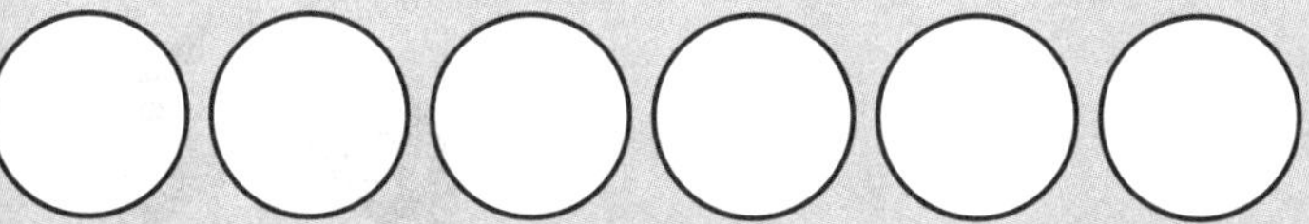

How many circles are **not** colored?

Directions: Circle your answer.

0 1 2 3 4 5 6 7 8

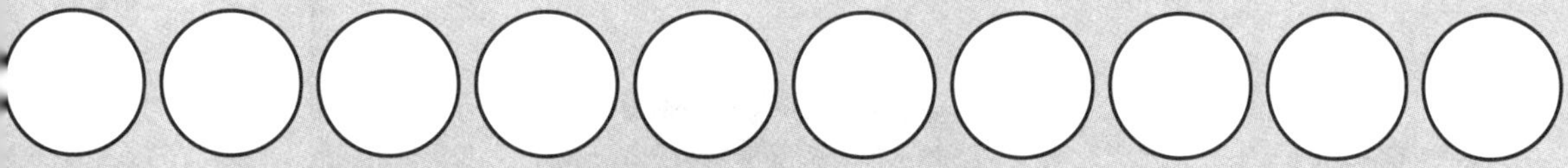

How many circles are **not** colored?

Directions: Circle your answer.

0 1 2 3 4 5 6 7 8

One Step Further

What is your favorite kind of pie?
How many slices of pie do you eat at once?

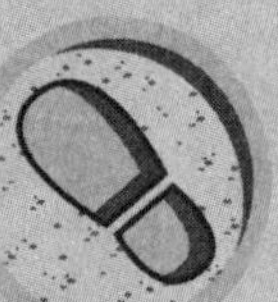

Face Clocks: Introduction

What is the best way to tell what time it is? Look at a clock. There are all kinds of clocks.

Directions: Circle the ones you have seen.

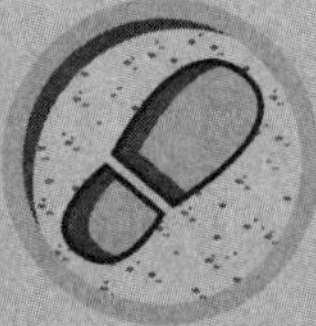

One Step Further

Look around you. How many types of clocks can you see right now?

Face Clocks: Identifying Parts

A clock can tell you what time it is. A clock has different parts.

Directions: Read and trace each part of the clock.

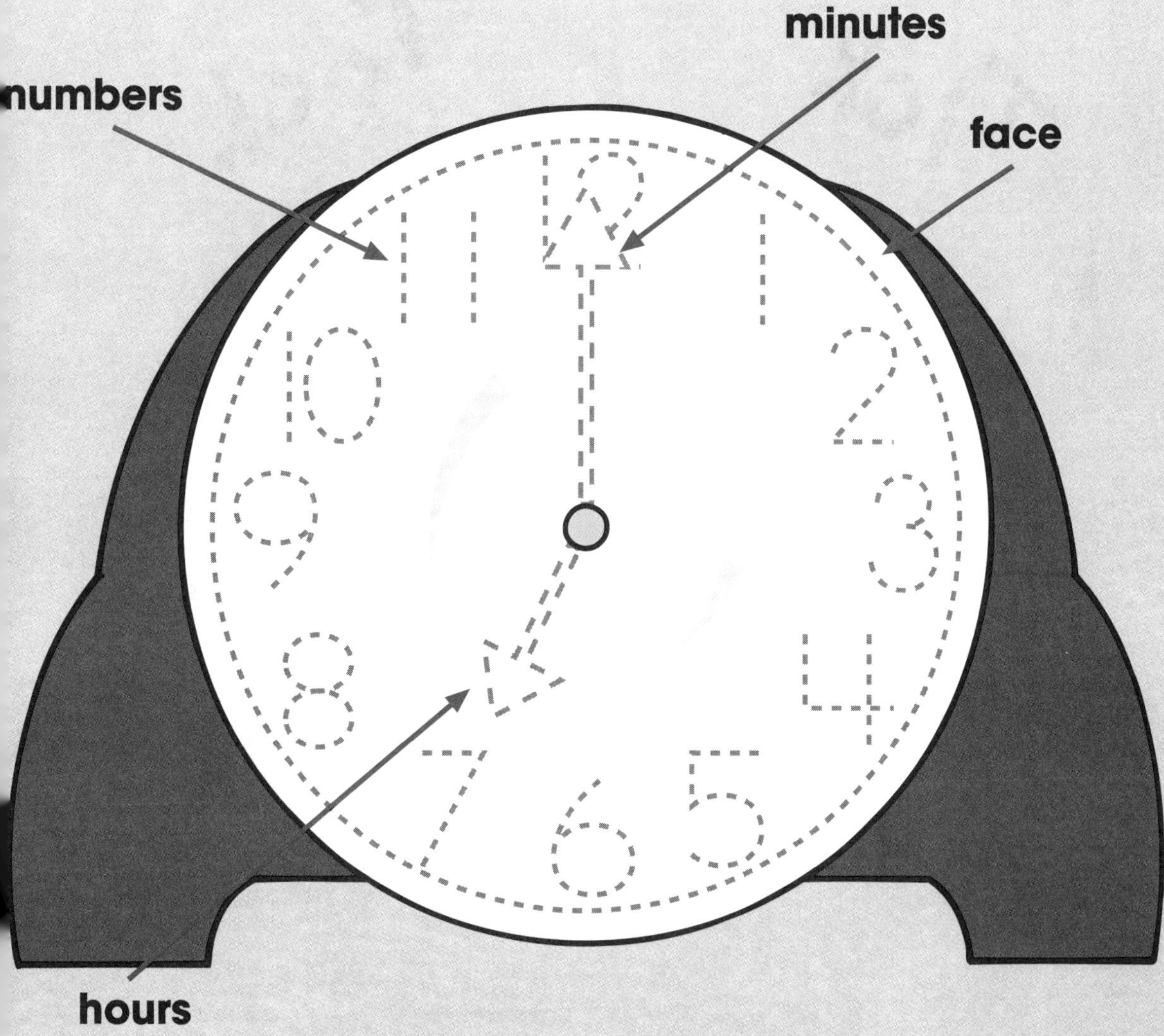

minutes

numbers

face

12 1 2 3 4 5 6 7 8 9 10 11

hours

The **BIG HAND** tells the minutes.
The **little hand** tells the hour.

One Step Further

Look at a clock. Where is the big hand right now? Where is the little hand?

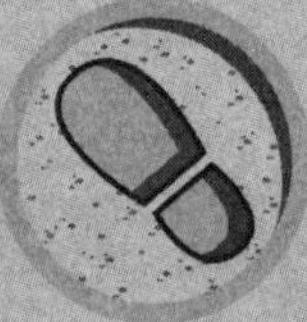

Face Clocks: Identifying Parts

Directions: A clock has numbers. Trace the numbers on the clock.

Tick Tock

12 1 2 3 4 5 6 7 8 9 10 11

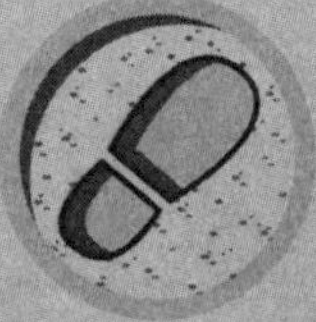

One Step Further

What time does your clock say when you get up in the morning?

Writing the Time

A clock tells us the time.

Directions: Write the numbers on the clock face. Draw the **BIG HAND** to **12**. Draw the **little hand** to **5**.

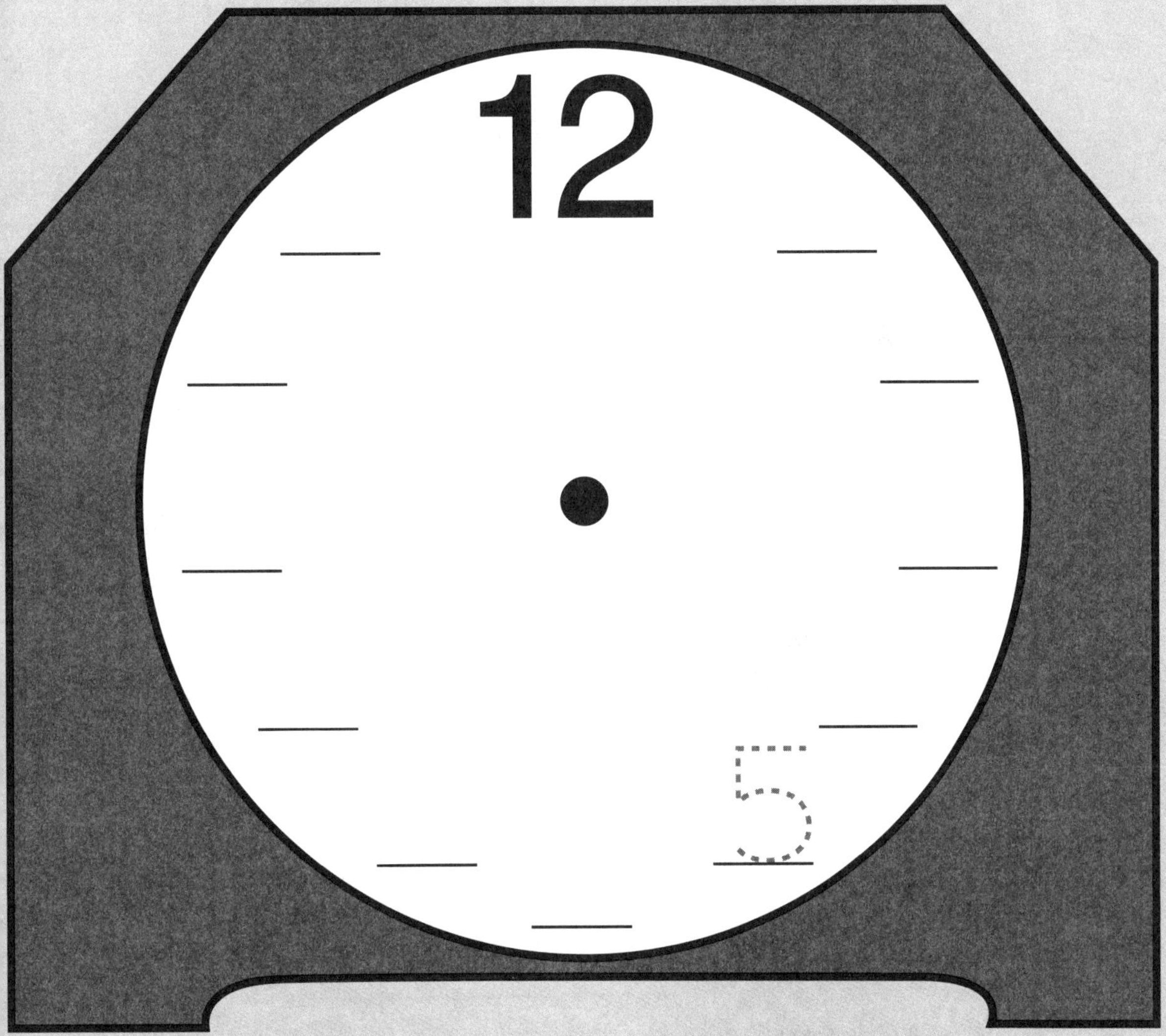

12

5

What time is it? ____________ o'clock.

One Step Further

Draw a clock. Draw where the big and little hands are when it is your bedtime.

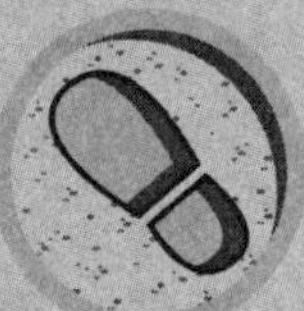

Writing the Time

An **hour** is **sixty minutes** long. It takes an hour for the **BIG HAND** to go around the clock. When the **BIG HAND** is on **12**, and the **little hand** points to a number, that is the **hour**!

Directions: The **BIG HAND** is on the **12**. Color it **red**. The **little hand** is on the **8**. Color it **blue**.

The **BIG HAND** is on ______________.

The **little hand** is on ______________.

It is ______8______ o'clock.

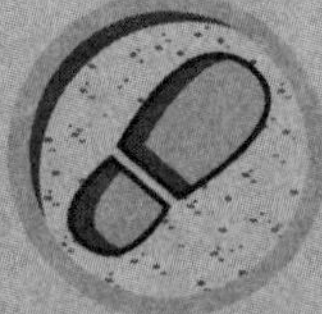

One Step Further

How many minutes does it take to brush your teeth? Watch the clock to time yourself.

Writing the Time

Directions: Color the **little hour hand red**. Fill in the blanks.

The **BIG HAND** is on ______.

The **little hand** is on ______.

It is ______ o'clock.

The **BIG HAND** is on ______.

The **little hand** is on ______.

It is ______ o'clock.

The **BIG HAND** is on ______.

The **little hand** is on ______.

It is ______ o'clock.

The **BIG HAND** is on ______.

The **little hand** is on ______.

It is ______ o'clock.

One Step Further

Look at the times on this page. On a normal day, where are you at these times?

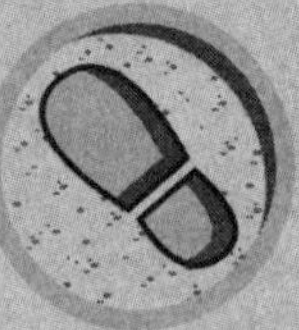

Drawing the Hour Hand

If the **BIG HAND** is on 12, it is easy to tell the time. Look and see the hour.

Directions: Trace the **little hand** to make the hour **10 o'clock**.

The **BIG HAND** is on ______________.

The **little hand** is on ______________.

It is ______________ o'clock.

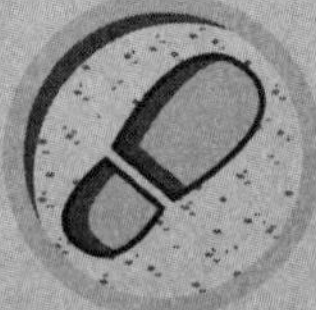

One Step Further

What time does your school start?
What time do you eat dinner?

Drawing the Hour Hand

Directions: Draw the **little hour hand** on each clock.

2 o'clock

12
1
2
3
4
5
6
7
8
9
10
11

10 o'clock

9 o'clock

One Step Further
What time do you eat lunch?
Have you eaten lunch yet today?

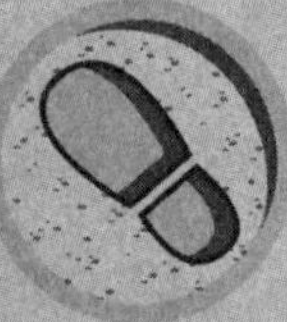

Drawing the Hour Hand

Directions: Draw the **little hour hand** on each clock.

4 o'clock

11 o'clock

5 o'clock

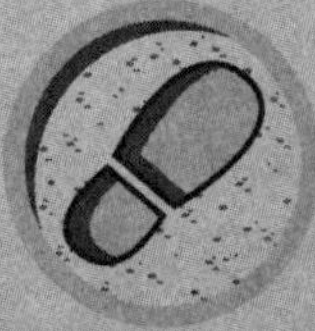

One Step Further

What time do you go to bed?
What do you do right before bedtime?

Circling the Hour Hand

Directions: Circle the **little hour hand** on each clock.
What time is it? Write the time below.

__________ o'clock

__________ o'clock

__________ o'clock

__________ o'clock

One Step Further

What is your favorite time of day?
What do you like about it?

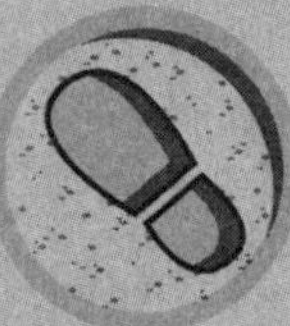

Time to the Half-Hour: Introduction

This clock face shows the time gone by since 8 o'clock. **Thirty minutes** or **half an hour** has gone by. There are three ways to say time to the half-hour. We say **eight thirty**, **thirty past eight**, or **half past eight**.

Directions: Write the times below.

9:00

9:30

30 minutes past 9 o'clock

____

____

__________ minutes past __________ o'clock

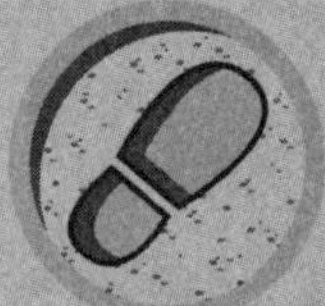

One Step Further

Draw a clock showing what time it is now. What activities have you done today?

Writing Time on the Half-Hour

Directions: Write the times below.

_______________ _______________

__________ minutes past __________ o'clock

_______________ _______________

__________ minutes past __________ o'clock

One Step Further

Look at the clock. Where will the big and little hands be 30 minutes from now?

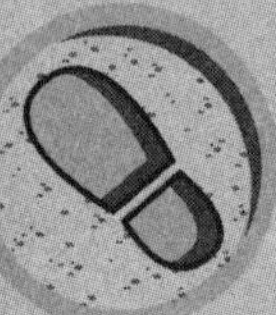

Writing Time on the Half-Hour

What time is it?

Directions: Write the times below.

half past ___________

half past ___________

half past ___________

half past ___________

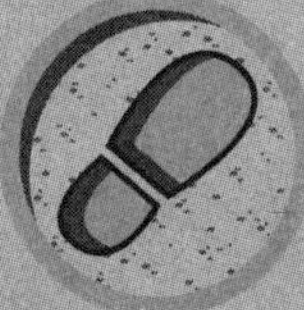

One Step Further

Where is the big hand on a clock right now?
What time is it?

Writing Time on the Half-Hour

Who "nose" these times?

Directions: Write the time under each clock. Color the noses.

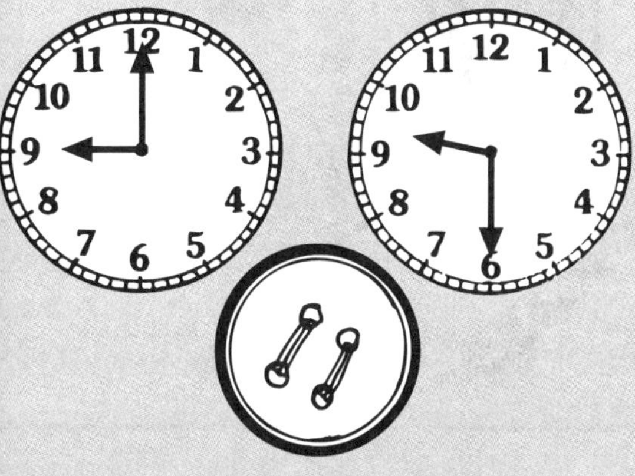

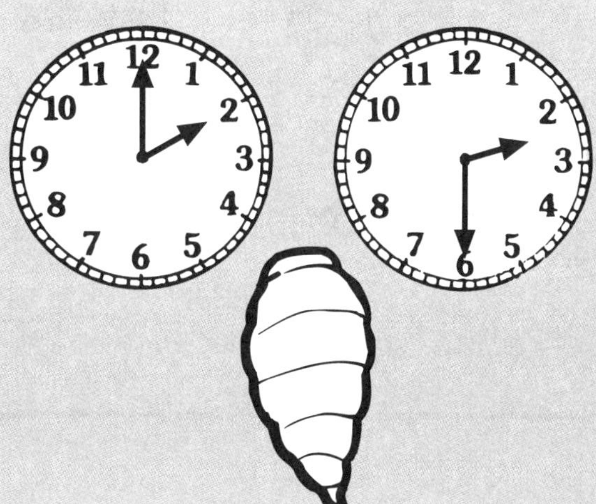

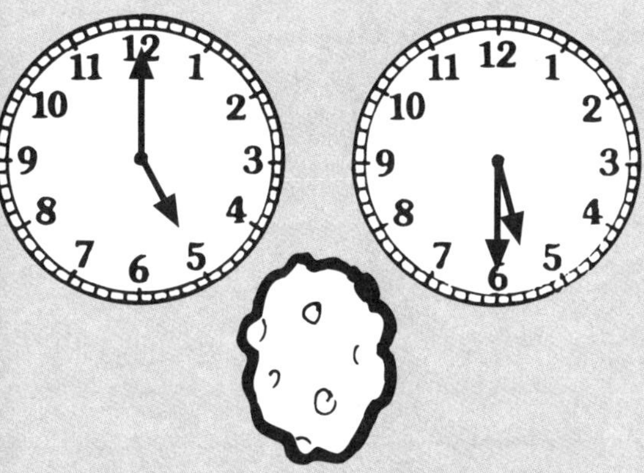

One Step Further

Where is the little hand on a clock right now? Touch your nose that number of times.

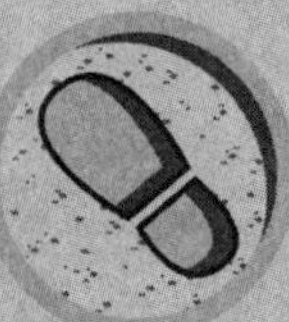

Favorite Time

Directions: Draw a special watch for yourself using some of these shapes. Show your favorite time of day.

My favorite time of day is ____________ o'clock.

One Step Further

Ask a friend about his or her favorite time of day. Draw a watch showing that time.

Important Hours

Directions: Write these important hours in your day.

_________ o'clock

_________ : 00

This is when I go to school.

_________ o'clock

_________ : 00

This is when I have dinner.

_________ o'clock

_________ : 00

This is when I watch my favorite TV program.

_________ o'clock

_________ : 00

This is when I would like to go to bed.

One Step Further

Ask a friend about his or her important hours. Are the answers the same as yours?

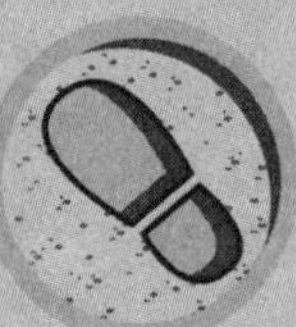

Pennies

A penny is worth **1** cent.

front **back**

Directions: Find each penny. Color it **brown**.

How many pennies did you find? ______________

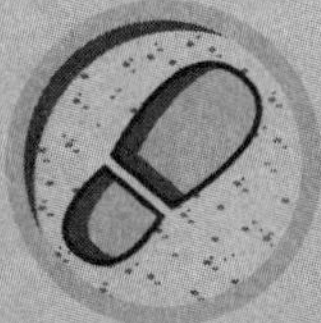

One Step Further

Look around the room you're in now.
How many pennies can you find?

Pennies

How much money is in the purse?

Directions: Circle the number that shows how many cents are in each purse.

2¢

3¢

4¢

5¢

6¢

7¢

One Step Further

Do you have a piggy bank?
How much money is in it?

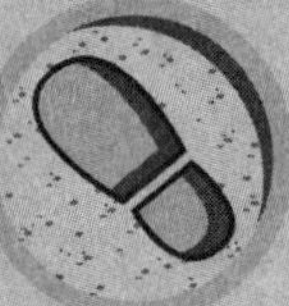

Counting Pennies

Count the pennies.

Directions: Write the number of cents in the blanks below.

___3___ pennies = ___3___ ¢

__________ pennies = __________ ¢

__________ penny = __________ ¢

One Step Further

Count the pennies you found.
How much money is there?

Nickels

A nickel is worth **5** cents.

front

back

Directions: Trace the number of cents in the blanks below. Color the nickel **silver**.

1 nickel = 5 pennies

1 nickel = 5 cents

1 nickel = 5 ¢

=

One Step Further
Look around the room you're in now.
How many nickels can you find?

Nickels and Pennies

Directions: Trace around the nickel to show it is worth **5¢**. Trace around the **5** pennies to show they are worth **5¢**. Circle the nickels. Circle the groups of **5** pennies.

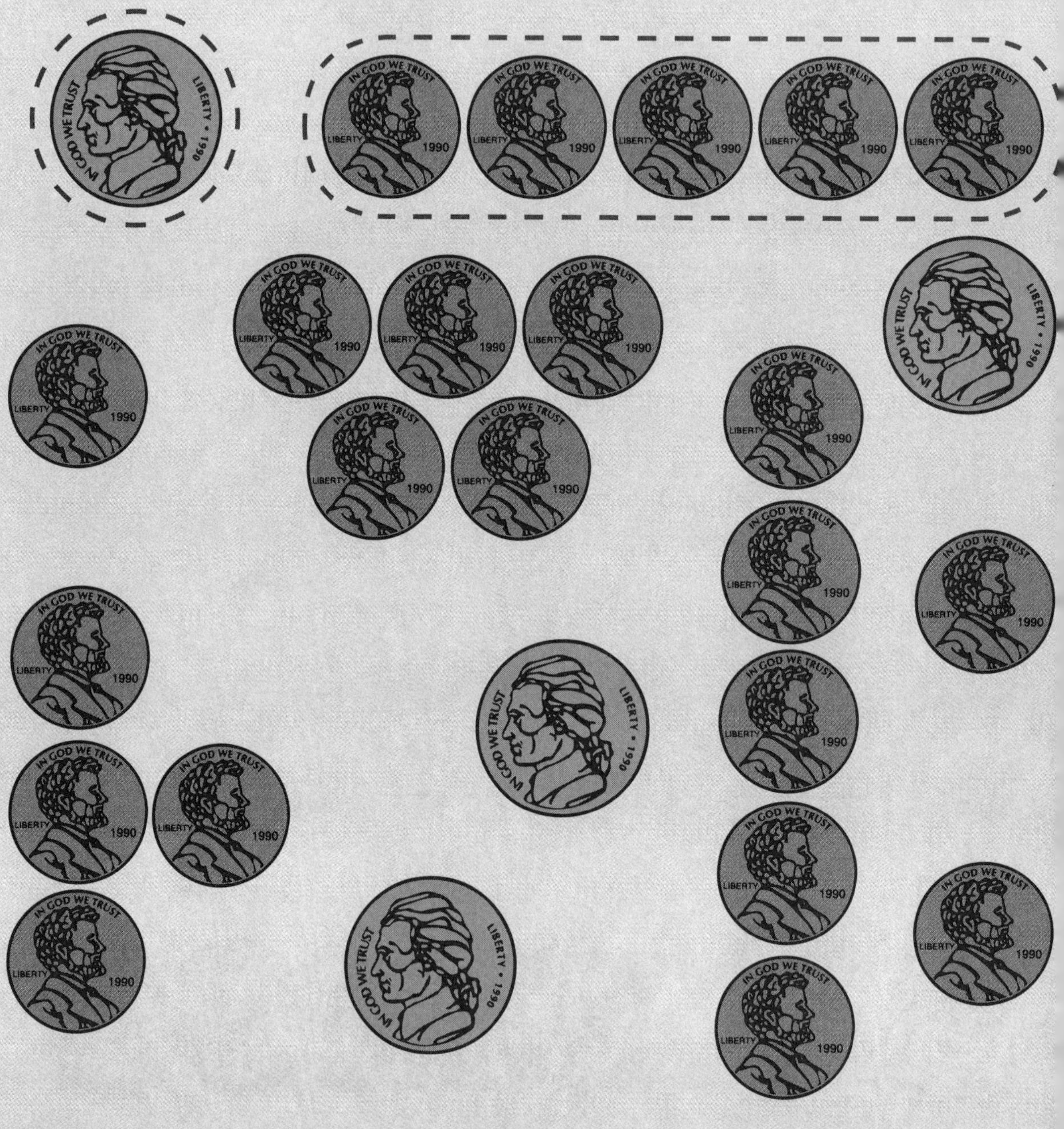

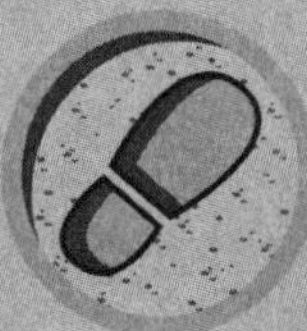

One Step Further

Ask an adult if he or she has any coins.
Ask if you can help count the coins.

Counting with Nickels and Pennies

Directions: Here is a **penny**. Color it **brown**.

Directions: Here is a **nickel**. Color it **silver**.

1 penny = __________ cent

1 penny = __________ ¢

1 nickel = __________ cents

1 nickel = __________ ¢

Directions: Write the cent symbol here: ________________

One Step Further
What makes a penny different from a nickel?
Name all the differences you can think of.

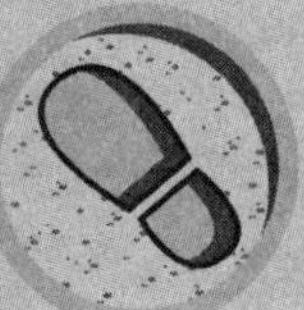

Dimes

A dime is worth **10** cents.

front

back

Directions: Trace the number of cents in the blanks below. Color the dime **silver**.

___1___ dime = ___10___ pennies

___1___ dime = ___10___ cents

___1___ dime = ___10___ ¢

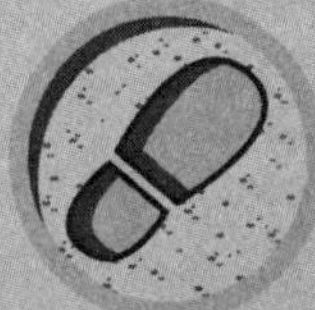

One Step Further

Look around the room you're in now.
How many dimes can you find?

Counting with Dimes and Pennies

Always begin with the dime. Then, add the pennies.

 +  = 12¢

10   1   1

Directions: Write the amount in the blanks below.

 +    = ____ 

____   ____ ____ ____

+   

____   ____ ____ ____

   = ____ ¢

____ ____ ____

One Step Further

With an adult's help, set up a lemonade stand. How much will each cup cost?

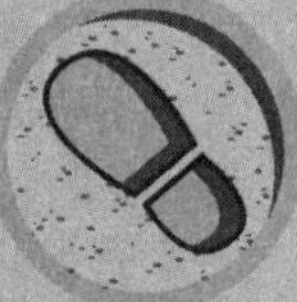

Counting with Dimes and Pennies

Directions: Count the money. Write the amount.

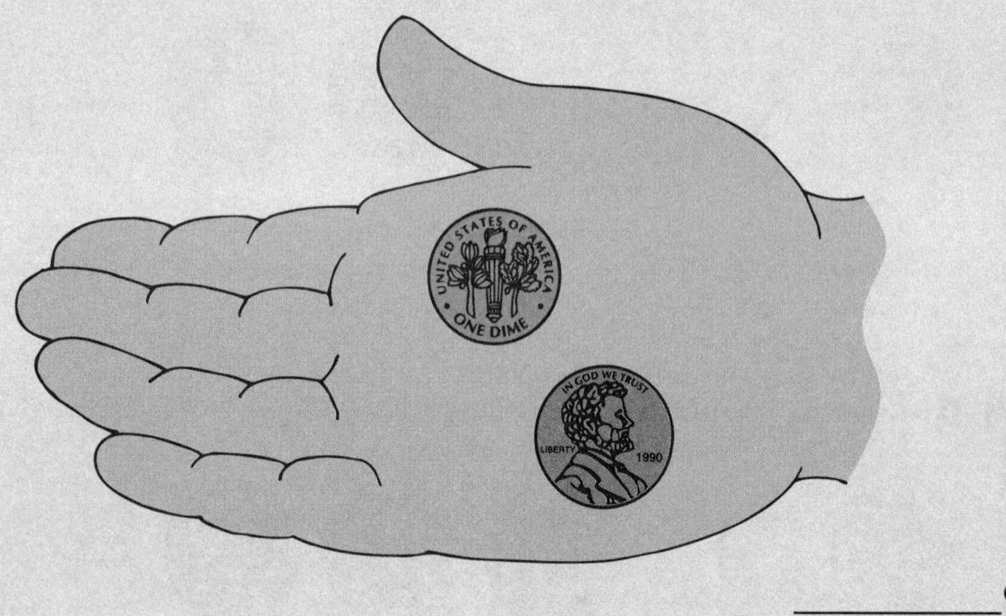

Child **1** __________ ¢

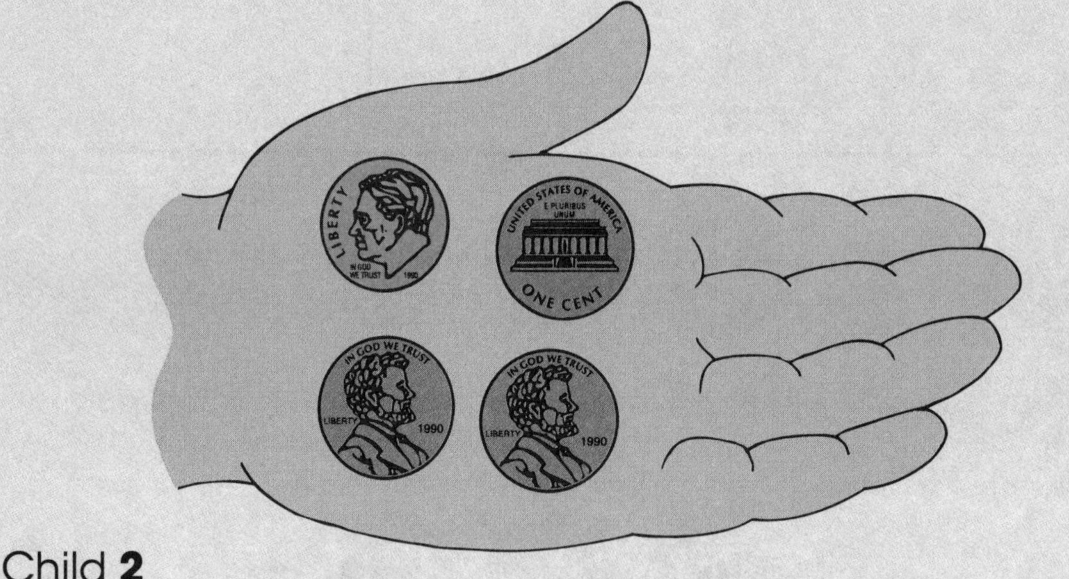

Child **2** __________ ¢

Who has more money? ____________________

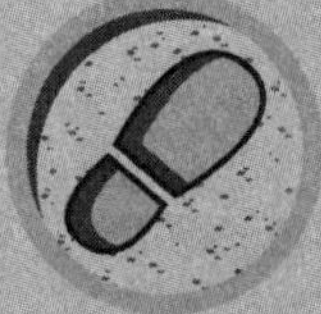

One Step Further
Grab a handful of coins. Divide the coins into equal piles.

Reading

Letter Aa

Directions: Trace and write the letter **Aa**.

UPPERCASE

lowercase

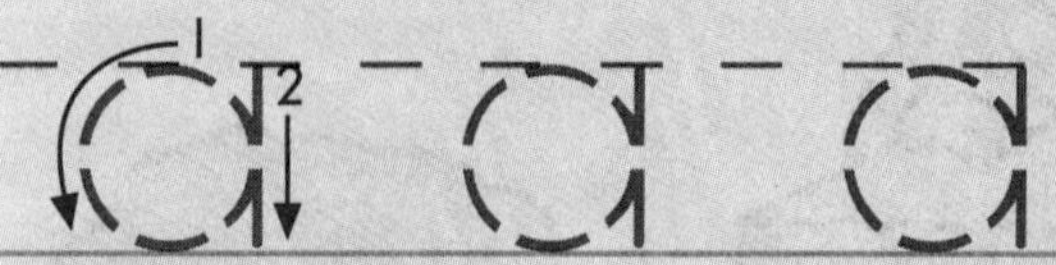

Directions: These pictures begin with the letter **Aa**. Color the pictures.

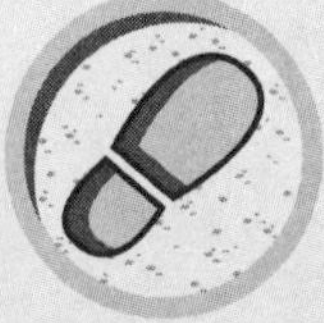

One Step Further

Look through a book or magazine for something that starts with the letter **A**.

Letter Bb

Directions: Trace and write the letter **Bb**.

UPPERCASE

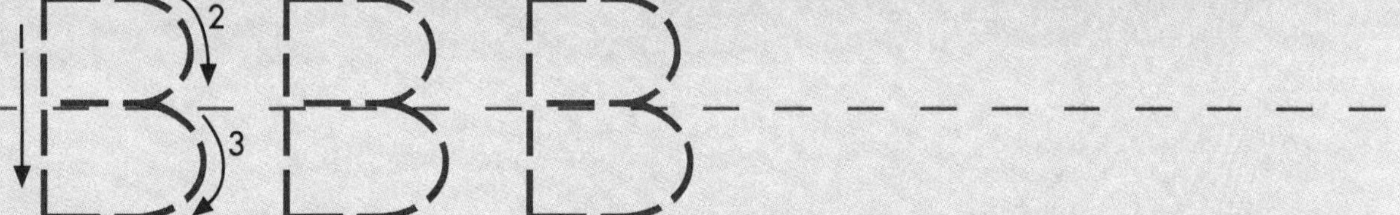

lowercase

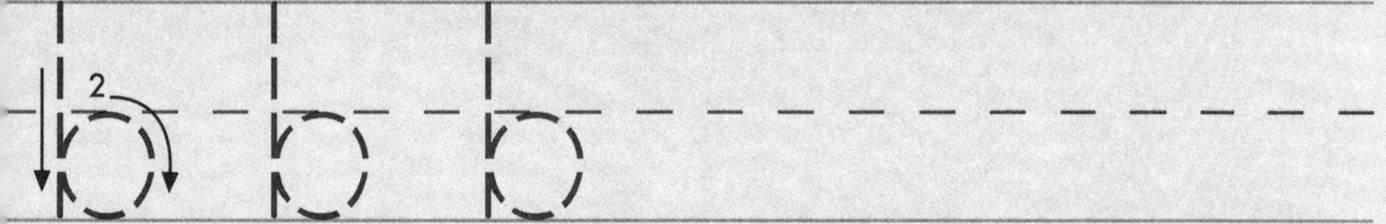

Directions: These pictures begin with the letter **Bb**.
Color the pictures.

One Step Further

Bounce starts with the letter **B**.
Bounce up and down five times.

Letter Cc

Directions: Trace and write the letter **Cc**.

UPPERCASE

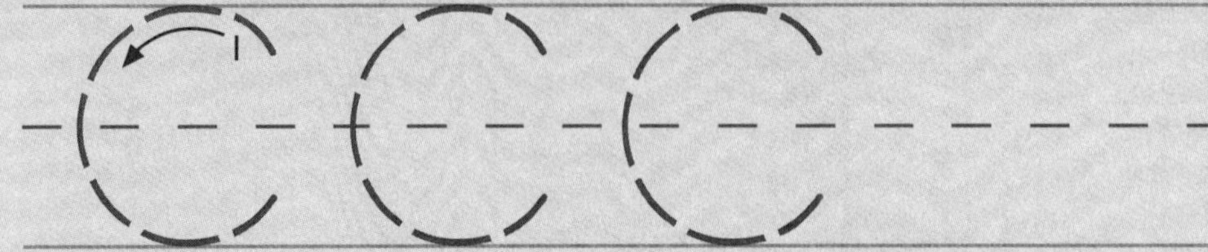

lowercase

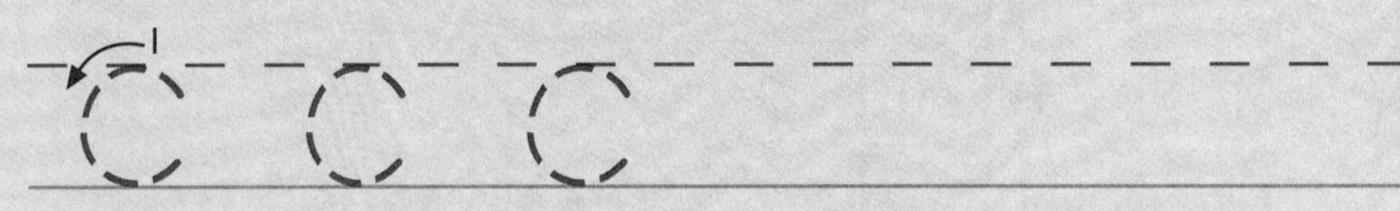

Directions: These pictures begin with the letter **Cc**. Color the pictures.

One Step Further

Clap starts with the letter **C**. Clap your hands 10 times.

Letter Dd

Directions: Trace and write the letter **Dd**.

UPPERCASE

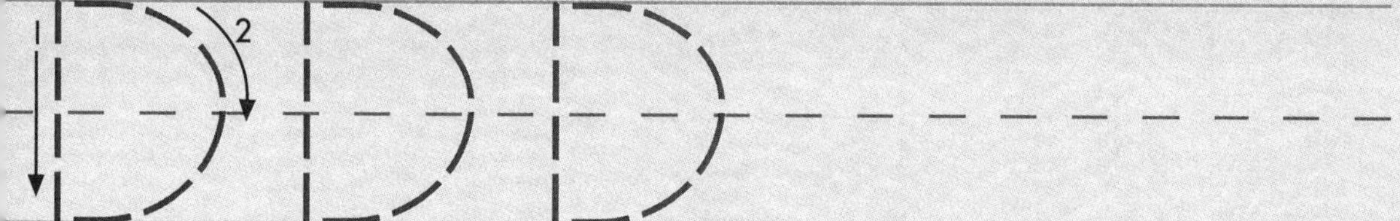

owercase

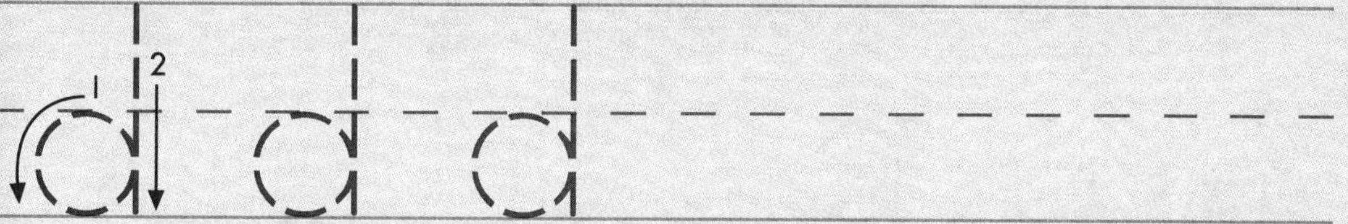

Directions: These pictures begin with the letter **Dd**. Color the pictures.

One Step Further

Name something else that starts with the letter **D**.

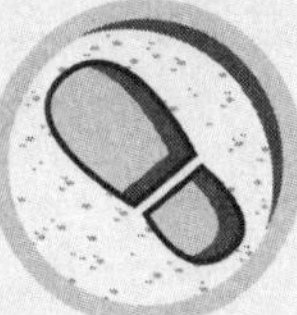

Letter Ee

Directions: Trace and write the letter **Ee**.

UPPERCASE

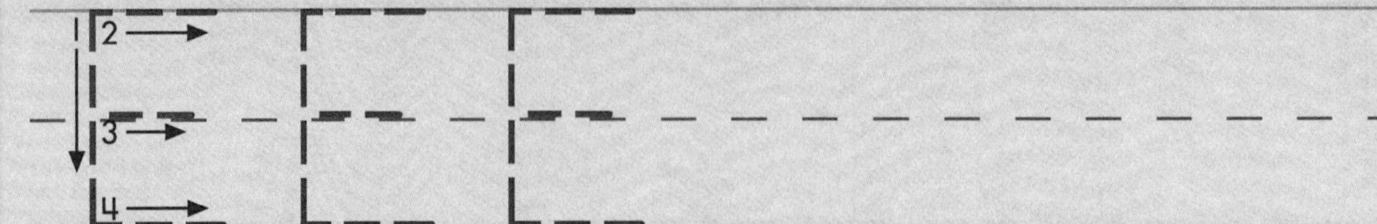

lowercase

Directions: These pictures begin with the letter **Ee**. Color the pictures.

One Step Further

Elephant starts with the letter **E**. Name another animal that starts with the letter **E**.

Letter Ff

Directions: Trace and write the letter **Ff**.

UPPERCASE

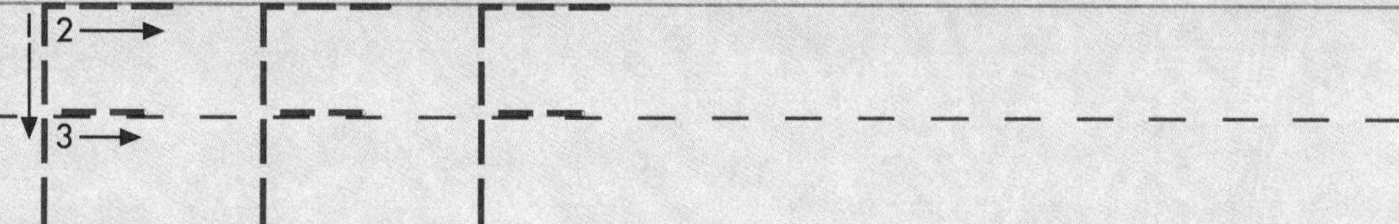

lowercase

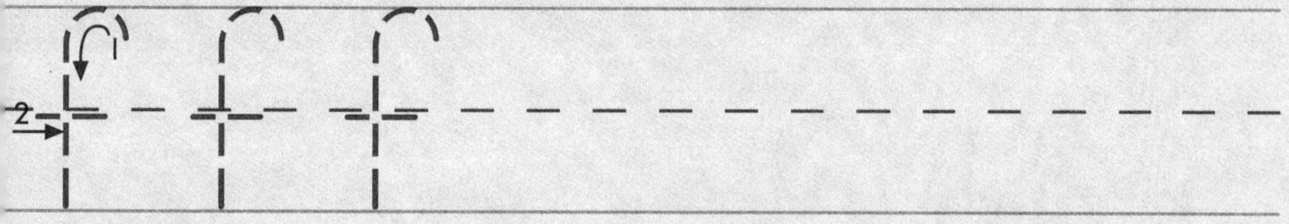

Directions: These pictures begin with the letter **Ff**.
Color the pictures.

One Step Further
Look at the pictures on this page. Can you find any of these objects in your home?

Letter Gg

Directions: Trace and write the letter **Gg**.

UPPERCASE

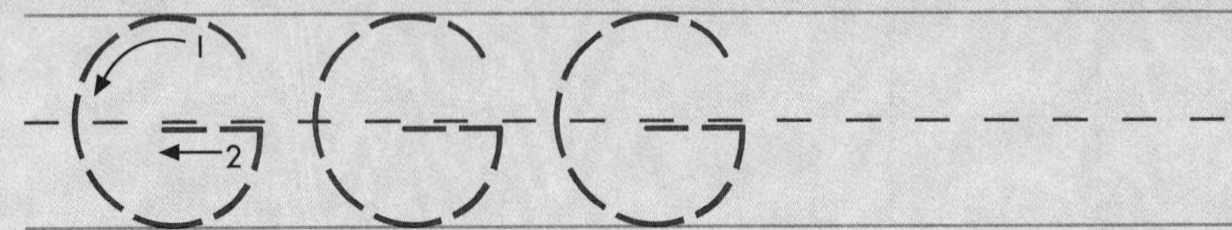

lowercase

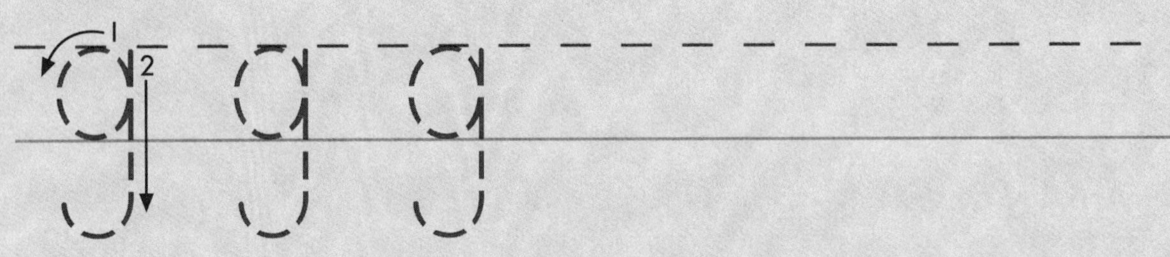

Directions: These pictures begin with the letter **Gg**. Color the pictures.

One Step Further

Look outside for objects that start with the letter **G**. What did you find?

Letter Hh

Directions: Trace and write the letter **Hh**.

UPPERCASE

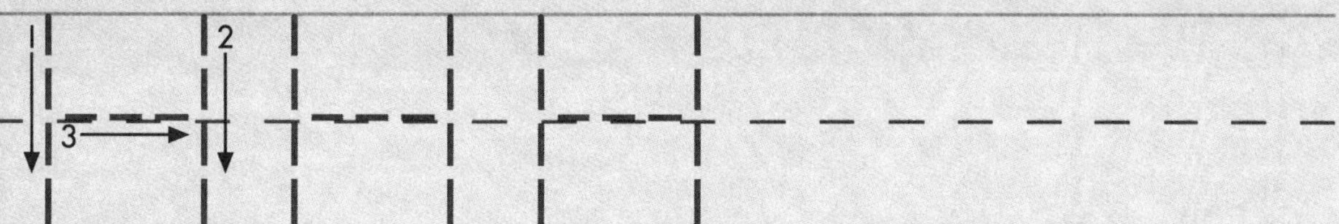

lowercase

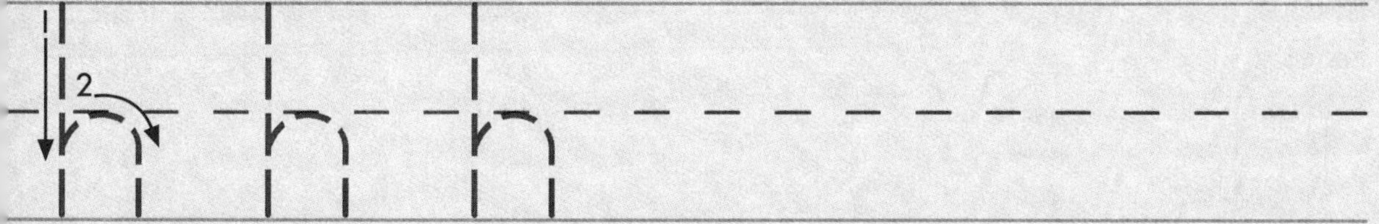

Directions: These pictures begin with the letter **Hh**.
Color the pictures.

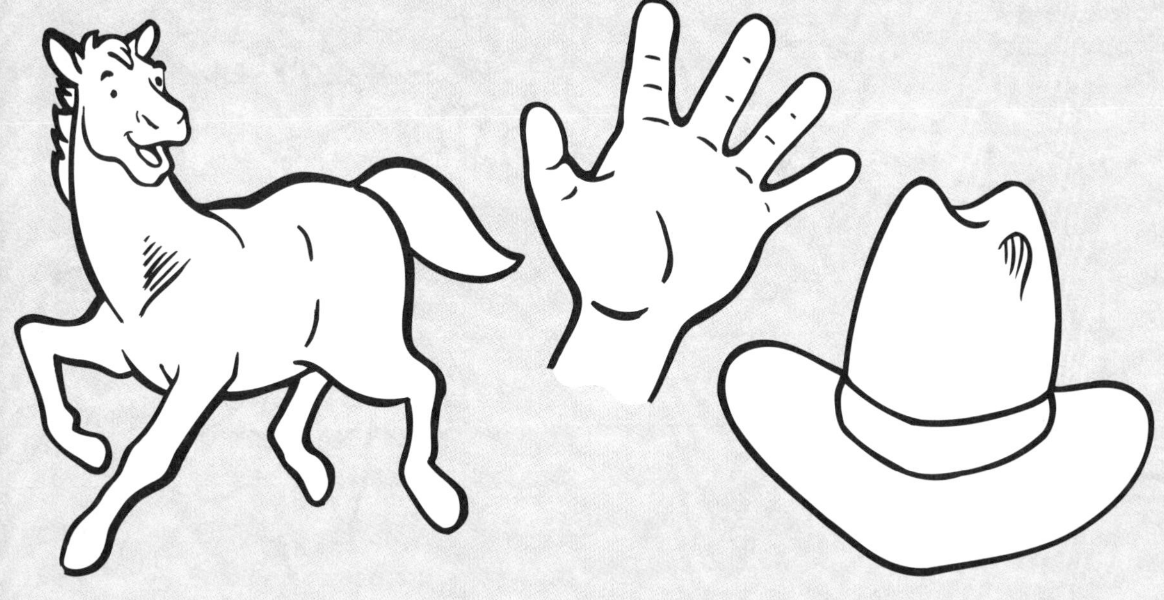

One Step Further

Hop starts with the letter **H**.
Hop like a rabbit 10 times.

Letter Ii

Directions: Trace and write the letter **Ii**.

UPPERCASE

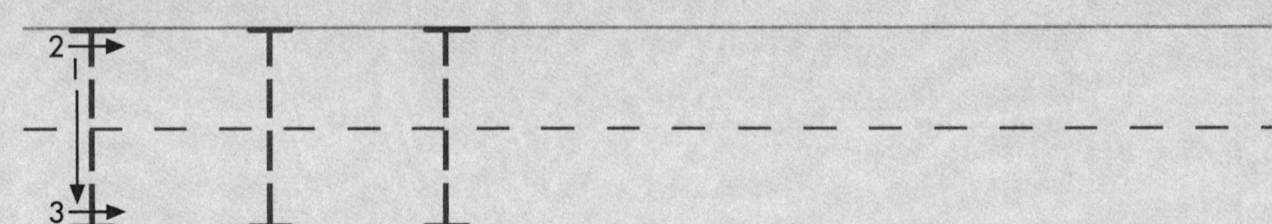

lowercase

Directions: These pictures begin with the letter **Ii**.
Color the pictures.

One Step Further

Ask an adult to help you make ice.
What letter does **ice** start with?

Letter Jj

Directions: Trace and write the letter **Jj**.

UPPERCASE

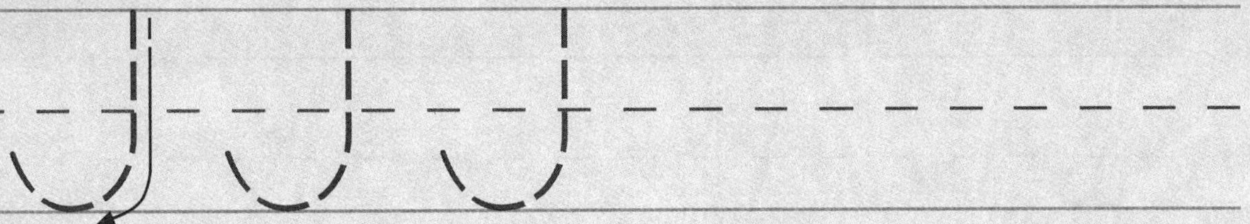

lowercase

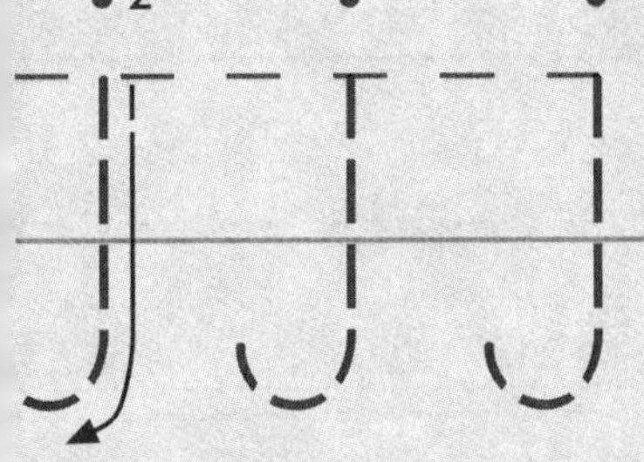

Directions: These pictures begin with the letter **Jj**.
Color the pictures.

One Step Further

Jump rope on your own or with a friend.
How long can you jump without missing?

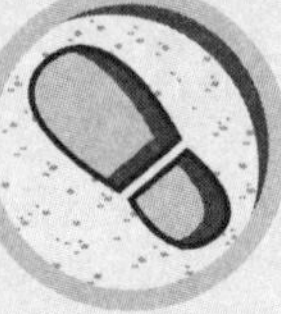

Review

Directions: Practice writing the letters **Aa–Jj** by tracing the **UPPER** and **lowercase** letters below.

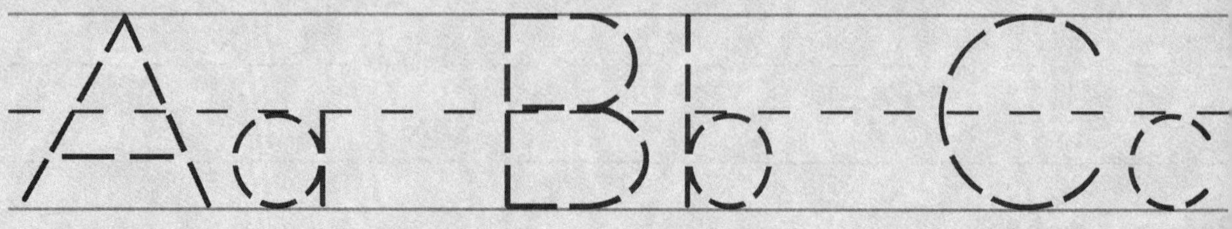

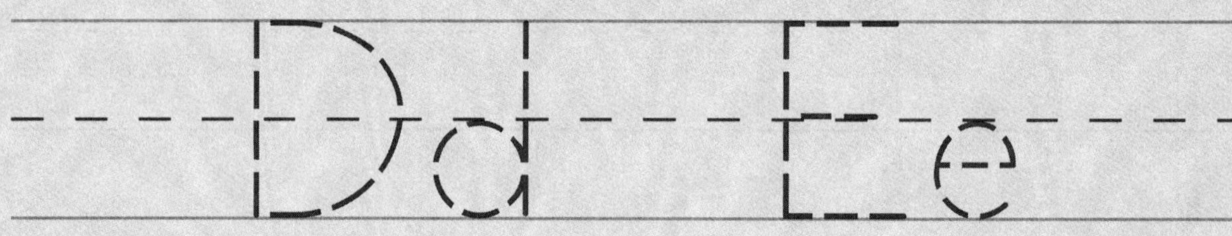

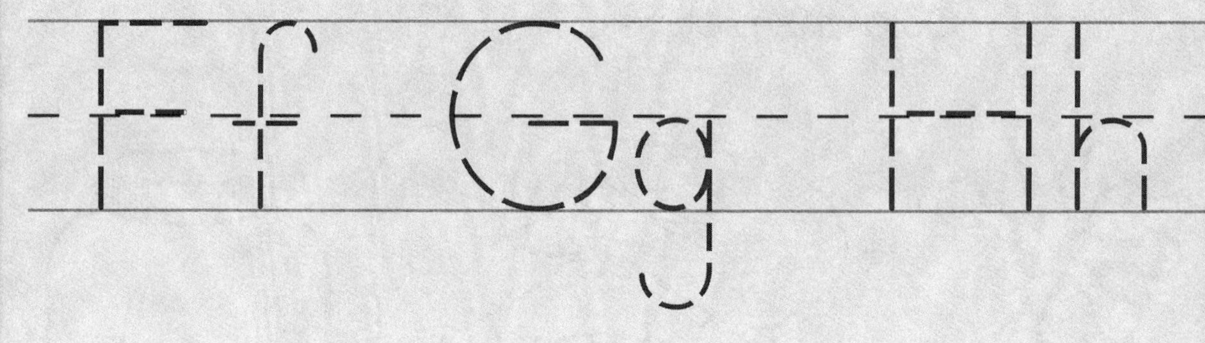

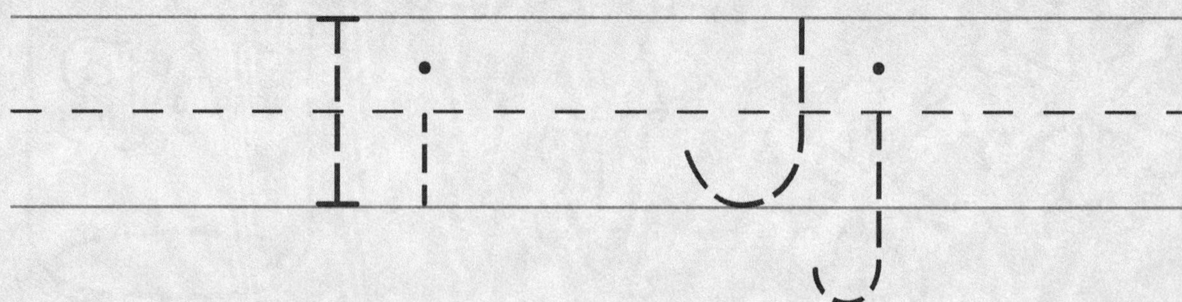

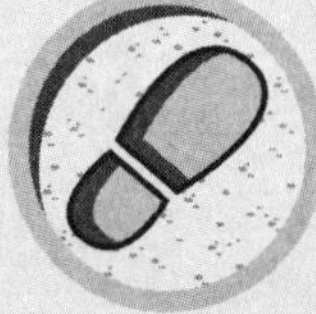

One Step Further

Choose a letter from this page.
Name an object that starts with that letter.

Letter Kk

Directions: Trace and write the letter **Kk**.

UPPERCASE

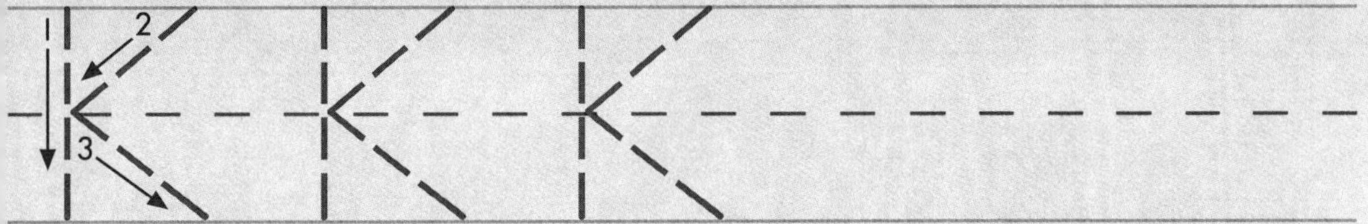

lowercase

Directions: These pictures begin with the letter **Kk**.
Color the pictures.

One Step Further

With a friend, go outside and fly a kite.
What color is your kite?

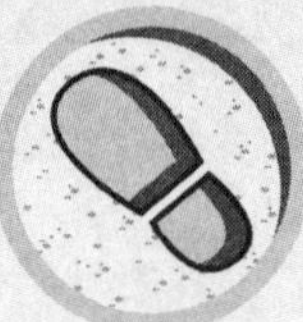

Letter Ll

Directions: Trace and write the letter **Ll**.

UPPERCASE

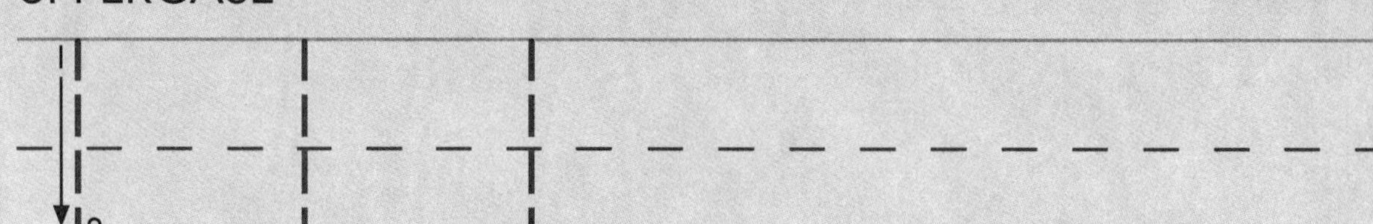

lowercase

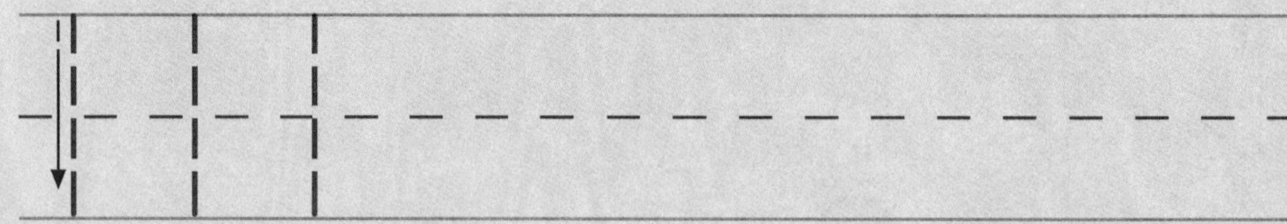

Directions: These pictures begin with the letter **Ll**.
Color the pictures.

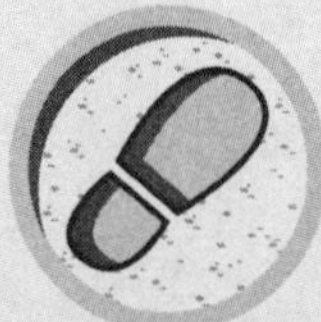

One Step Further

Turn the lights off, and back on again.
How many lamps are in your home?

Letter Mm

Directions: Trace and write the letter **Mm**.

UPPERCASE

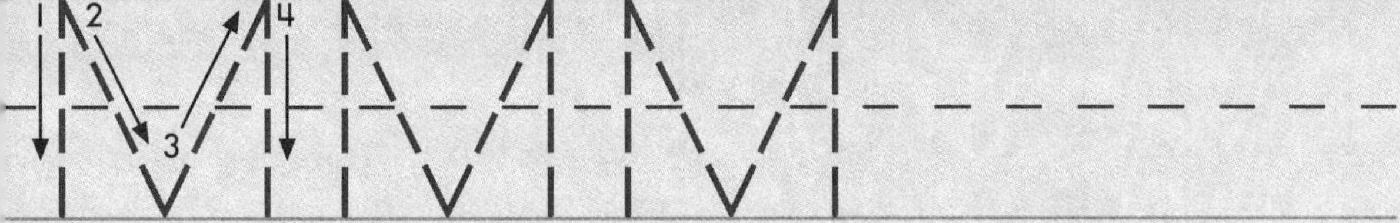

lowercase

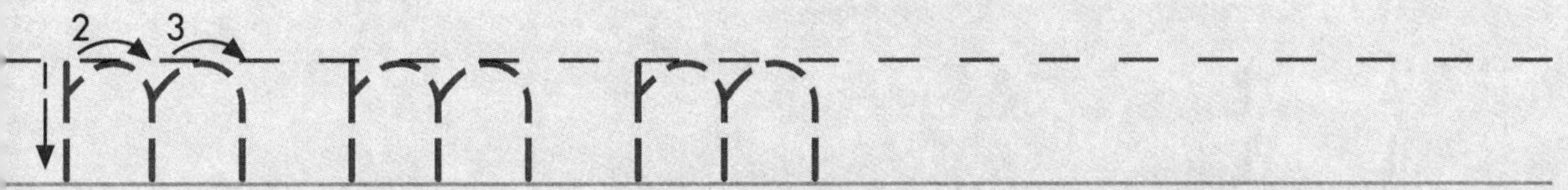

Directions: These pictures begin with the letter **Mm**. Color the pictures.

One Step Further

Milk is good for you! What is your favorite thing to drink with breakfast?

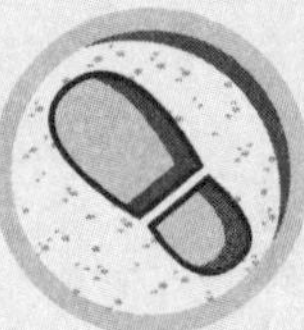

Letter Nn

Directions: Trace and write the letter **Nn**.

UPPERCASE

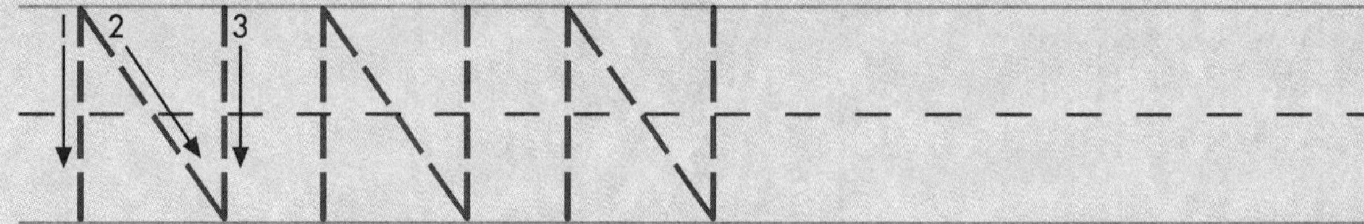

lowercase

Directions: These pictures begin with the letter **Nn**. Color the pictures.

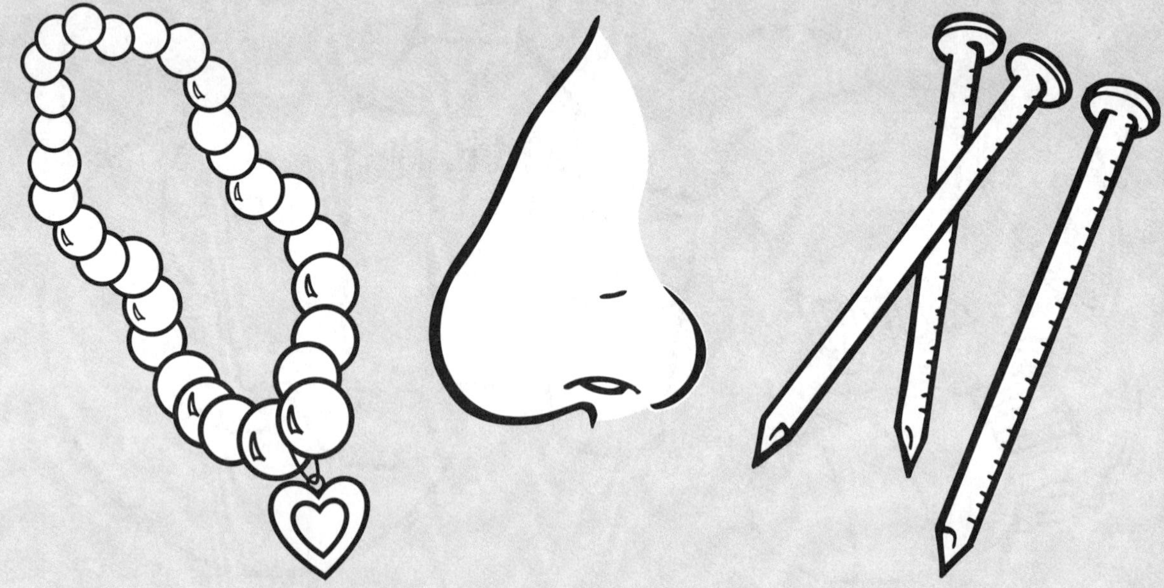

One Step Further

Point to your nose. Point to your mouth. Which starts with the letter **N**?

Letter Oo

Directions: Trace and write the letter **Oo**.

UPPERCASE

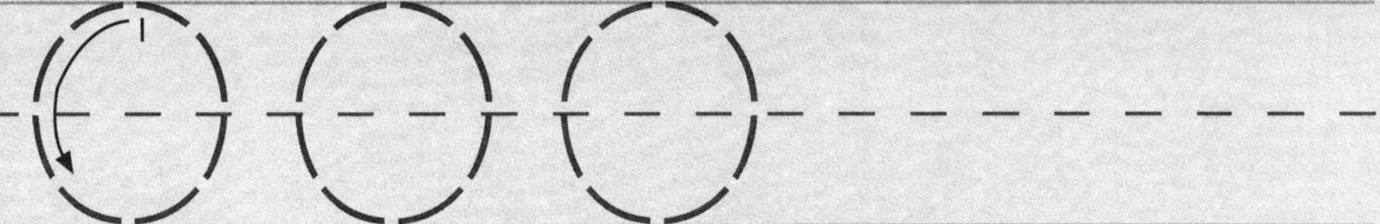

lowercase

Directions: These pictures begin with the letter **Oo**. Color the pictures.

One Step Further

Think about shapes you've learned. What shape starts with an **O**? Draw that shape.

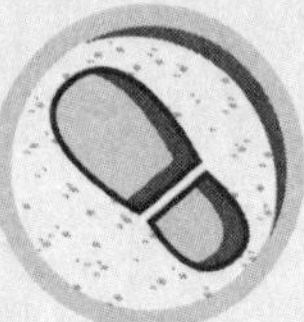

Letter Pp

Directions: Trace and write the letter **Pp**.

UPPERCASE

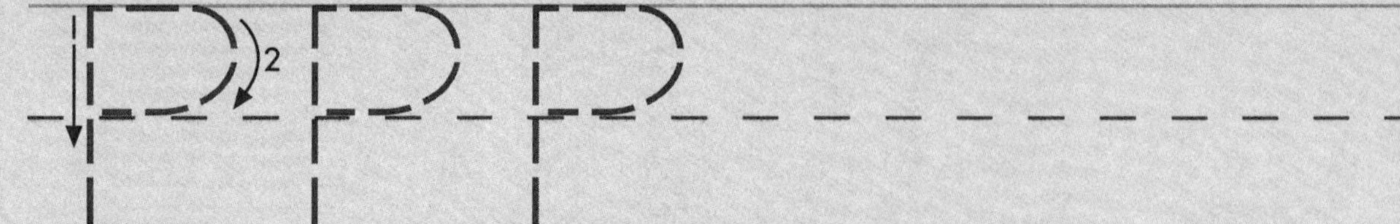

lowercase

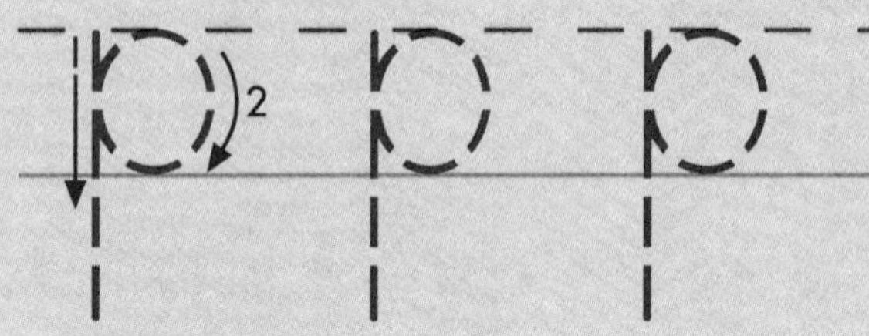

Directions: These pictures begin with the letter **Pp**. Color the pictures.

One Step Further

Get with a friend and see how many **P** words you can come up with.

Letter Qq

Directions: Trace and write the letter **Qq**.

JPPERCASE

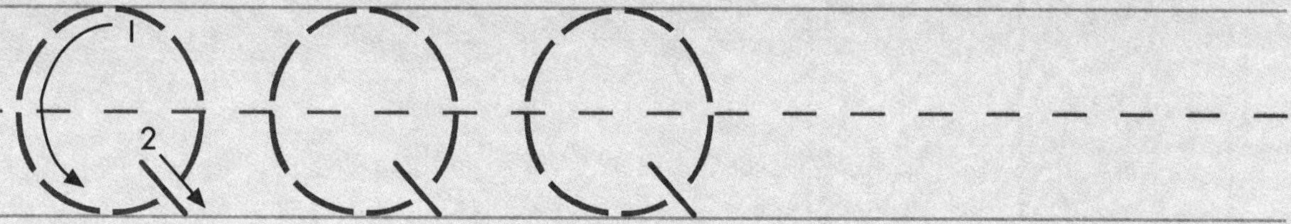

owercase

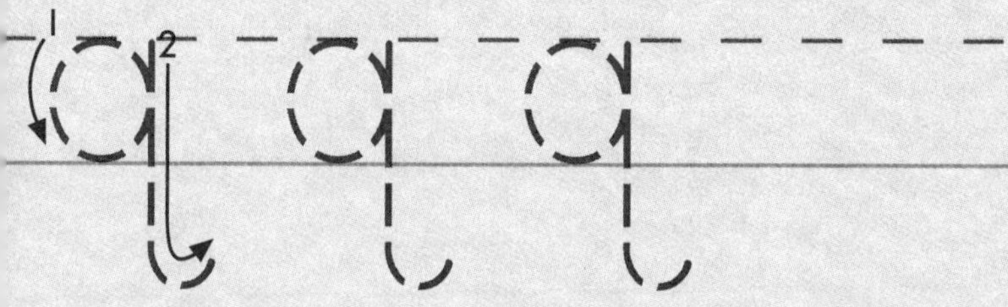

Directions: These pictures begin with the letter **Qq**. Color the pictures.

One Step Further
Look around your home.
How many quarters can you find?

Letter Rr

Directions: Trace and write the letter **Rr**.

UPPERCASE

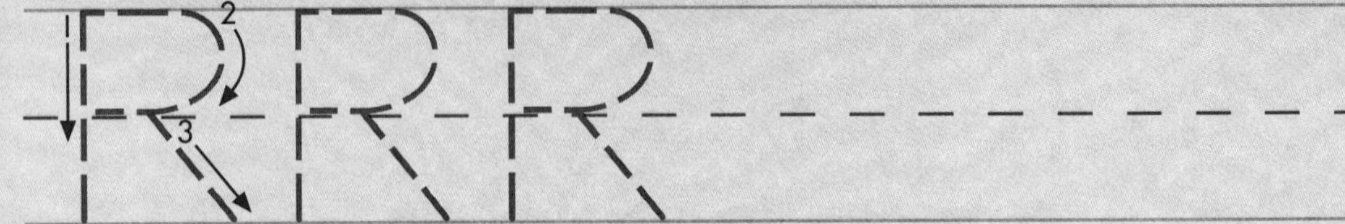

lowercase

Directions: These pictures begin with the letter **Rr**. Color the pictures.

One Step Further

Look through a book or magazine for something that starts with the letter **R**.

Letter Ss

Directions: Trace and write the letter **Ss**.

UPPERCASE

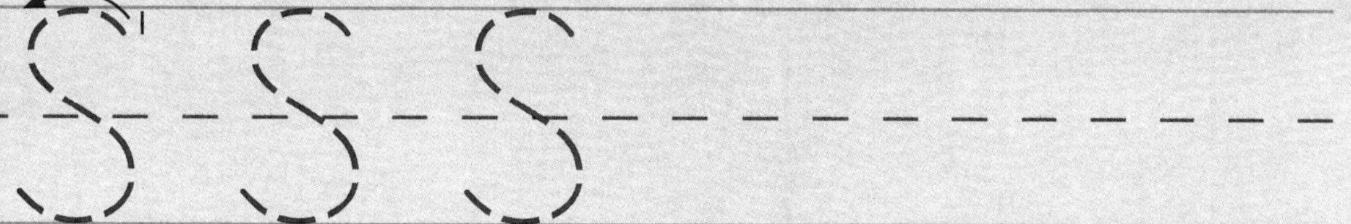

lowercase

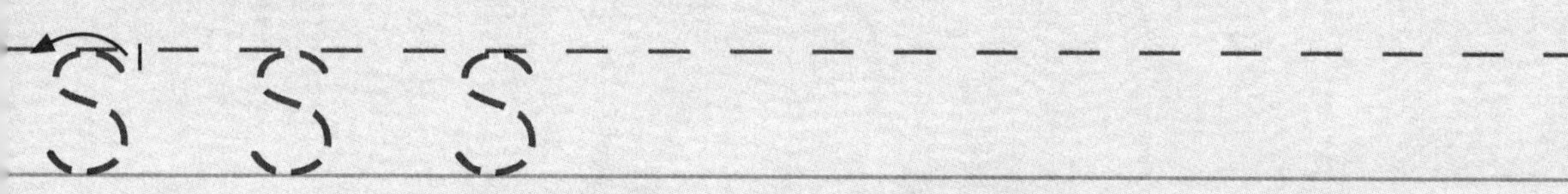

Directions: These pictures begin with the letter **Ss**. Color the pictures.

One Step Further
Look around the room. Can you find anything that starts with the letter **S**?

Letter Tt

Directions: Trace and write the letter **Tt**.

UPPERCASE

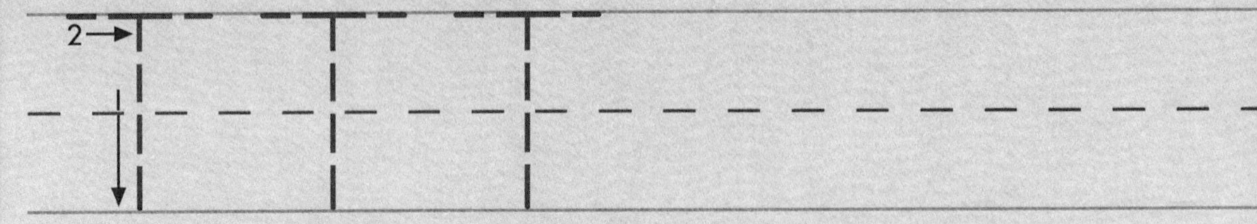

lowercase

Directions: These pictures begin with the letter **Tt**.
Color the pictures.

One Step Further

Do you know how to tap dance?
Practice by tapping your feet on the ground.

Letter Uu

Directions: Trace and write the letter **Uu**.

UPPERCASE

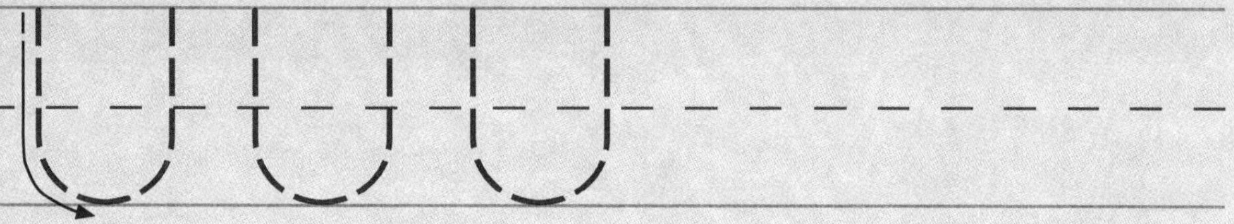

lowercase

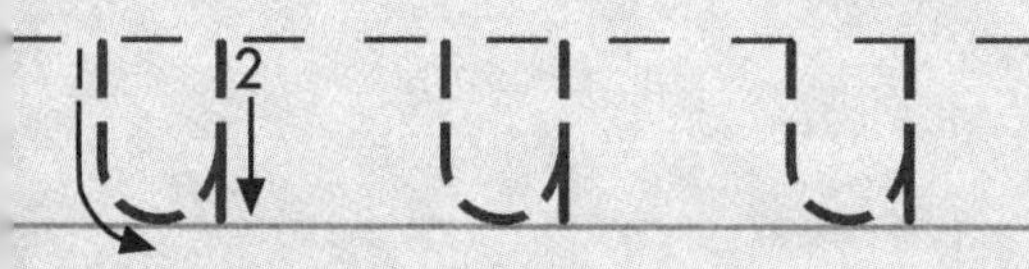

Directions: These pictures begin with the letter **Uu**.
Color the pictures.

One Step Further

What can you crawl under?

What animals live under the sea?

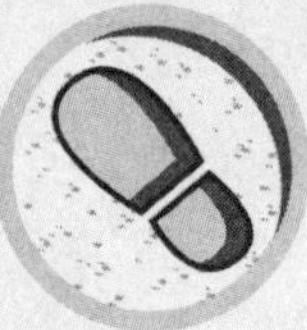

Letter Vv

Directions: Trace and write the letter **Vv**.

UPPERCASE

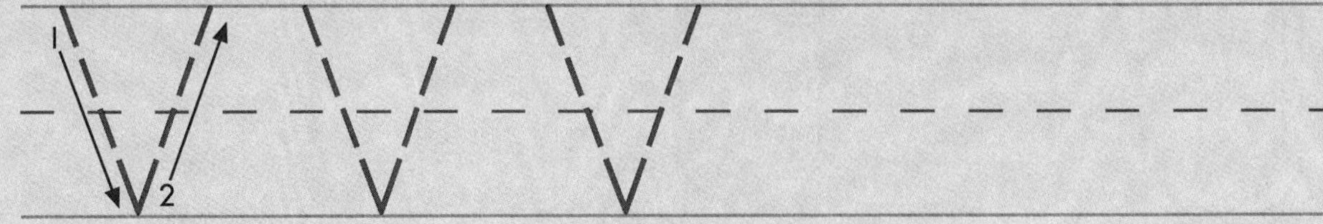

lowercase

Directions: These pictures begin with the letter **Vv**. Color the pictures.

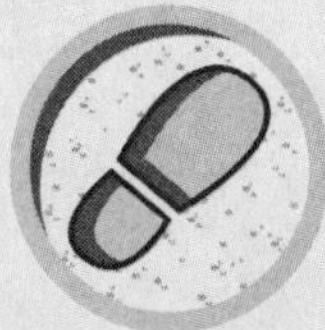

One Step Further

How many vegetables can you name?
Which one is your favorite?

Letter Ww

Directions: Trace and write the letter **Ww**.

UPPERCASE

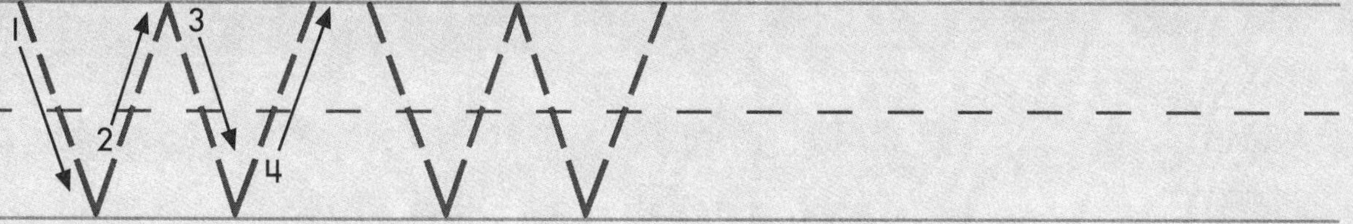

owercase

Directions: These pictures begin with the letter **Ww**. Color the pictures.

One Step Further

Go to the sink and run some water. What letter does **water** start with?

Letter Xx

Directions: Trace and write the letter **Xx**.

UPPERCASE

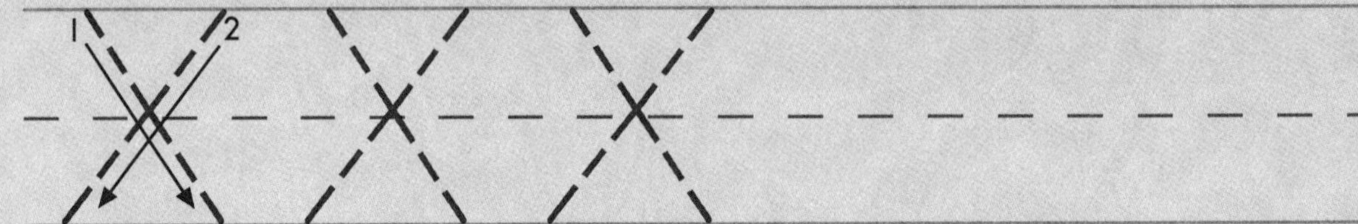

lowercase

Directions: These pictures contain the letter **Xx**.
Color the pictures.

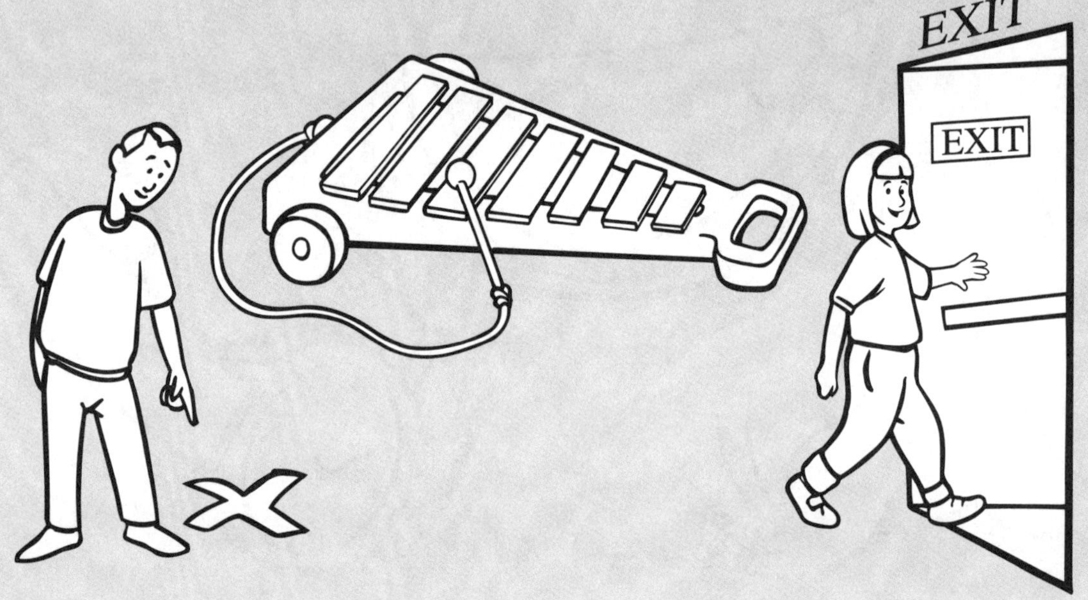

One Step Further

Create a treasure map, where **X** marks the spot of the hidden treasure.

Letter Yy

Directions: Trace and write the letter **Yy**.

UPPERCASE

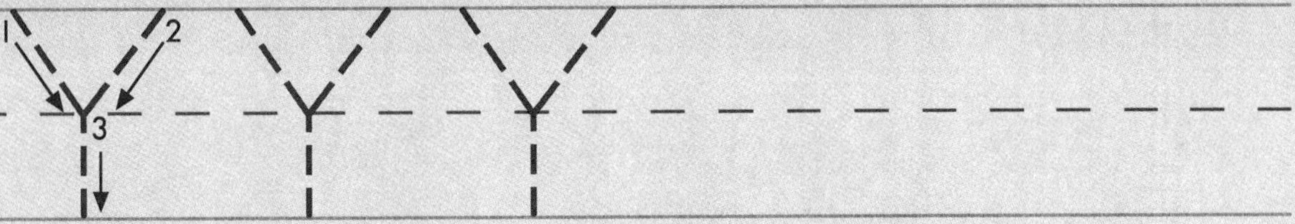

lowercase

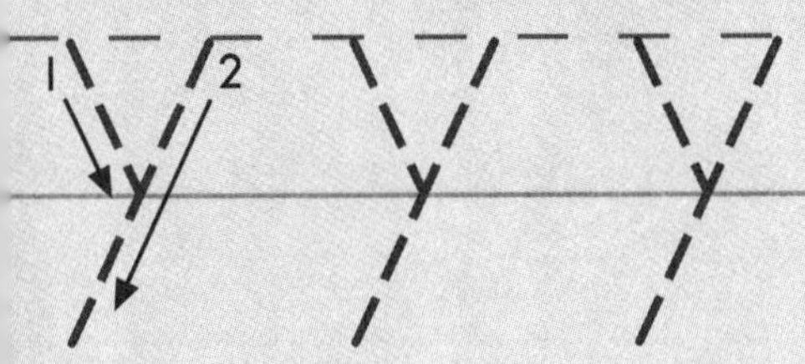

Directions: These pictures begin with the letter **Yy**.
Color the pictures.

One Step Further

What color is the sun?
Draw a picture of the sun and color it.

Letter Zz

Directions: Trace and write the letter **Zz**.

UPPERCASE

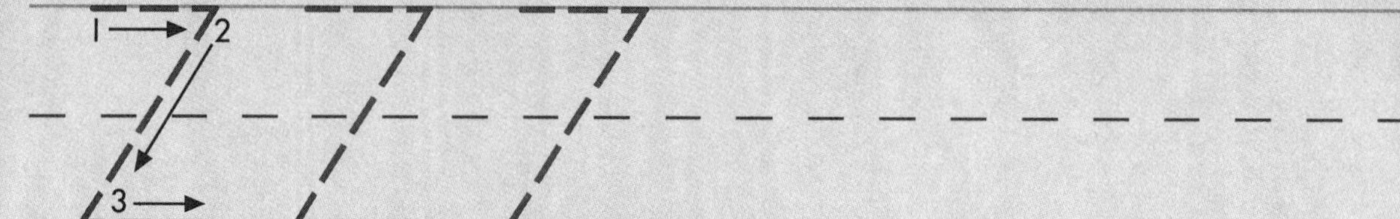

lowercase

Directions: These pictures begin with the letter **Zz**. Color the pictures.

One Step Further

Name your favorite zoo animal.
What letter does that animal start with?

Review

Directions: Help the zebra find its way back to the zoo. Color the boxes from **A-Z**.

A B C D E F G H I J K L M N O P Q R S T U V W X Y Z

ZOO

One Step Further

What does the zebra see on the way? What letter do those objects start with?

Letter Aa

Directions: Circle the **A** or **a** in these words:

apple	alligator	angel
Amy	art	Andy

The letter **Aa** can have more than one sound.

Directions: Color the pictures that start with the sound of **Aa**.

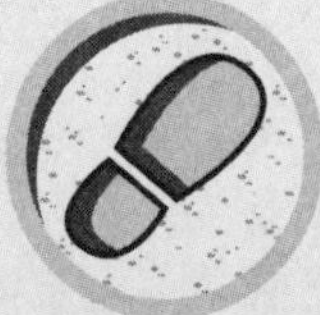

One Step Further

Do you have a friend whose name starts with the letter **A**? What is it?

Letter Bb

Directions: Circle the **B** or **b** in these words:

Bill	**brown**	**Bonnie**
boy	**baby**	**balloon**

Directions: Color the pictures that start with the sound of **Bb**.

One Step Further

Read a book. What words in the book start with the letter **B**?

Letter Cc

Directions: Circle the **C** or **c** in these words:

cat	**Casey**	**can**
cow	**corn**	**Carol**

Directions: Color the pictures that start with the sound of **Cc**.

One Step Further

Look at the cars outside.
What color are the cars?

Letter Dd

Directions: Circle the **D** or **d** in these words:

doll	Darcy	desk
door	David	dog

Directions: Color the pictures that start with the sound of **Dd**.

One Step Further

Dog starts with the letter **D**. Name another animal that starts with the letter **D**.

Letter Ee

Directions: Circle the **E** or **e** in these words:

ear	Elizabeth	eleven
earth	Eric	elf

The letter **Ee** can have more than one sound.

Directions: Color the pictures that start with the sound of **Ee**.

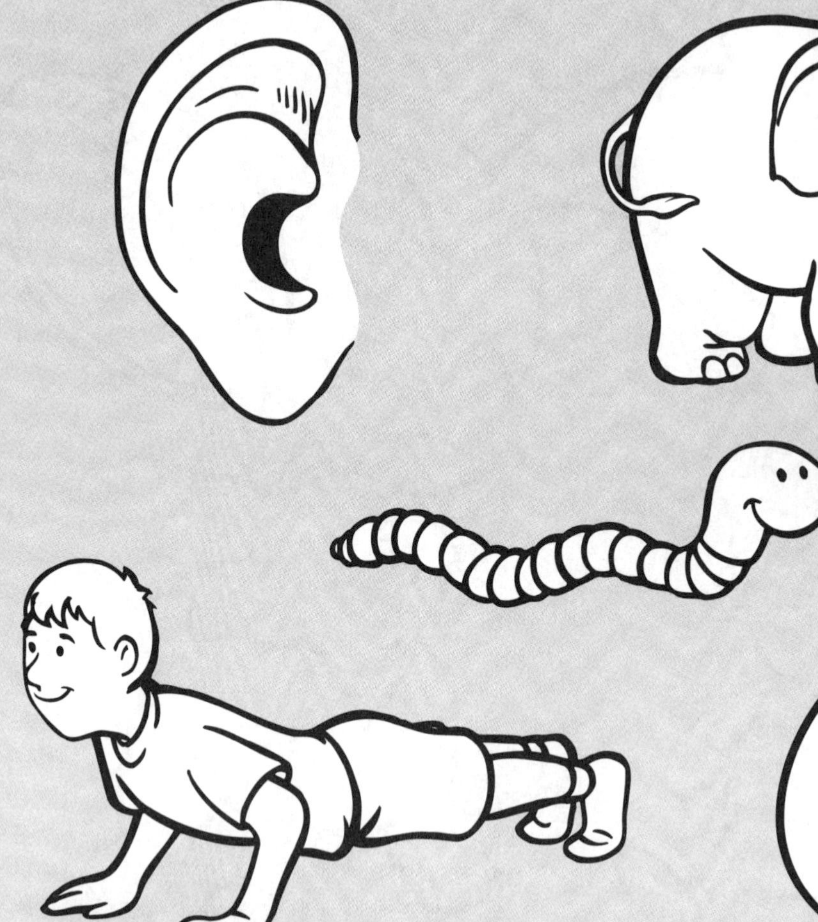

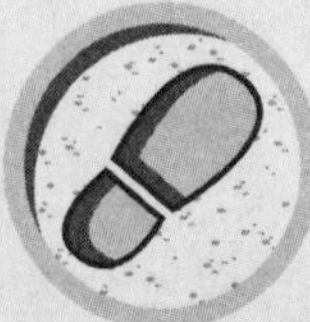

One Step Further

Draw a picture of Earth.
How many countries can you name?

Letter Ff

Directions: Circle the **F** or **f** in these words:

fire	**Faye**	**fork**
Fred	**farm**	**fish**

Directions: Color the pictures that start with the sound of **Ff**.

One Step Further

Look for these objects. What else can you find that starts with the letter **F**?

Letter Recognition

READING

Letter Gg

Directions: Circle the **G** or **g** in these words:

goat	Gregory	gate
great	Gloria	gift

Directions: Color the pictures that start with the sound of **Gg**.

One Step Further

Look through a book or magazine for something that starts with the letter **G**.

Letter Hh

Directions: Circle the **H** or **h** in these words:

Heather	**hose**	**house**
Henry	**horse**	**hand**

Directions: Color the pictures that start with the sound of **Hh**.

Welcome

One Step Further

Hand starts with the letter **H**.
Clap your hands five times.

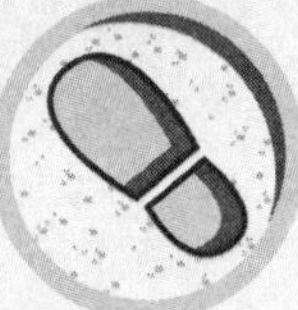

Letter Ii

Directions: Circle the **I** or **i** in these words:

is	**ice cream**	**igloo**
Ivan	**icing**	**Indian**

The letter **Ii** can have more than one sound.

Directions: Color the pictures that start with the sound of **Ii**.

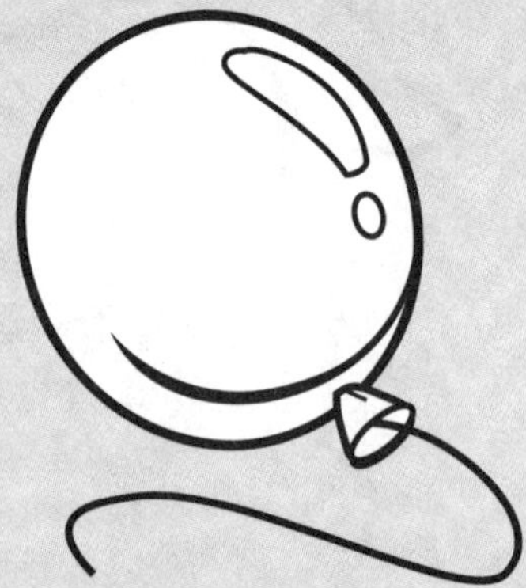

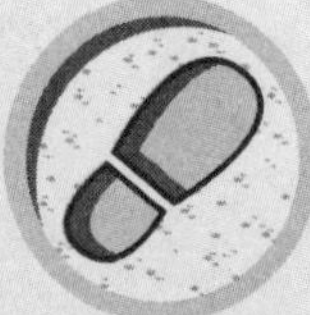

One Step Further

Look at the **I** words on this page.
Tell a story using these words.

Letter Jj

Directions: Circle the **J** or **j** in these words:

Jamal	**jump**	**Jennifer**
jug	**jar**	**joke**

Directions: Color the pictures that start with the sound of **Jj**.

One Step Further

Find three small balls or other objects. Go outside and try to juggle.

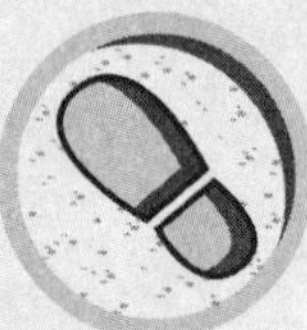

Letter Kk

Directions: Circle the **K** or **k** in these words:

key	**kite**	**kangaroo**
Kim	**karate**	**Kelly**

Directions: Color the pictures that start with the sound of **Kk**.

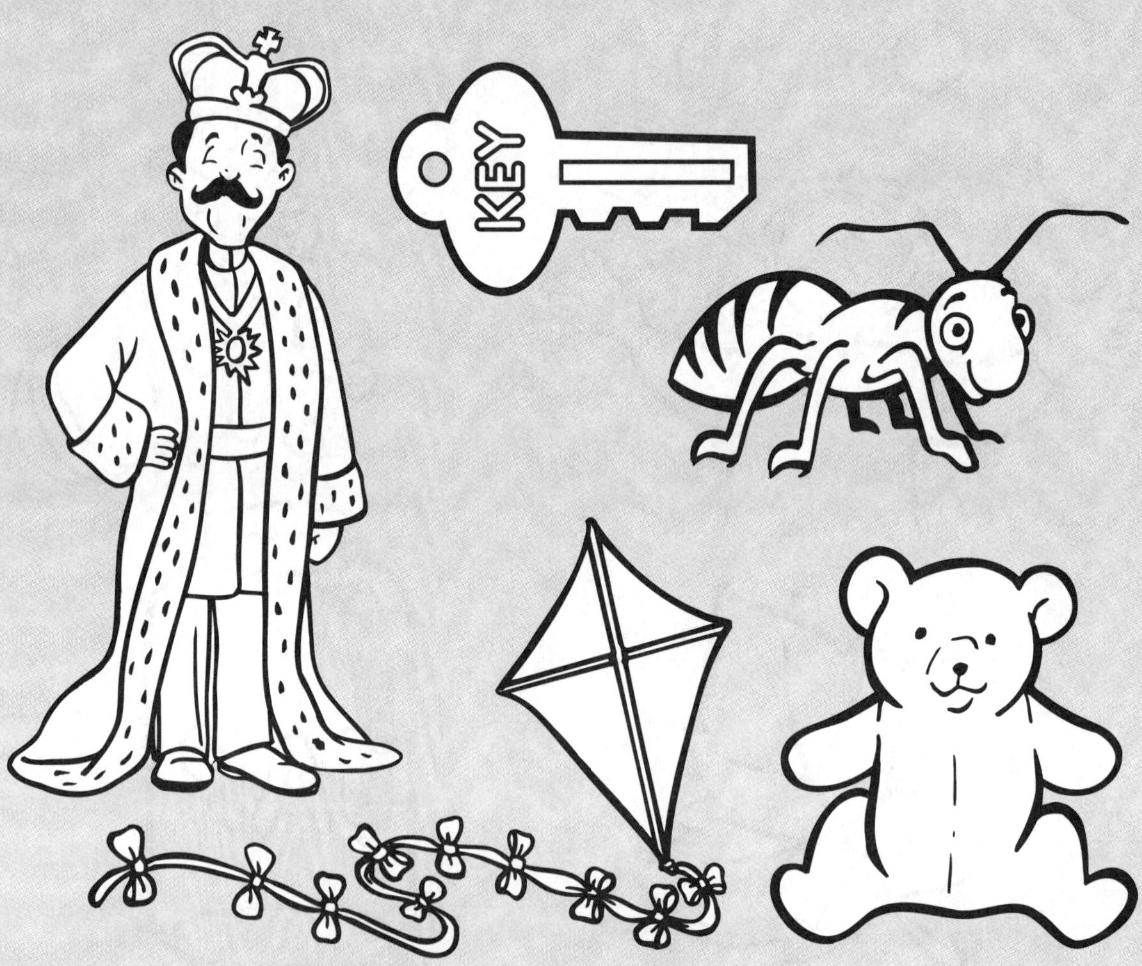

One Step Further

Ask an adult to give you a key.
Find out what it unlocks.

Letter Ll

Directions: Circle the **L** or **l** in these words:

letter	**Larry**	**lion**
Leah	**lamp**	**ladder**

Directions: Color the pictures that start with the sound of **Ll**.

One Step Further

Find five leaves. What letter does **leaf** start with?

Letter Mm

Directions: Circle the **M** or **m** in these words:

man	monkey	Maria
mask	make	Martin

Directions: Color the pictures that start with the sound of **Mm**.

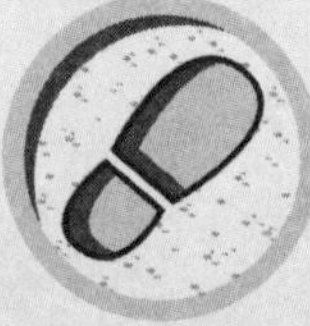

One Step Further

With an adult's help, create a mask to wear. Put on a show wearing the mask.

Letter Nn

Directions: Circle the **N** or **n** in these words:

Nathan	**net**	**nine**
no	**nest**	**Nancy**

Directions: Color the pictures that start with the sound of **Nn**.

One Step Further

What can you catch in a net?
Go outside and see what you can find.

Letter Oo

Letter Recognition

Directions: Circle the **O** or **o** in these words:

Olivia	**owl**	**octopus**
once	**only**	**Owen**

The letter **Oo** can have more than one sound.

Directions: Color the pictures that start with the sound of **Oo**.

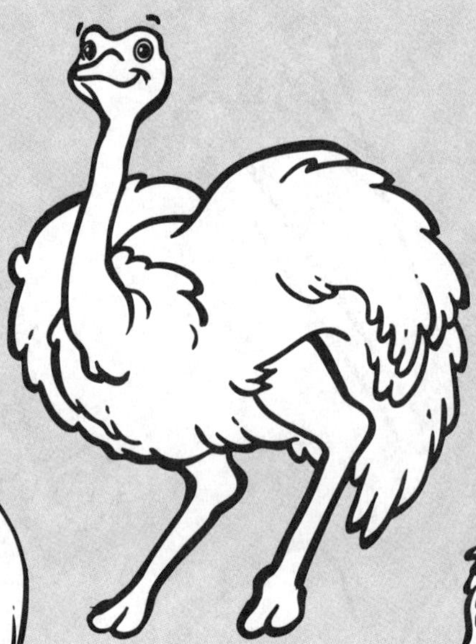

READING

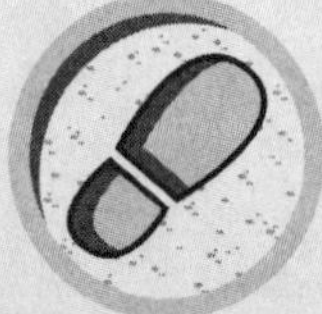

One Step Further

Walk around your home.
Name things that you can open.

Letter Pp

Directions: Circle the **P** or **p** in these words:

pencil	**Paul**	**pig**
party	**penny**	**Patty**

Directions: Color the pictures that start with the sound of **Pp**.

PENCIL

One Step Further

Look at the **P** words on this page.
Tell a story using these words.

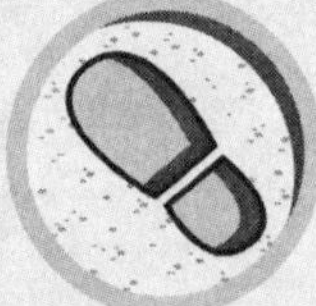

Letter Qq

Directions: Circle the **Q** or **q** in these words:

Quincy	**quarter**	**quilt**
quit	**Quake**	**quiet**

Directions: Color the pictures that start with the sound of **Qq**.

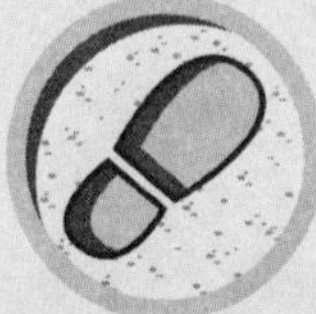

One Step Further

What can you buy with a quarter?
What can you buy with four quarters?

Letter Rr

Directions: Circle the **R** or **r** in these words:

rain	**rose**	**Robert**
rake	**rabbit**	**Renee**

Directions: Color the pictures that start with the sound of **Rr**.

One Step Further
What is your favorite thing to do when it rains?

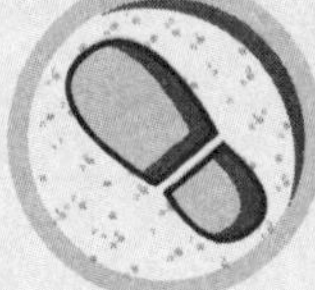

Letter Ss

Directions: Circle the **S** or **s** in these words:

sun	**see**	**six**
Sam	**sailboat**	**Susie**

Directions: Color the pictures that start with the sound of **Ss**.

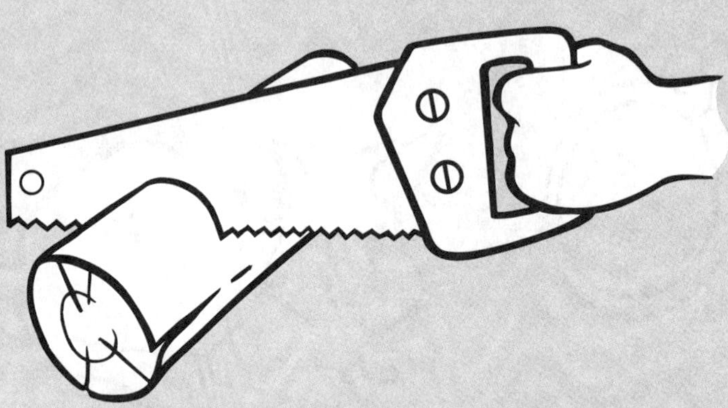

One Step Further

State starts with the letter **S**.
What state do you live in?

Letter Tt

Directions: Circle the **T** or **t** in these words:

Taylor	table	tiger
Timothy	two	television

Directions: Color the pictures that start with the sound of **Tt**.

One Step Further
Call someone on the telephone.
Tell them a story using words on this page.

Letter Uu

Directions: Circle the **U** or **u** in these words:

under	**unicorn**	**unless**
umbrella	**up**	**use**

The letter **Uu** can have more than one sound.

Directions: Color the pictures that start with the sound of **Uu**.

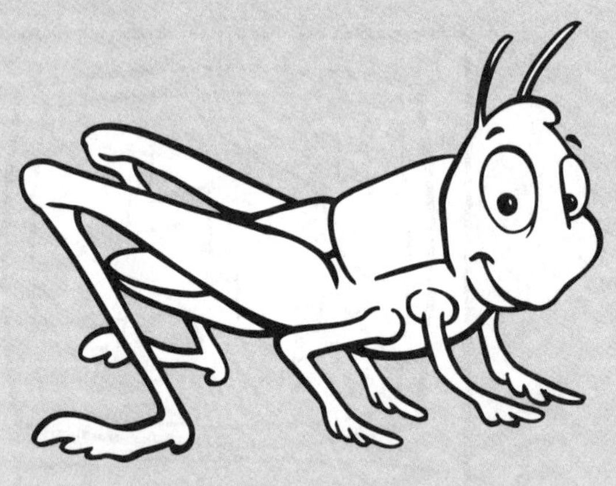

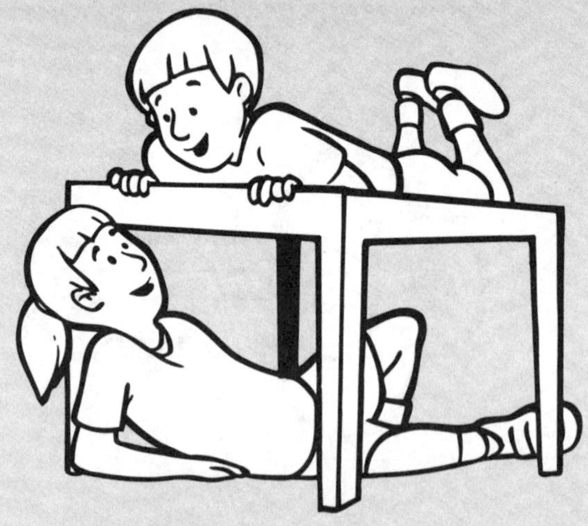

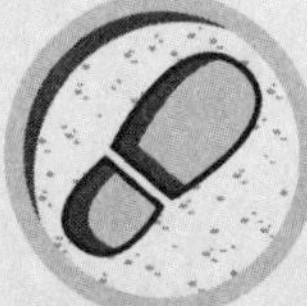

One Step Further

Look up. What do you see? Look under your bed. What do you see there?

Letter Vv

Directions: Circle the **V** or **v** in these words:

Valerie	violin	vest
Victor	valentine	van

Directions: Color the pictures that start with the sound of **Vv**.

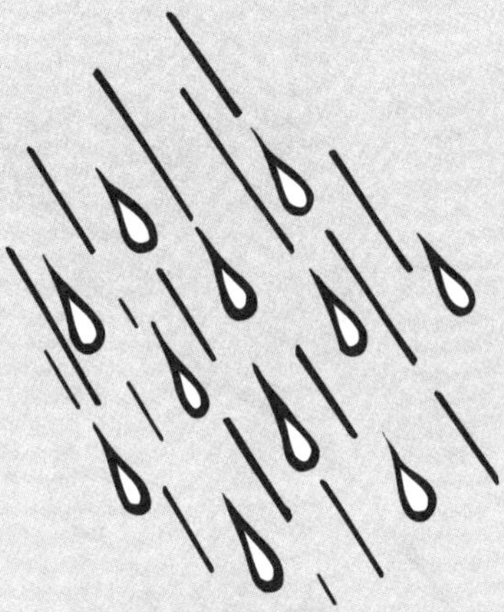

One Step Further

Make a valentine to give to a friend. Decorate it using your favorite colors.

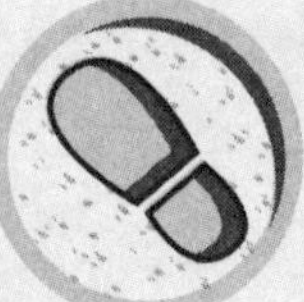

Letter Recognition

READING

Letter Ww

Directions: Circle the **W** or **w** in these words:

window	Walter	walk
win	white	Wendy

Directions: Color the pictures that start with the sound of **Ww**.

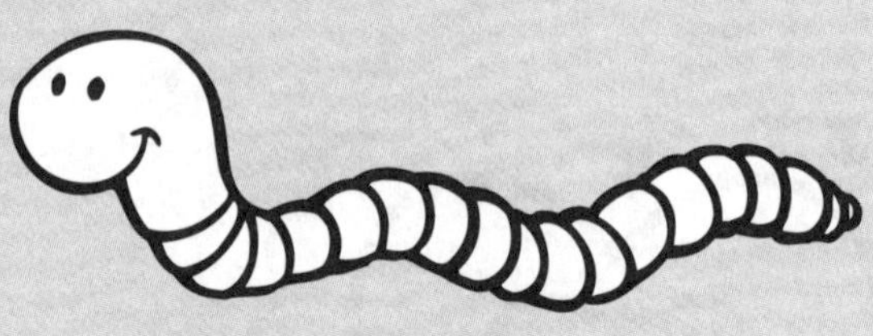

One Step Further

Go for a walk around your home.
Do you see anything that starts with a **W**?

Letter Xx

Directions: Circle the **X** or **x** in these words:

Xavier	X-ray	exit
Rex	xylophone	tax

Directions: Color the pictures that start with the sound of **Xx**.

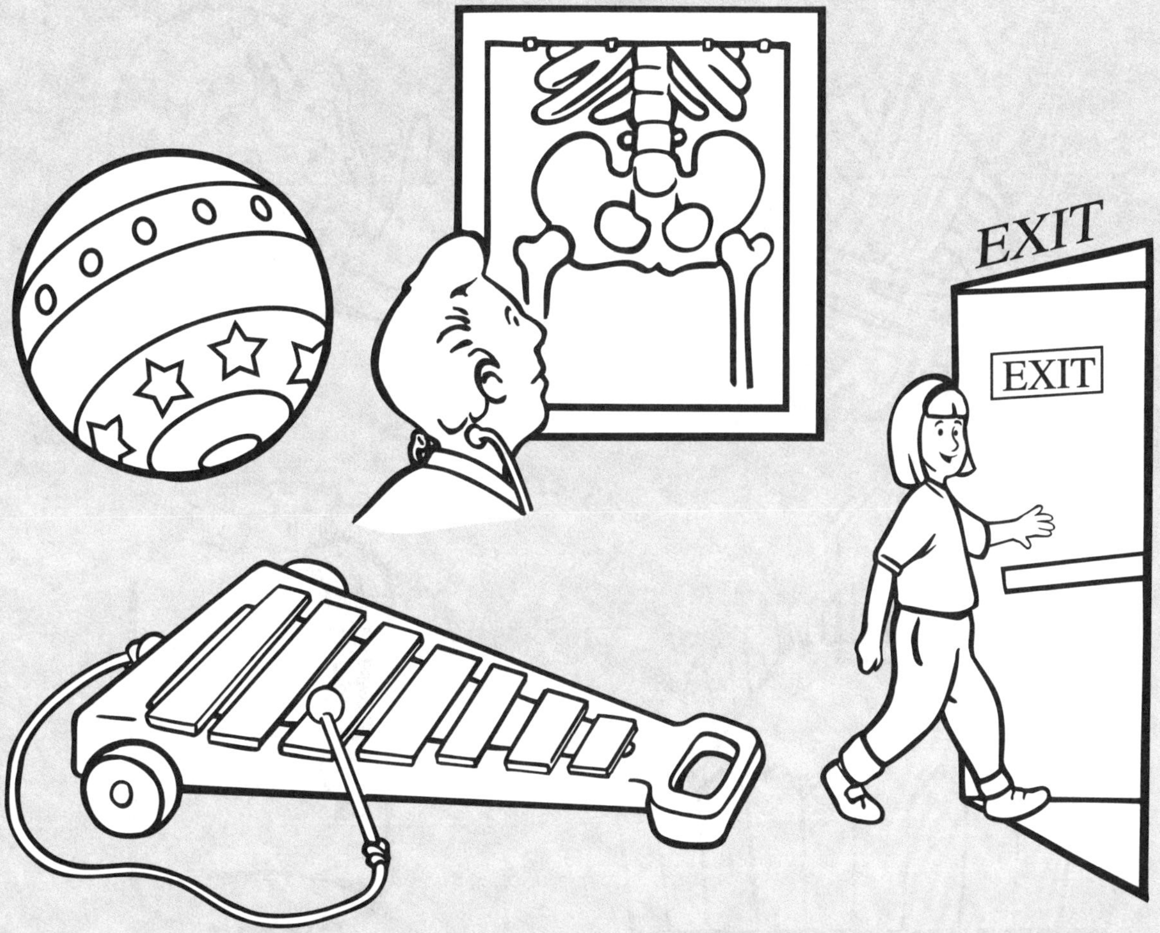

EXIT

EXIT

One Step Further

Draw an **X** on the first red object you see in this book.

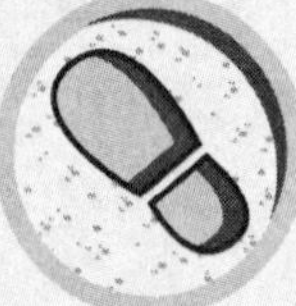

Letter Yy

Directions: Circle the **Y** or **y** in these words:

yarn	yo-yo	yard
Yuri	Yvonne	yes

Directions: Color the pictures that start with the sound of **Yy**.

JAR

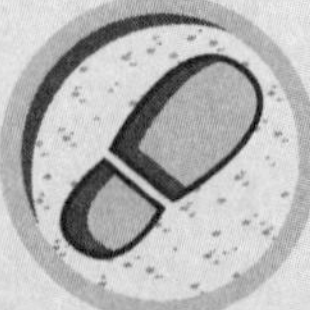

One Step Further

Ask an adult to cut a piece of yarn. How many shapes can you make with the yarn?

Letter Zz

Directions: Circle the **Z** or **z** in these words:

zipper	**zebra**	**zig-zag**
Zelda	**zero**	**zoo**

Directions: Color the pictures that start with the sound of **Zz**.

ZOOM!

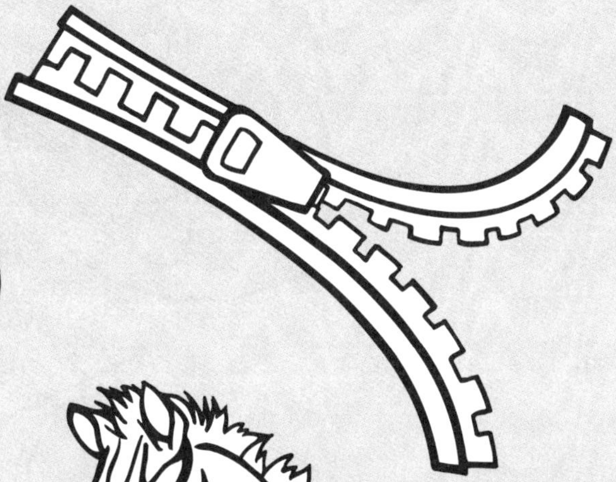

One Step Further

Find a shirt or jacket that has a zipper. Put it on and zip it all the way up.

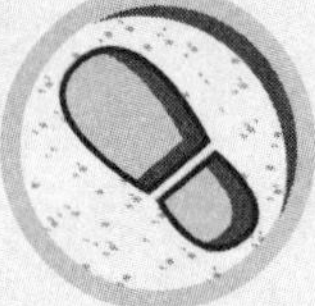

Letter Recognition

READING

Review Letters A–Z

Directions: Draw a line to connect the dots from **A–Z**. Use the correct color for each part of the line.

A–F = **red** F–I = **yellow** I–N = **blue** N–T = **green** T–Z = **purple**

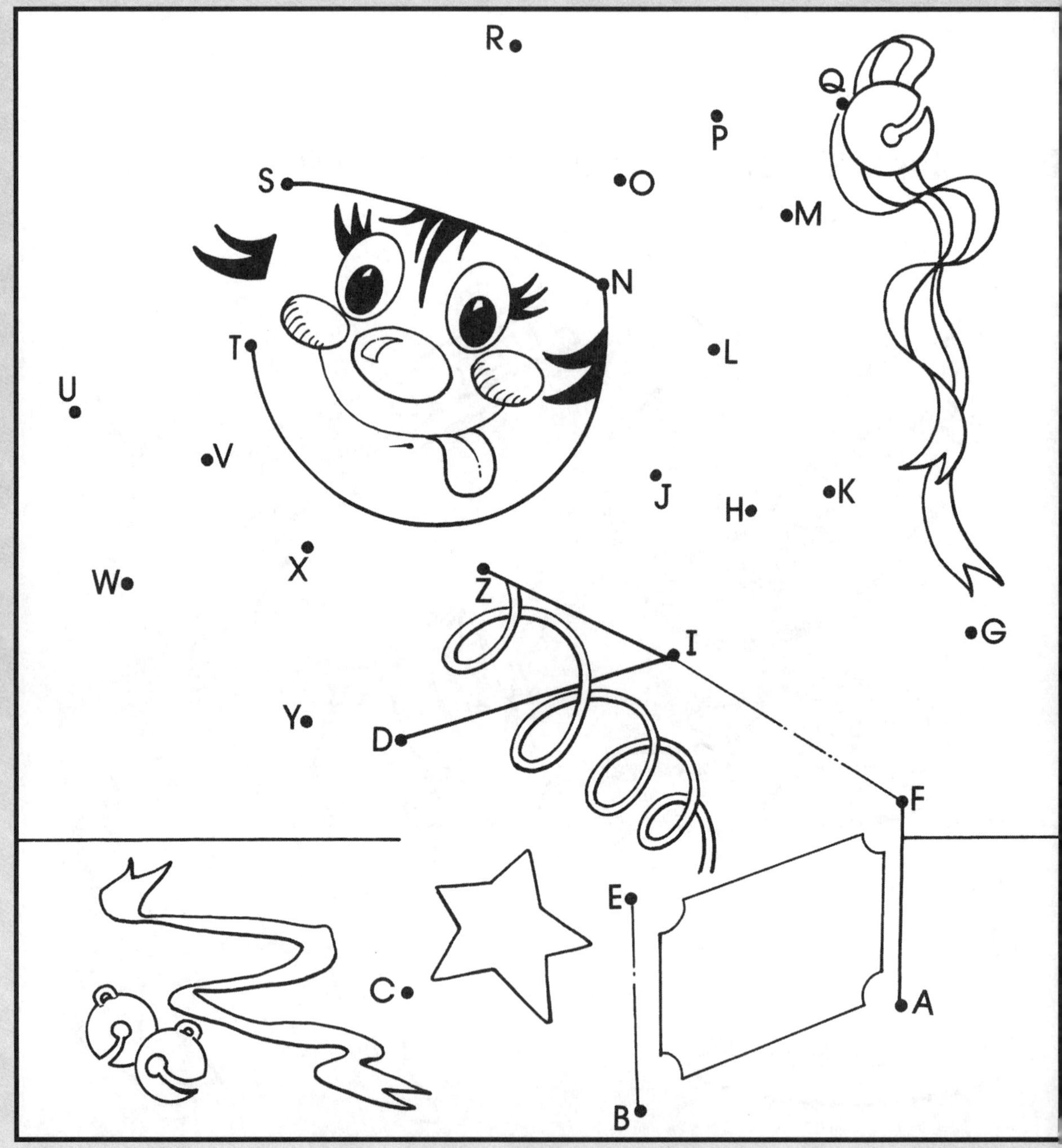

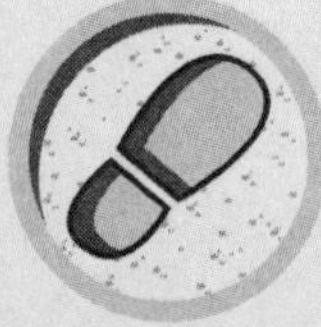

One Step Further

Draw a rainbow. Color it using the colors you used in the activity on this page.

Review Letters A–Z

Directions: Draw lines to match the **UPPER** and **lowercase** letters that go together.

m

f

b

S

T

a

A

t

F

B

s

M

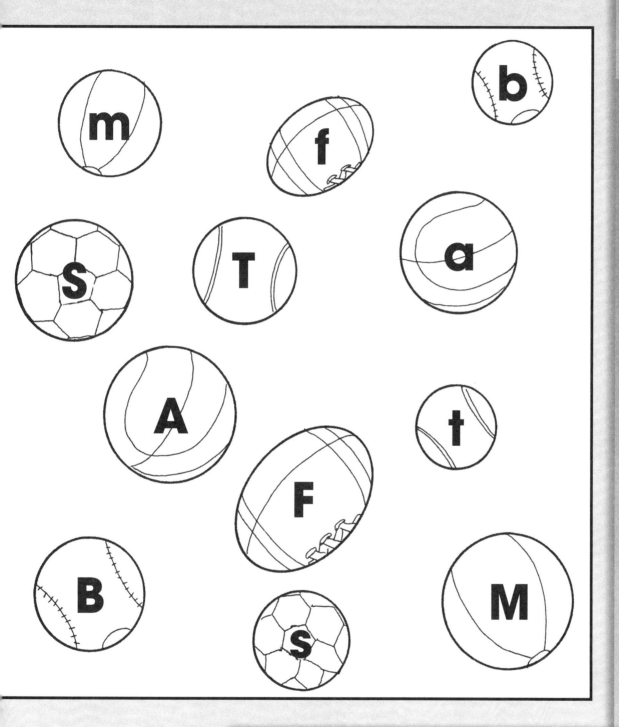

One Step Further

Pick one of these sports balls. Find a friend and play a game with just the two of you.

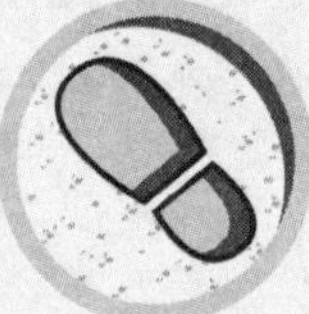

Review Letters A–Z

Directions: Draw lines to match the **UPPER** and **lowercase** letters that go together.

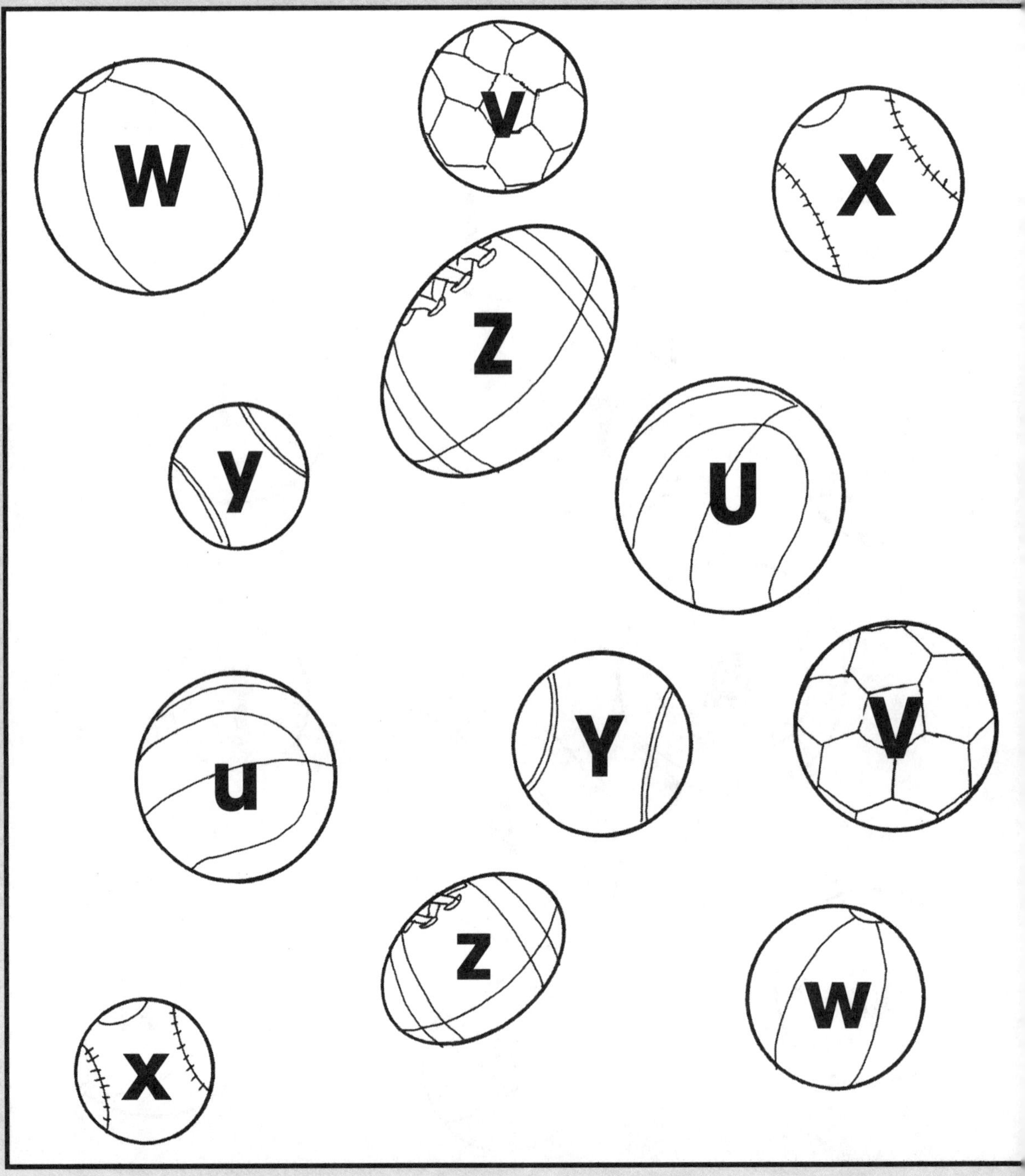

W v X

Z

y U

u Y V

z w

x

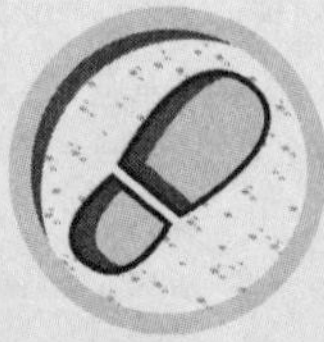

One Step Further

Think of your favorite sport.
What letter does that sport start with?

Review Letters A-Z

Directions: Draw a line from **A-Z** to show the way to the grandparents' house.

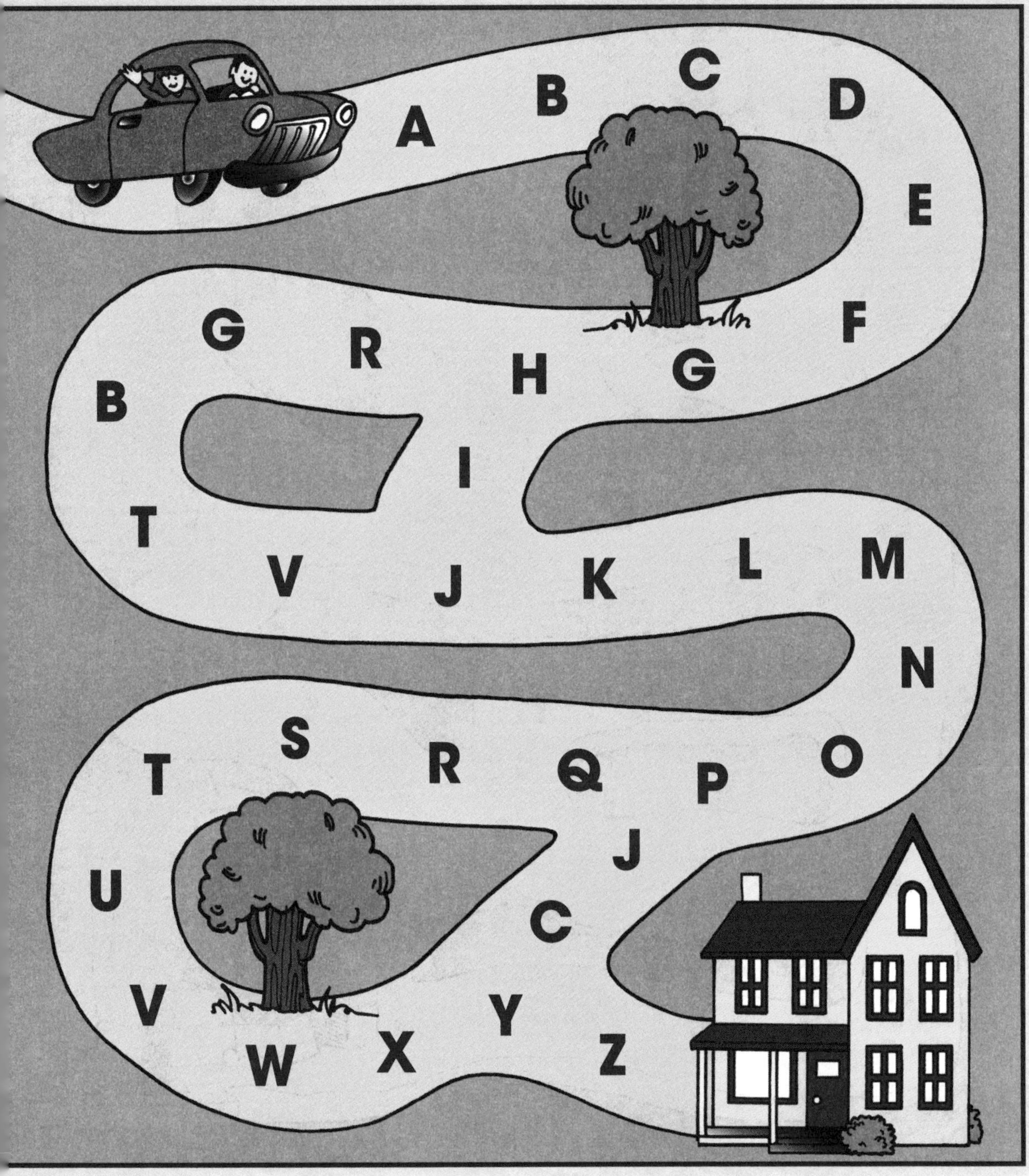

One Step Further

Who do you most like to visit?
What do you do when you visit that person?

Review Letters A-Z

Directions: Draw a line from **A-Z** to show the way to Penguin's house.

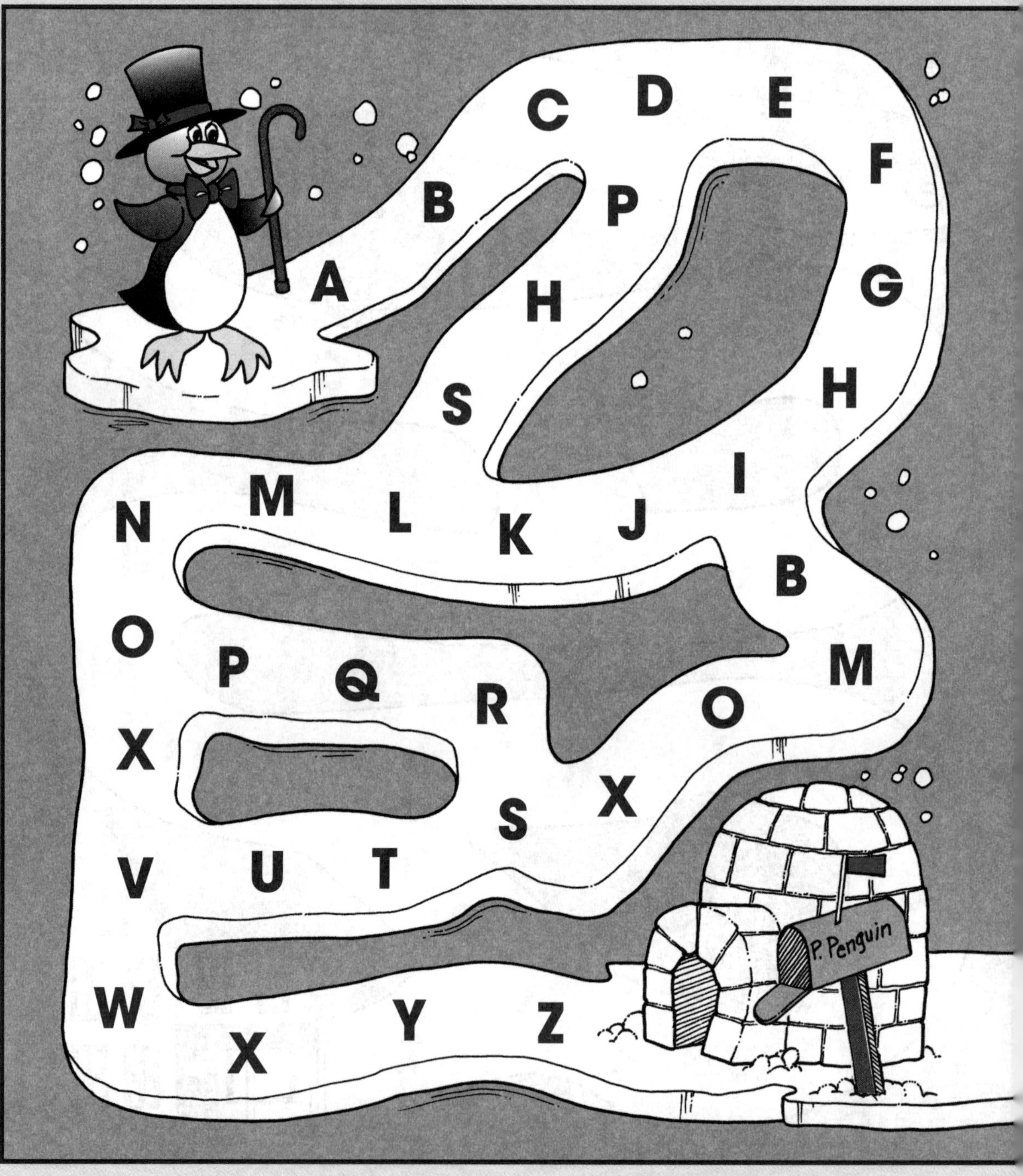

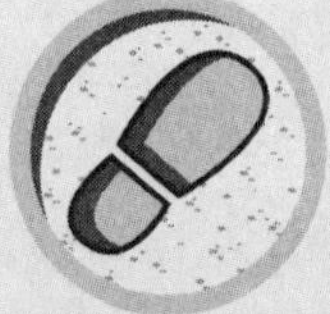

One Step Further

Draw a picture of you doing your favorite activity. Mail it to someone special.

Color These Cows

Directions: Color the cows using the clues below.

The **brown** cow is hiding.
The **black**-and-**pink** spotted cow is eating.
The **blue** cow is fat!

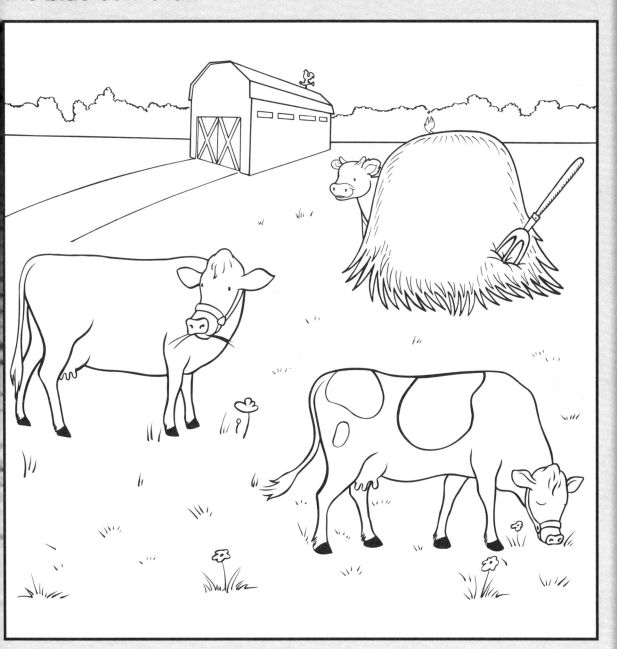

One Step Further

Pretend you are on a farm.
What are some fun things you would do?

Stop Making Sense!

Reading Comprehension

READING

Directions: Look at the picture. A lot of silly things are happening! Circle all of the things that do **not** make sense.

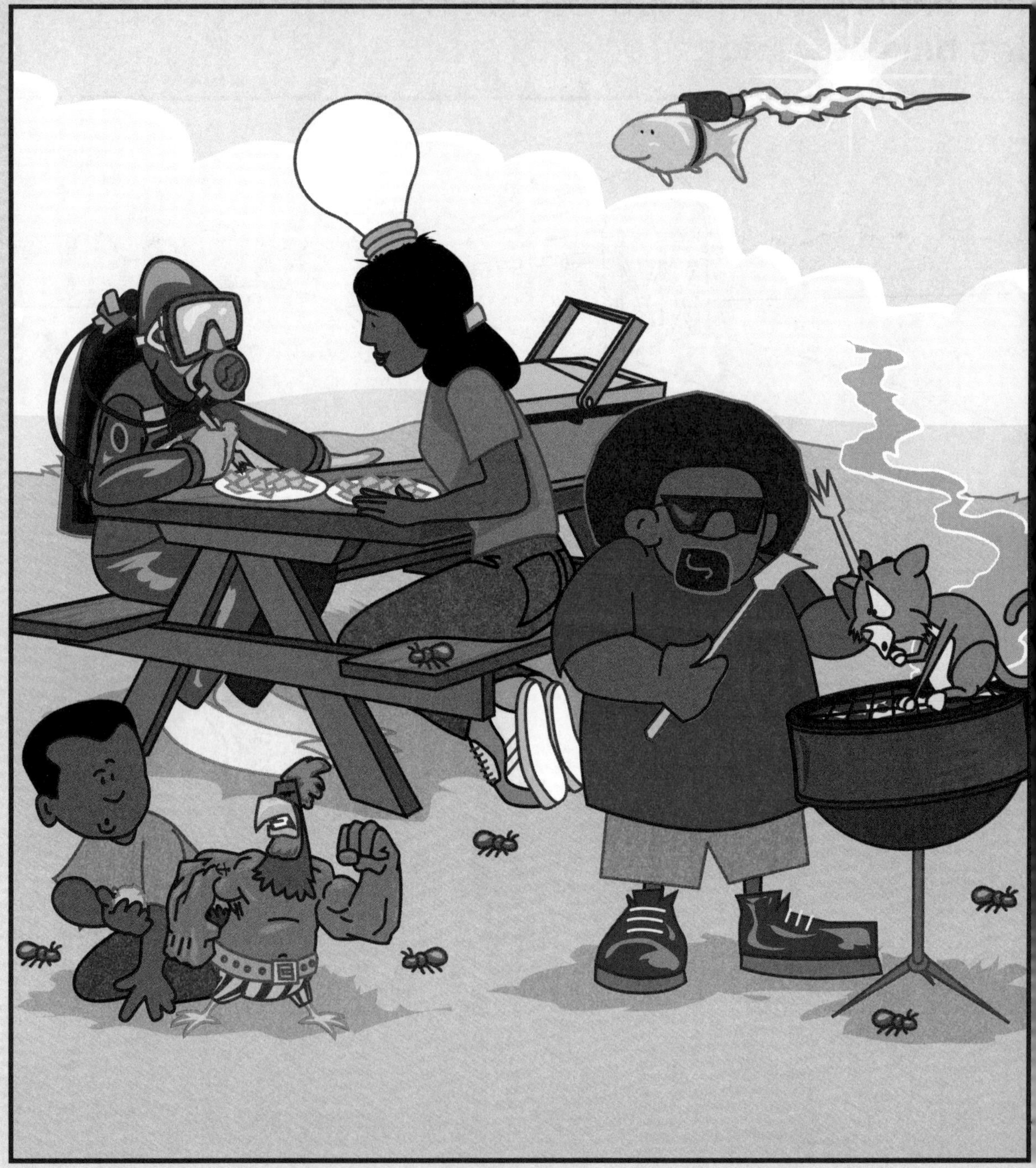

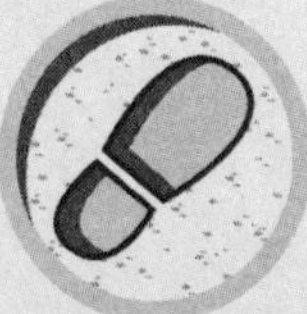

One Step Further

Make up a story about a picnic. Tell it to a friend.

Ben's New Sister

Directions: Ben is going to see his new baby sister for the first time! Ben and his dad are at the hospital looking at all the sleeping babies. Use the clues to find out which baby is Ben's new sister. Then, circle your choice.

Ben's sister is **not** bald.
Ben's sister has a yellow blanket.
Ben's sister has dark hair.

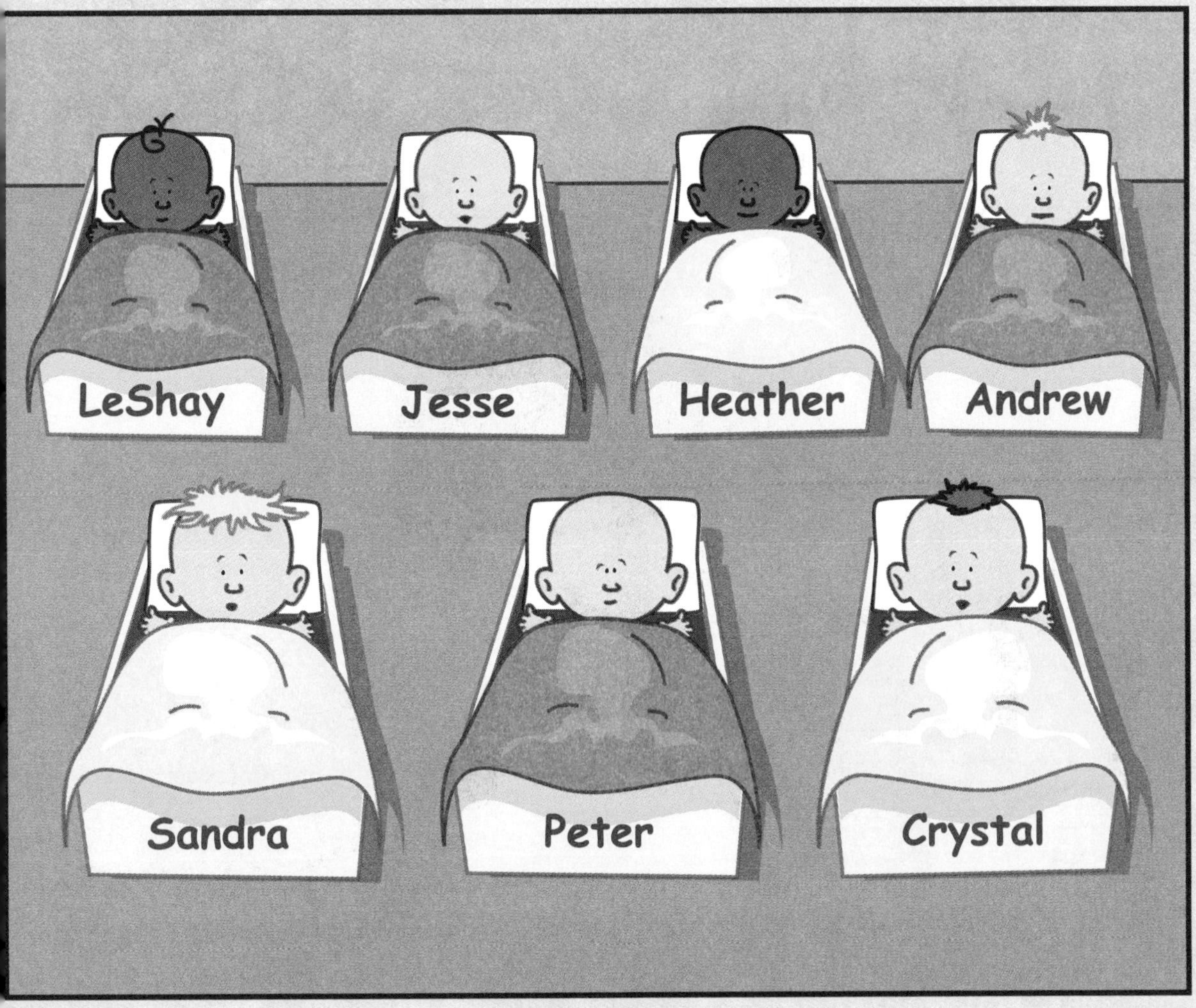

LeShay | Jesse | Heather | Andrew

Sandra | Peter | Crystal

One Step Further

Tell a story about the babies in this picture. What are the babies doing?

Reading Comprehension

READING

Tim's Turtle

Directions: Help Tim pick out a turtle at the pet shop.

Tim does **not** want a turtle with circles on its back.
Tim does **not** want a **green** turtle.
Tim does **not** want a turtle with triangles on its back.

Circle the turtle that Tim should pick.

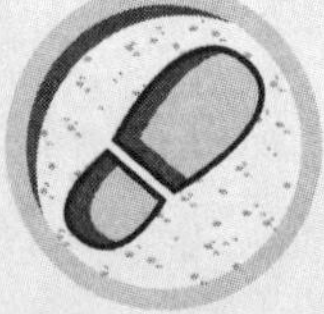

One Step Further
Which turtle would you pick?
What would you name it?

Find the Right Picture

Directions: Which picture goes with the sentence? Circle the correct picture.

The three little pigs had a picnic in the tree to escape from the big bad wolf.

One Step Further

Look at the third picture.
Tell a story about what is happening.

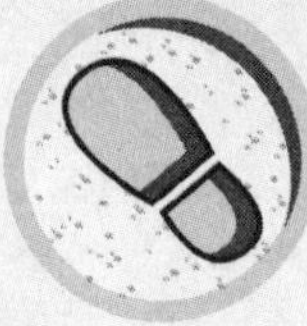

Find the Right Picture

Directions: Which picture goes with the sentence? Circle the correct picture.

Marilyn and Mindy went on a Ferris wheel ride with their parents.

One Step Further

What is your favorite ride at the fair?
What else do you like about the fair?

Find the Right Picture

Directions: Which picture goes with the sentence? Circle the correct picture.

Raju and her mom spent Saturday alone. They painted pictures together.

One Step Further

Paint a picture with a friend.
What did you paint?

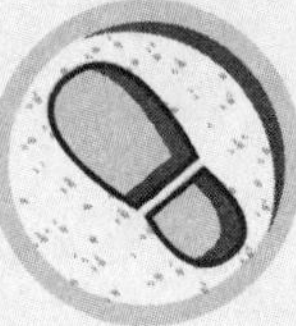

Which Picture is Missing?

Directions: Look at the pictures below. There is a picture missing.

Directions: Circle the missing picture.

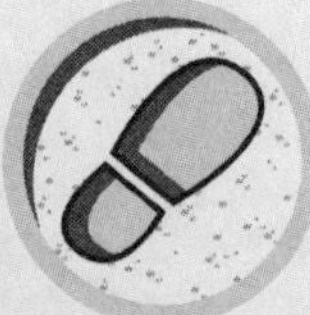

One Step Further

Think about your bath time.
What do you do first?

Which Picture is Missing?

Directions: Look at the pictures below. There is a picture missing.

Directions: Circle the missing picture.

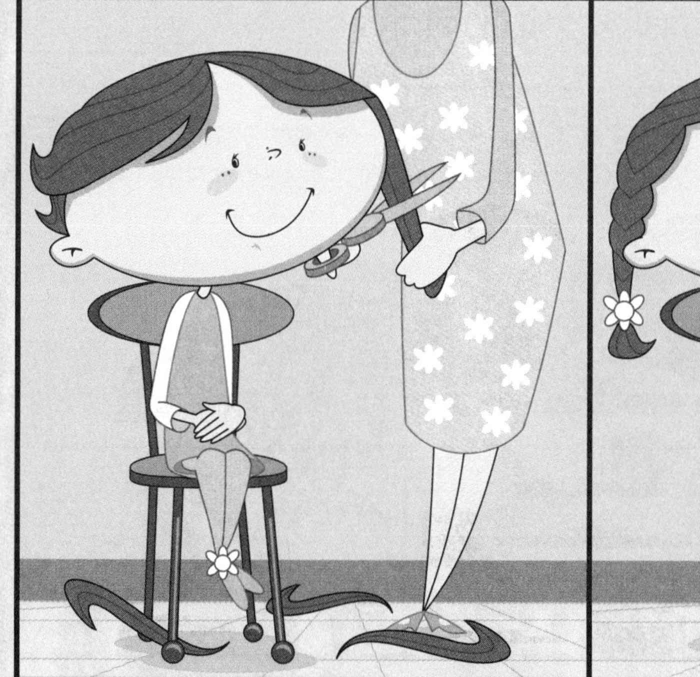

One Step Further

Tell a story about getting a haircut.
Do you like getting your hair cut?

Which Picture is Missing?

Directions: Look at the pictures below. There is a picture missing.

Directions: Circle the missing picture.

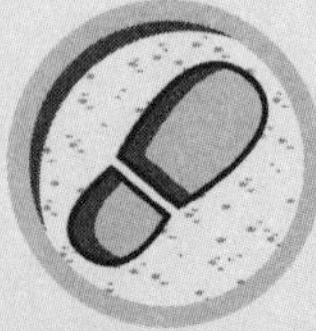

One Step Further

Work with a friend to draw a beautiful picture. What did you draw?

I'm Hungry!

Directions: Draw a line to match each animal to the food it likes to eat.

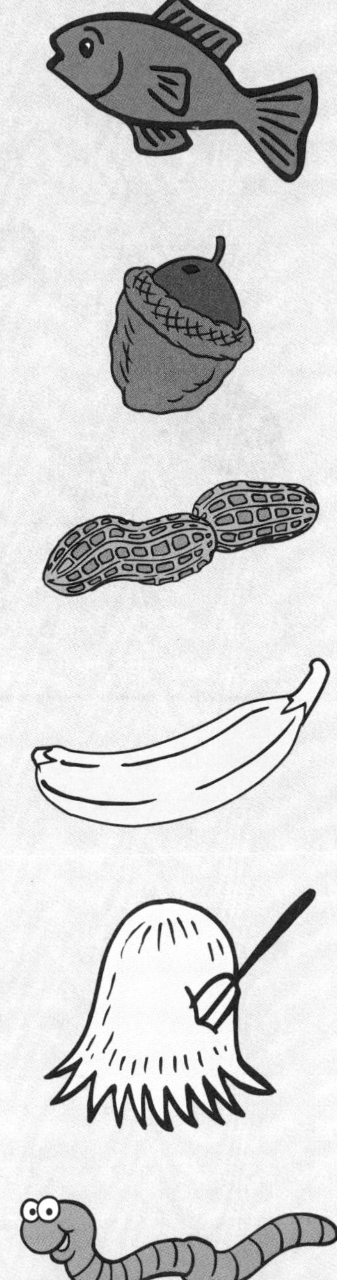

One Step Further

What is your favorite afternoon snack? Is it the same snack these animals like to eat?

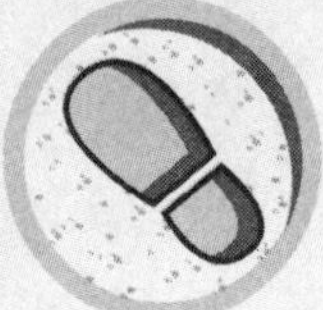

Not in the Nest

Directions: A mother robin wants to build a nest for her new babies. Draw an **X** on the things they will **not** need. Then, draw a picture of some other things she might need.

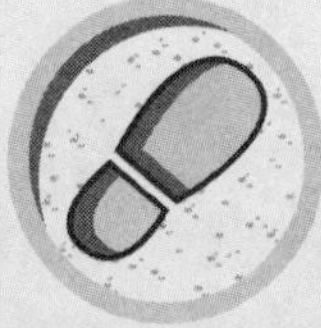

One Step Further

Look up in some trees around your neighborhood. Do you see any nests?

Puppy Needs

Directions: Marcy and her dad want to build a doghouse for their new puppy. Draw an **X** on the things they will **not** need. Then, draw a picture of some other things they might need.

One Step Further

What other things do puppies need, besides a doghouse? Draw them.

Super Ice-Cream Sundaes!

Directions: Janet and her mom want to make ice-cream sundaes. Draw an **X** on the things they will **not** need. Then, draw a picture of some other things they might need.

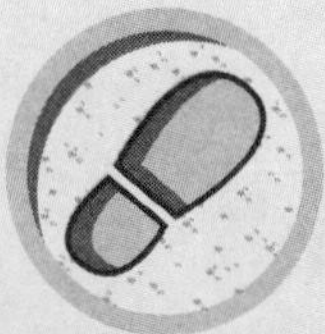

One Step Further

Look around your kitchen. What items can you find for an ice-cream sundae?

What's Missing?

Directions: Look at the pictures below. They start to tell a story. The last box is empty.

Directions: Which of these pictures helps finish the story? Circle it.

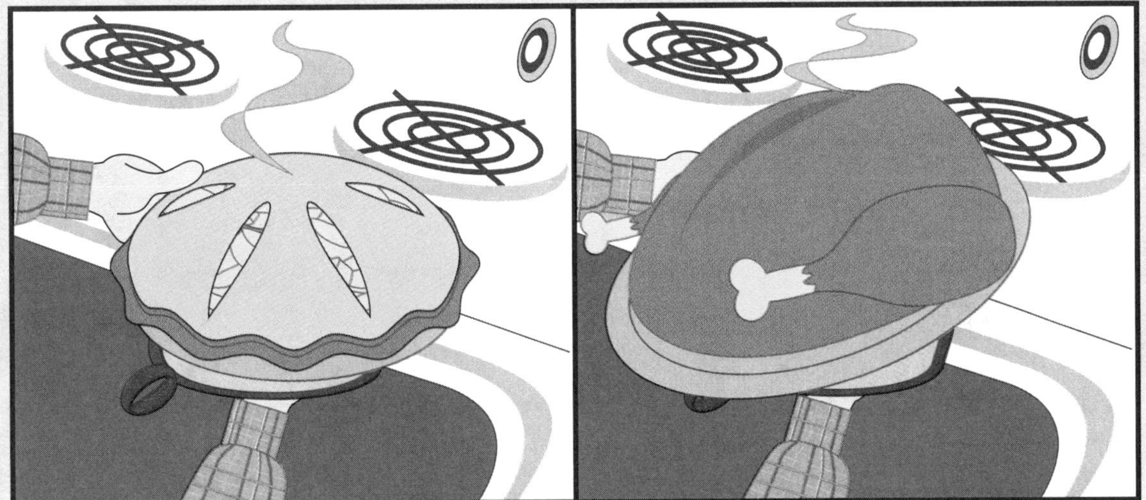

One Step Further

Help an adult bake a pie.
What should you do first?

The Big Finish!

Directions: Look at the pictures below. They start to tell a story. The last box is empty.

Directions: Which of these pictures helps finish the story? Circle it.

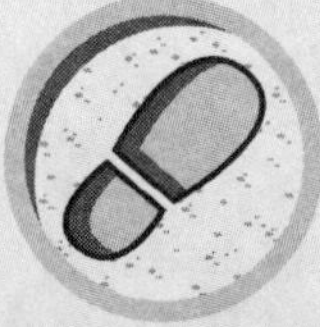

One Step Further
Look at the pictures in this activity.
What do you think will happen next?

What Will Happen Next?

Directions: Look at the picture above. Now, circle the picture below that shows what happens next.

One Step Further

Perform a magic trick for a friend by making a quarter disappear.

Answer Key

6

Shapes

BASIC SKILLS

Circle

Directions: Trace the **circles**.

Directions: Trace the word.

circle

One Step Further
Draw a silly face using circles.
What else can you draw using circles?

Everyday Success Preschool

7

Shapes

BASIC SKILLS

Circle

Directions: This picture has **circles** in it. Trace the circles.

One Step Further
What is your favorite thing to do when it snows? Tell a story about it.

Everyday Success Preschool

8

Shapes

BASIC SKILLS

Square

Directions: Trace the **squares**.

Directions: Trace the word.

square

One Step Further
Pretend the squares on this page are boxes.
Draw a picture inside each box.

Everyday Success Preschool

9

Shapes

BASIC SKILLS

Square

Directions: This picture has **squares** in it. Trace the squares.

One Step Further
Look around you for objects that are squares.
What did you find?

Everyday Success Preschool

10

Shapes

BASIC SKILLS

Triangle

Directions: Trace the **triangles**.

Directions: Trace the word.

triangle

One Step Further
Draw a house using squares and triangles.
What other shapes could you use?

Everyday Success Preschool

11

Shapes

BASIC SKILLS

Triangle

Directions: This picture has **triangles** in it. Trace the triangles.

One Step Further
What is happening in the picture?
Tell a story about it.

Everyday Success Preschool

ANSWER KEY

12

Shapes

BASIC SKILLS

Rectangle

Directions: Trace the **rectangles**.

Directions: Trace the word.

rectangle

One Step Further
Draw a picture using the shapes you have learned so far. What did you draw?

Everyday Success Preschool

13

Shapes

BASIC SKILLS

Rectangle

Directions: This picture has **rectangles** in it. Trace the rectangles.

One Step Further
What is happening in the picture?
Where do you think the train is going?

Everyday Success Preschool

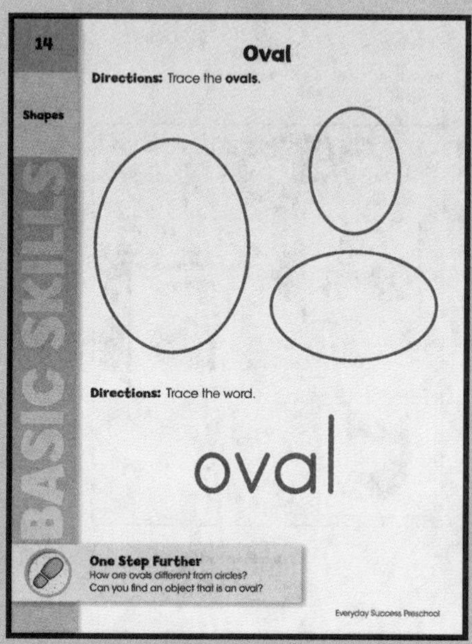

14

Shapes

BASIC SKILLS

Oval

Directions: Trace the **ovals**.

Directions: Trace the word.

oval

One Step Further
How are ovals different from circles?
Can you find an object that is an oval?

Everyday Success Preschool

15

Shapes

BASIC SKILLS

Oval

Directions: This picture has **ovals** in it. Trace the ovals.

One Step Further
What color are your eyes? Find a friend.
Are your eyes the same color?

Everyday Success Preschool

16

Shapes

BASIC SKILLS

Rhombus

Directions: Trace the **rhombuses**.

Directions: Trace the word.

rhombus

One Step Further
Draw a rhombus. Ask a friend to name the shape.

Everyday Success Preschool

17

Shapes

BASIC SKILLS

Rhombus

Directions: This picture has a **rhombus** in it. Trace the rhombus.

One Step Further
What is your favorite sport to play? What do you like about playing that sport?

Everyday Success Preschool

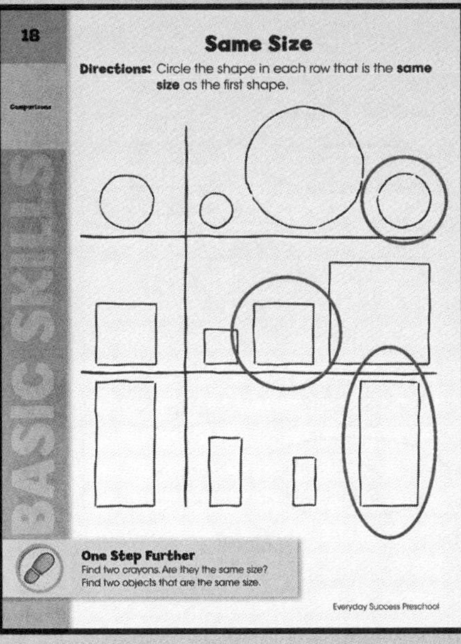

18

Comparisons

BASIC SKILLS

Same Size

Directions: Circle the shape in each row that is the **same size** as the first shape.

One Step Further
Find two crayons. Are they the same size?
Find two objects that are the same size.

Everyday Success Preschool

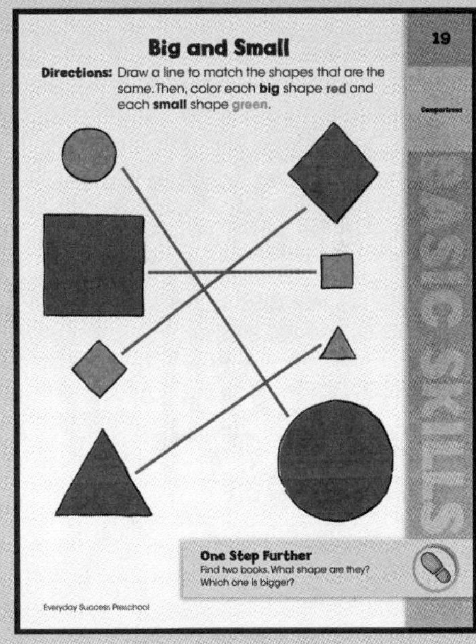

19

Comparisons

BASIC SKILLS

Big and Small

Directions: Draw a line to match the shapes that are the same. Then, color each **big** shape red and each **small** shape green.

One Step Further
Find two books. What shape are they?
Which one is bigger?

Everyday Success Preschool

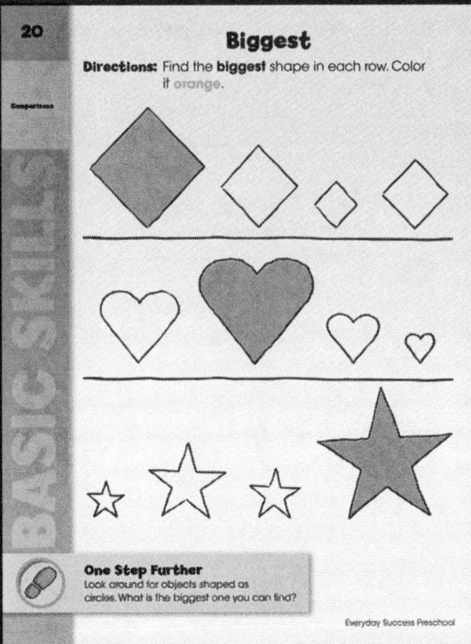

20

Comparisons

BASIC SKILLS

Biggest

Directions: Find the **biggest** shape in each row. Color it orange.

One Step Further
Look around for objects shaped as circles. What is the biggest one you can find?

Everyday Success Preschool

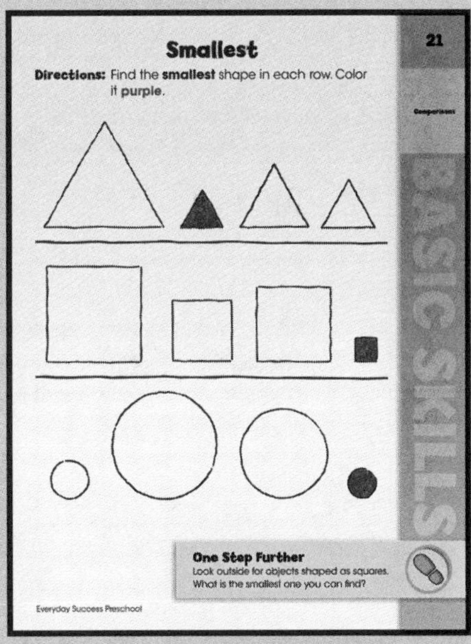

21

Comparisons

BASIC SKILLS

Smallest

Directions: Find the **smallest** shape in each row. Color it **purple**.

One Step Further
Look outside for objects shaped as squares.
What is the smallest one you can find?

Everyday Success Preschool

22

Comparisons

BASIC SKILLS

Short and Tall

Directions: Circle each **short** person below. Draw a line under each **tall** person.

One Step Further
Ask two friends to stand next to each other.
Which one is shorter? Which one is taller?

Everyday Success Preschool

23

Comparisons

BASIC SKILLS

Shorter

Directions: Look at the flagpole and flag below. Draw another flagpole and flag beside it. Make your flagpole **shorter** than the first one.

One Step Further
Stand next to a friend. Who is shorter?
How much shorter?

Everyday Success Preschool

24

Comparisons

BASIC SKILLS

Taller

Directions: Look at the table below. Draw another table beside it. Make your table **taller** than the first one.

One Step Further
Find something in your home that is taller than you. What is it?

Everyday Success Preschool

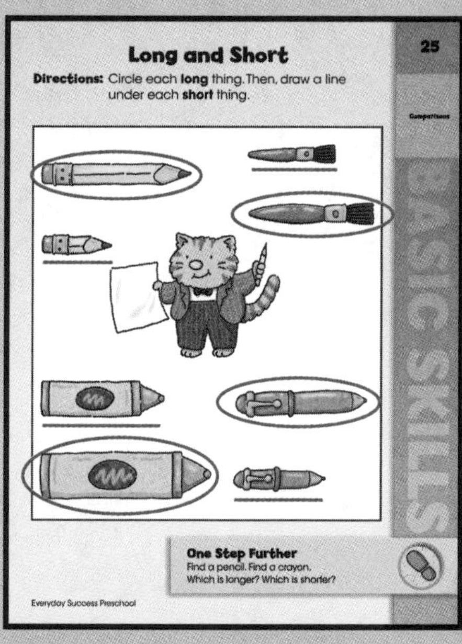

25

Comparisons

BASIC SKILLS

Long and Short

Directions: Circle each **long** thing. Then, draw a line under each **short** thing.

One Step Further
Find a pencil. Find a crayon. Which is longer? Which is shorter?

Everyday Success Preschool

26

Comparisons

BASIC SKILLS

Longer

Directions: Look at the snake. Draw a **longer** snake below it.

One Step Further
Ask a friend to draw a ruler. Then, draw a longer ruler next to it.

Everyday Success Preschool

27

Comparisons

BASIC SKILLS

Shorter

Directions: Look at the top cat. Draw a **shorter** tail on the bottom cat.

One Step Further
What is happening in the picture? Tell a story about it.

Everyday Success Preschool

28

Opposites

BASIC SKILLS

Big

Directions: Look at the picture. Trace the word.

big

One Step Further
Look around your room for a big object. What did you find?

Everyday Success Preschool

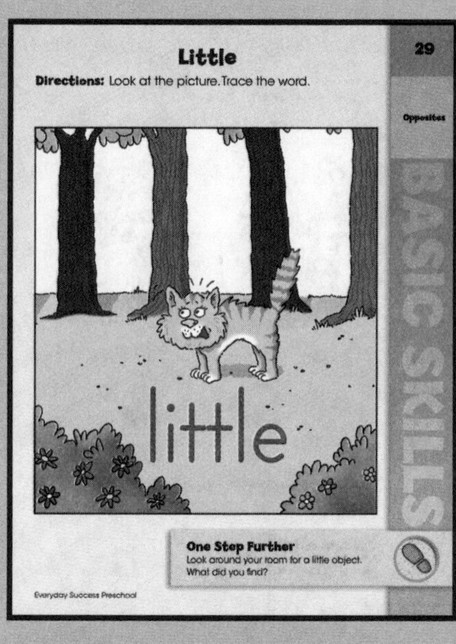

29

Opposites

BASIC SKILLS

Little

Directions: Look at the picture. Trace the word.

little

One Step Further
Look around your room for a little object. What did you find?

Everyday Success Preschool

30

Opposites

BASIC SKILLS

Slow

Directions: Look at the picture. Trace the word.

slow

One Step Further
Turtles walk slow. Walk slowly around a table or desk.

Everyday Success Preschool

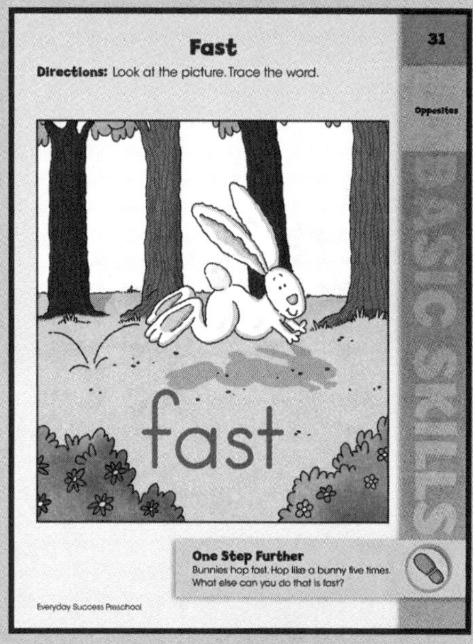

31

Opposites

BASIC SKILLS

Fast

Directions: Look at the picture. Trace the word.

fast

One Step Further
Bunnies hop fast. Hop like a bunny five times. What else can you do that is fast?

Everyday Success Preschool

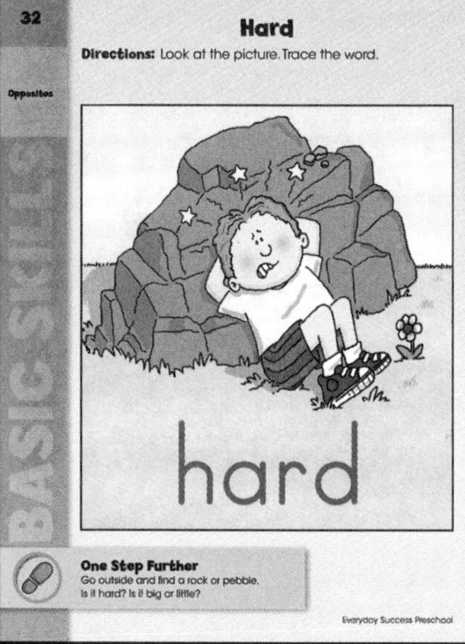

32

Opposites

BASIC SKILLS

Hard

Directions: Look at the picture. Trace the word.

hard

One Step Further
Go outside and find a rock or pebble. Is it hard? Is it big or little?

Everyday Success Preschool

33

Opposites

BASIC SKILLS

Soft

Directions: Look at the picture. Trace the word.

soft

One Step Further
Find your favorite stuffed animal. Does it feel soft?

Everyday Success Preschool

34

Opposites

BASIC SKILLS

In

Directions: Look at the picture. Trace the word.

in

One Step Further
What is your favorite game to play inside? Ask a friend to play it with you.

Everyday Success Preschool

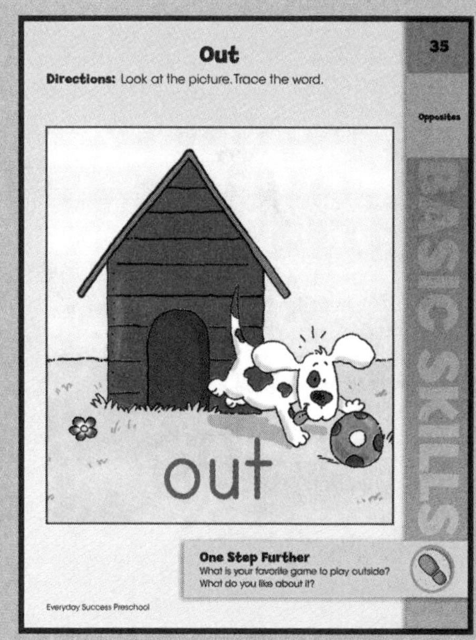

35

Opposites

BASIC SKILLS

Out

Directions: Look at the picture. Trace the word.

out

One Step Further
What is your favorite game to play outside? What do you like about it?

Everyday Success Preschool

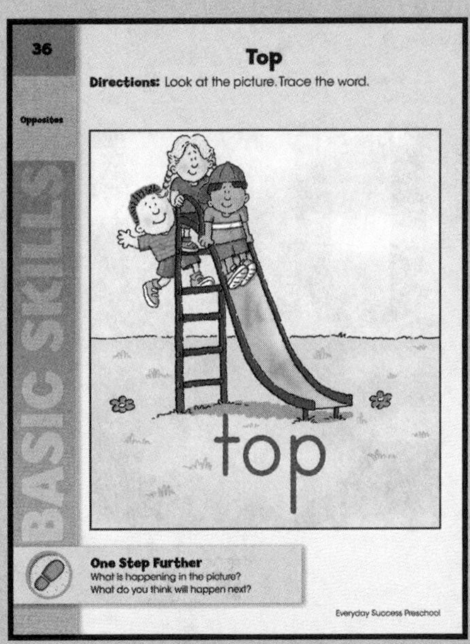
36

Opposites

BASIC SKILLS

Top

Directions: Look at the picture. Trace the word.

top

One Step Further
What is happening in the picture?
What do you think will happen next?

Everyday Success Preschool

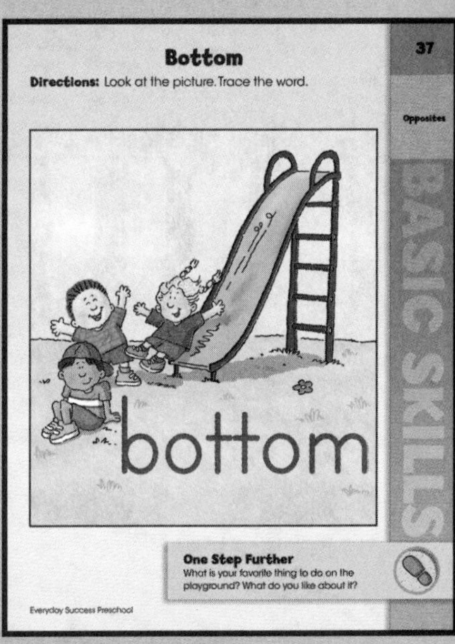
37

Opposites

BASIC SKILLS

Bottom

Directions: Look at the picture. Trace the word.

bottom

One Step Further
What is your favorite thing to do on the playground? What do you like about it?

Everyday Success Preschool

38

Opposites

BASIC SKILLS

Full

Directions: Look at the picture. Trace the word.

full

One Step Further
Ask an adult to give you a cup of water.
Is the cup full?

Everyday Success Preschool

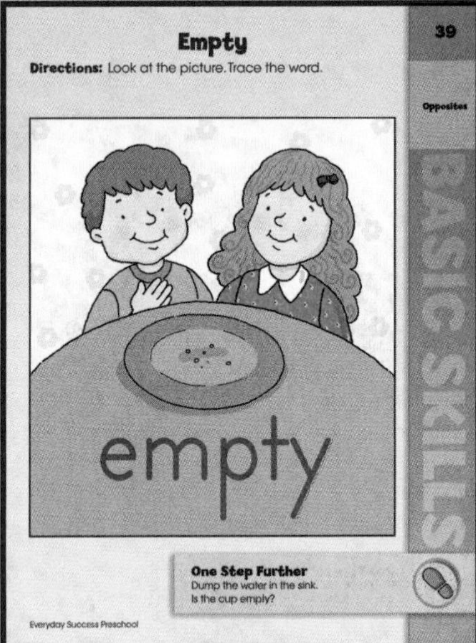
39

Opposites

BASIC SKILLS

Empty

Directions: Look at the picture. Trace the word.

empty

One Step Further
Dump the water in the sink.
Is the cup empty?

Everyday Success Preschool

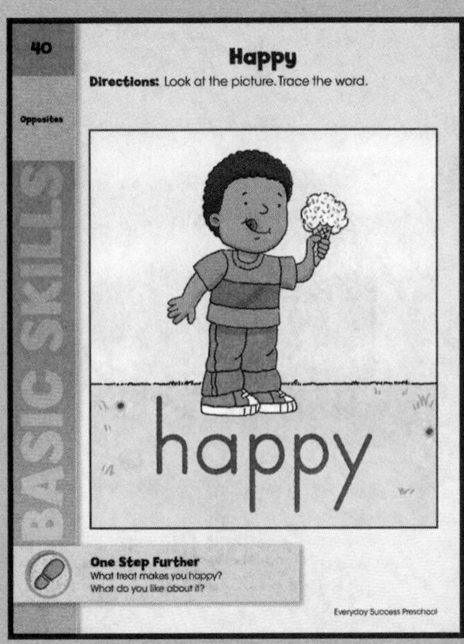
40

Opposites

BASIC SKILLS

Happy

Directions: Look at the picture. Trace the word.

happy

One Step Further
What treat makes you happy?
What do you like about it?

Everyday Success Preschool

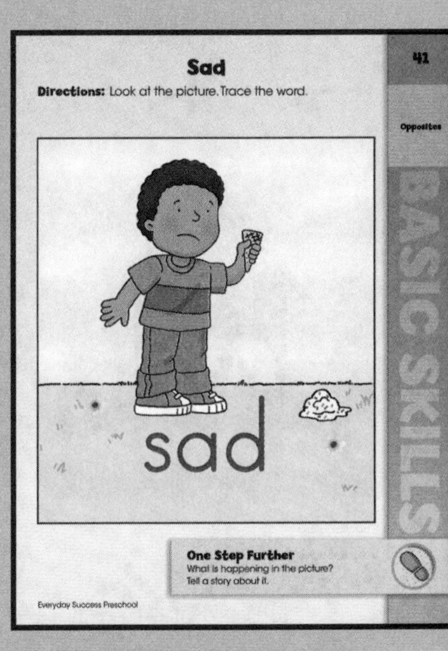
41

Opposites

BASIC SKILLS

Sad

Directions: Look at the picture. Trace the word.

sad

One Step Further
What is happening in the picture?
Tell a story about it.

Everyday Success Preschool

42 Opposites BASIC SKILLS

Up

Directions: Look at the picture. Trace the word.

up

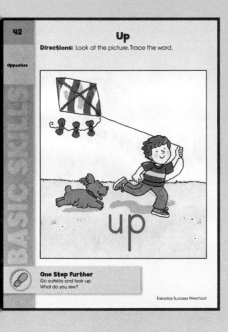

One Step Further
Go outside and look up.
What do you see?

Everyday Success Preschool

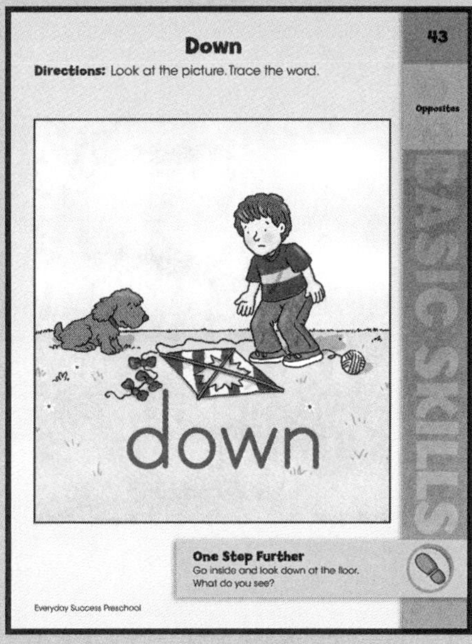

43
Opposites
BASIC SKILLS
Down
Directions: Look at the picture. Trace the word.
down
One Step Further
Go inside and look down at the floor.
What do you see?
Everyday Success Preschool

44 Opposites BASIC SKILLS

On

Directions: Look at the picture. Trace the word.

on

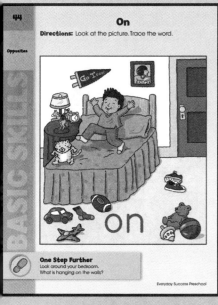

One Step Further
Look around your bedroom.
What is hanging on the walls?

Everyday Success Preschool

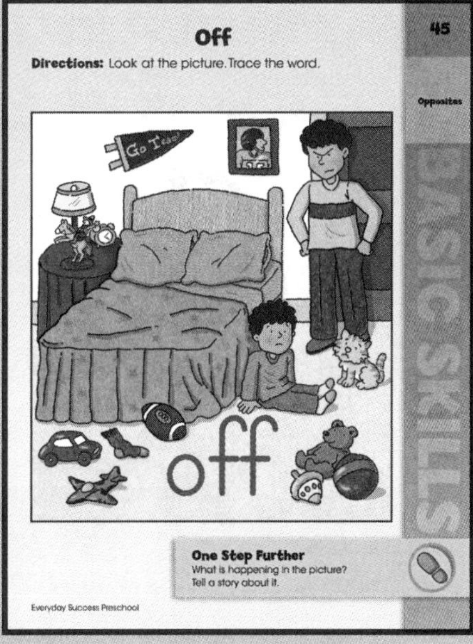

46 Opposites BASIC SKILLS

Over

Directions: Look at the picture. Trace the word.

over

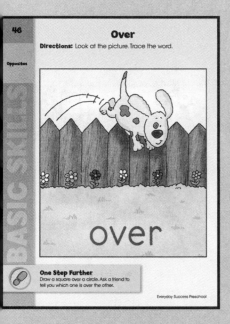

One Step Further
Draw a square over a circle. Ask a friend to tell you which one is over the other.

Everyday Success Preschool

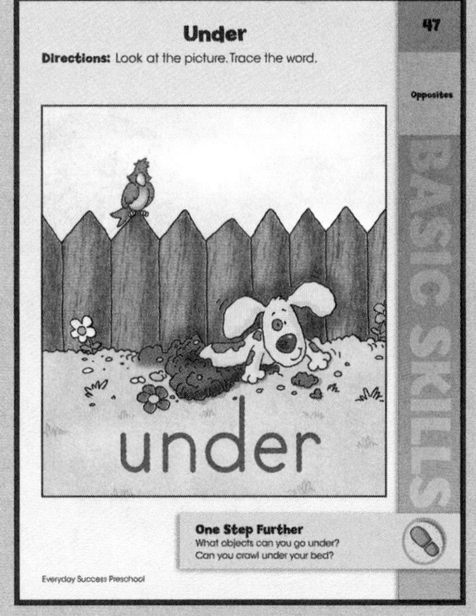

47
Opposites
BASIC SKILLS
Under
Directions: Look at the picture. Trace the word.
under
One Step Further
What objects can you go under?
Can you crawl under your bed?
Everyday Success Preschool

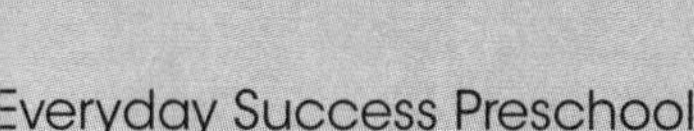

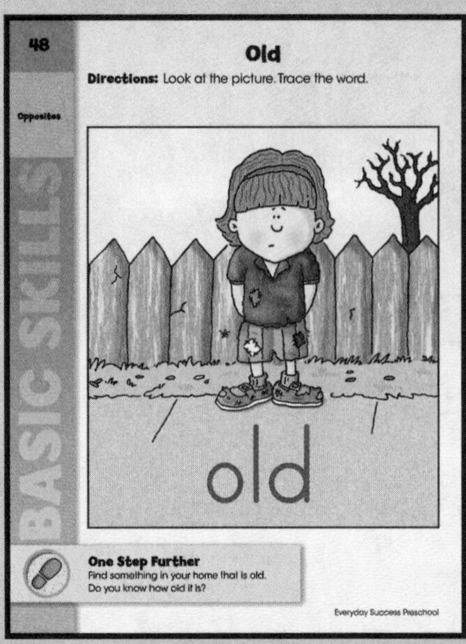
48

Opposites

BASIC SKILLS

Old

Directions: Look at the picture. Trace the word.

One Step Further
Find something in your home that is old. Do you know how old it is?

Everyday Success Preschool

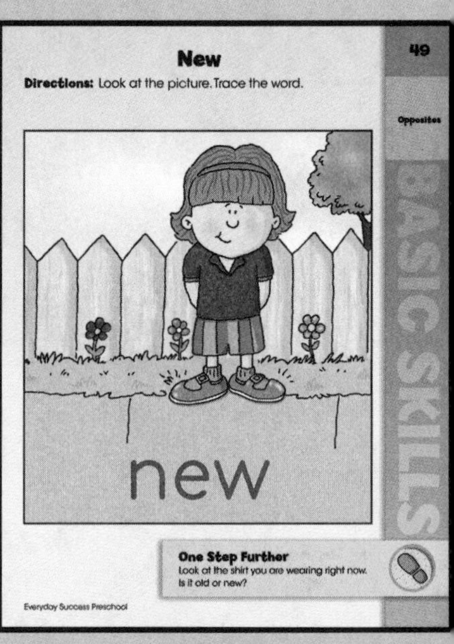
49

Opposites

BASIC SKILLS

New

Directions: Look at the picture. Trace the word.

One Step Further
Look at the shirt you are wearing right now. Is it old or new?

Everyday Success Preschool

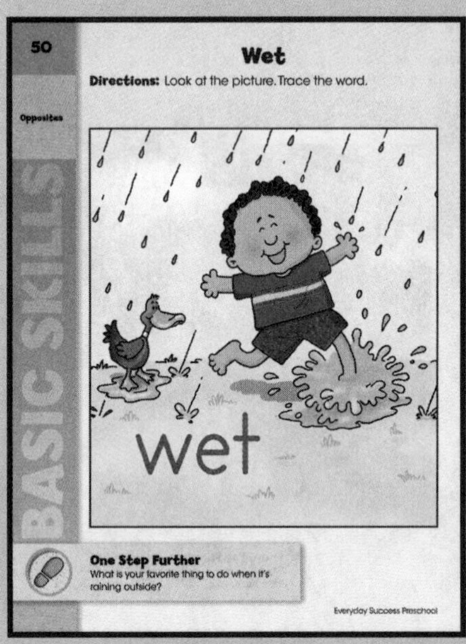
50

Opposites

BASIC SKILLS

Wet

Directions: Look at the picture. Trace the word.

One Step Further
What is your favorite thing to do when it's raining outside?

Everyday Success Preschool

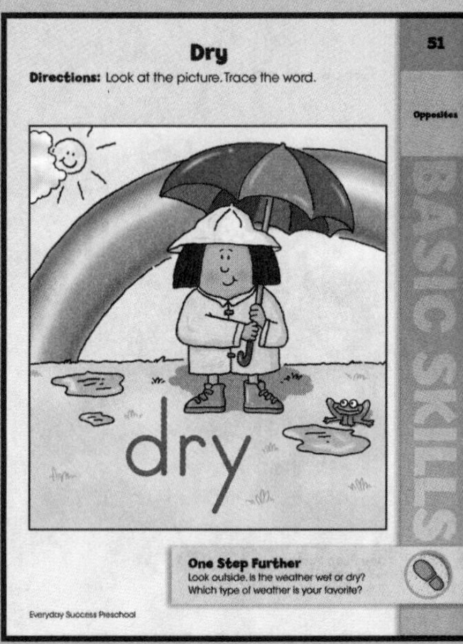
51

Opposites

BASIC SKILLS

Dry

Directions: Look at the picture. Trace the word.

One Step Further
Look outside. Is the weather wet or dry? Which type of weather is your favorite?

Everyday Success Preschool

52

Opposites

BASIC SKILLS

Hot

Directions: Look at the picture. Trace the word.

One Step Further
What is happening in the picture? What do you think will happen next?

Everyday Success Preschool

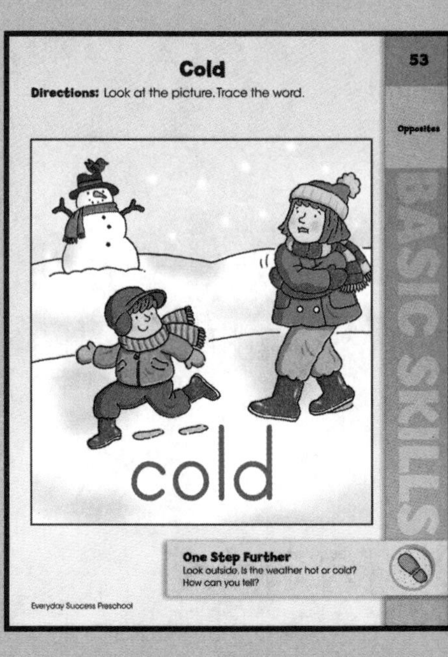
53

Opposites

BASIC SKILLS

Cold

Directions: Look at the picture. Trace the word.

One Step Further
Look outside. Is the weather hot or cold? How can you tell?

Everyday Success Preschool

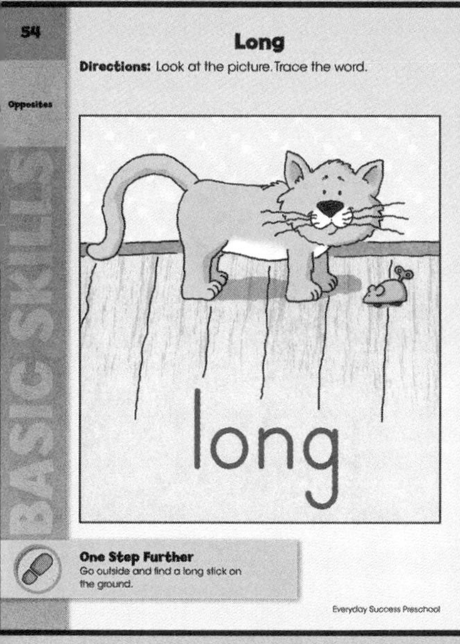
54
Long
Directions: Look at the picture. Trace the word.
Opposites
BASIC SKILLS
long
One Step Further
Go outside and find a long stick on the ground.
Everyday Success Preschool

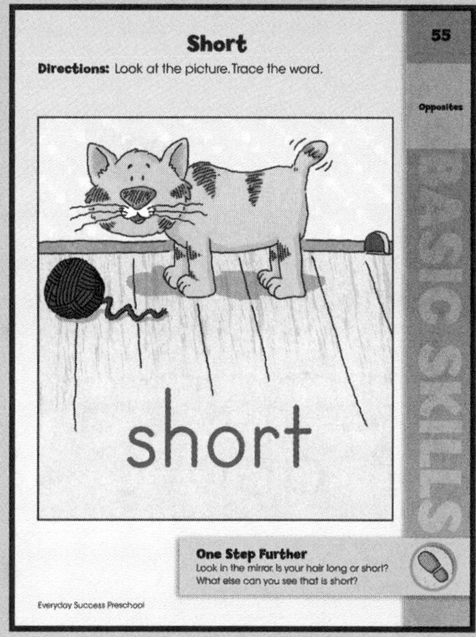
55
Short
Directions: Look at the picture. Trace the word.
Opposites
BASIC SKILLS
short
One Step Further
Look in the mirror. Is your hair long or short? What else can you see that is short?
Everyday Success Preschool

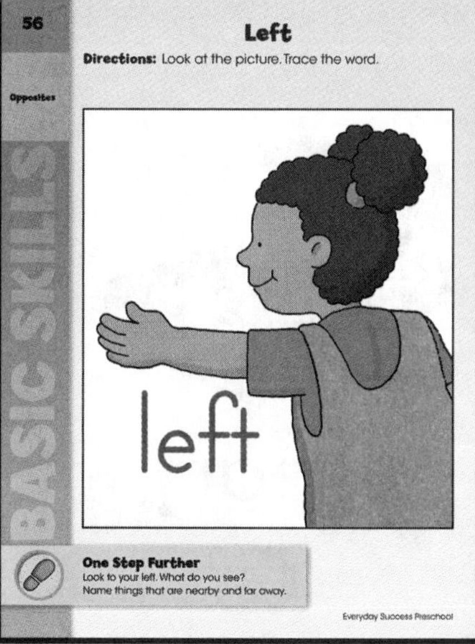
56
Left
Directions: Look at the picture. Trace the word.
Opposites
BASIC SKILLS
left
One Step Further
Look to your left. What do you see? Name things that are nearby and far away.
Everyday Success Preschool

57
Right
Directions: Look at the picture. Trace the word.
Opposites
BASIC SKILLS
right
One Step Further
Look to your right. What do you see? Is it different from what you saw on your left?
Everyday Success Preschool

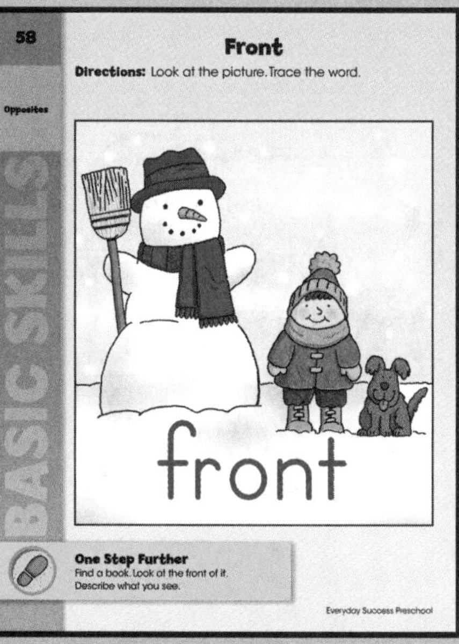
58
Front
Directions: Look at the picture. Trace the word.
Opposites
BASIC SKILLS
front
One Step Further
Find a book. Look at the front of it. Describe what you see.
Everyday Success Preschool

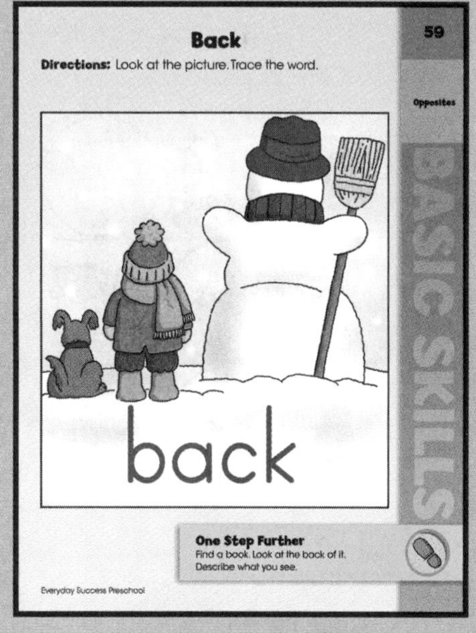
59
Back
Directions: Look at the picture. Trace the word.
Opposites
BASIC SKILLS
back
One Step Further
Find a book. Look at the back of it. Describe what you see.
Everyday Success Preschool

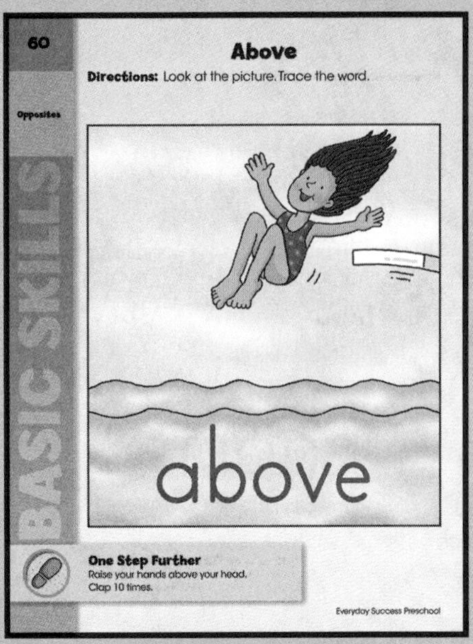
60
Above
Directions: Look at the picture. Trace the word.
Opposites
BASIC SKILLS
above
One Step Further
Raise your hands above your head.
Clap 10 times.
Everyday Success Preschool

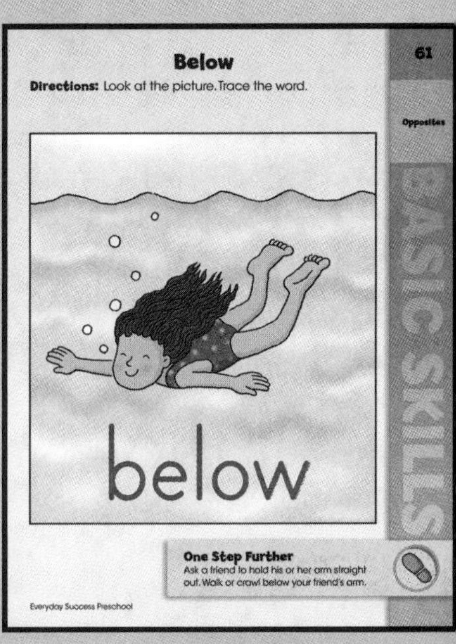
61
Below
Directions: Look at the picture. Trace the word.
Opposites
BASIC SKILLS
below
One Step Further
Ask a friend to hold his or her arm straight out. Walk or crawl below your friend's arm.
Everyday Success Preschool

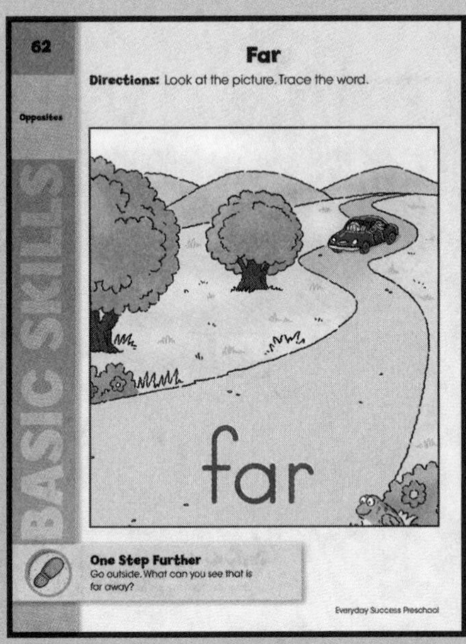
62
Far
Directions: Look at the picture. Trace the word.
Opposites
BASIC SKILLS
far
One Step Further
Go outside. What can you see that is far away?
Everyday Success Preschool

63
Near
Directions: Look at the picture. Trace the word.
Opposites
BASIC SKILLS
near
One Step Further
Look around you. What can you see that is near?
Everyday Success Preschool

64
Go-Togethers
Directions: Look at the pictures in each row. Circle the picture that goes together with the first picture.
Same and Different
BASIC SKILLS
One Step Further
Choose one object on this page.
What goes together with that object?
Everyday Success Preschool

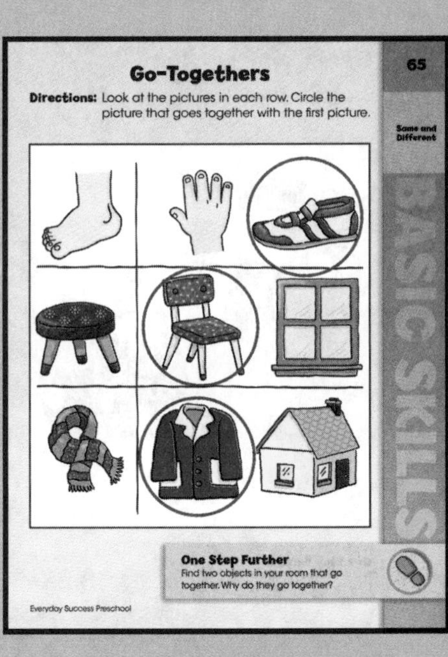
65
Go-Togethers
Directions: Look at the pictures in each row. Circle the picture that goes together with the first picture.
Same and Different
BASIC SKILLS
One Step Further
Find two objects in your room that go together. Why do they go together?
Everyday Success Preschool

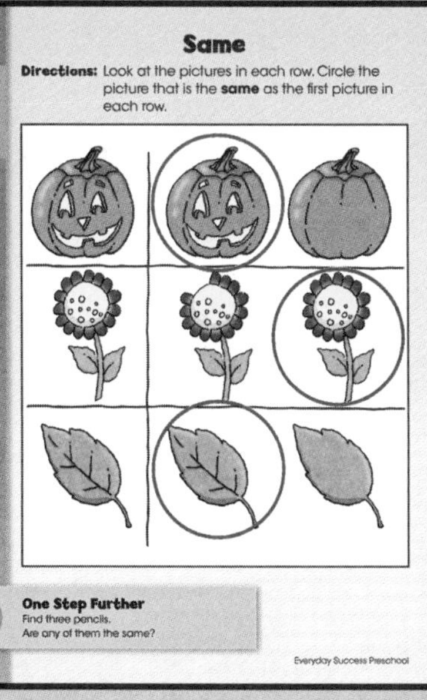

66 Same and Different

Same

Directions: Look at the pictures in each row. Circle the picture that is the **same** as the first picture in each row.

One Step Further
Find three pencils.
Are any of them the same?

Everyday Success Preschool

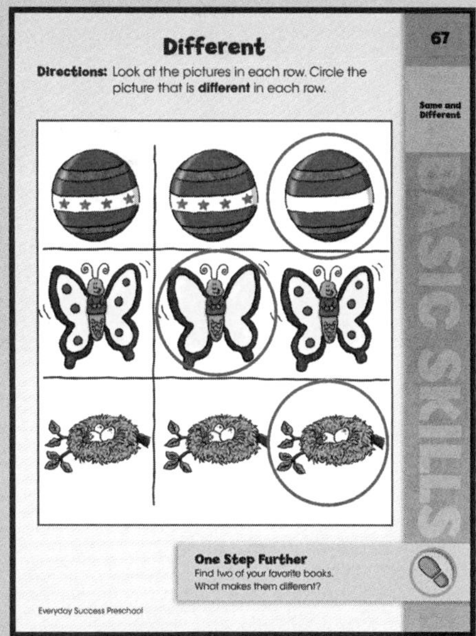

67 Same and Different

Different

Directions: Look at the pictures in each row. Circle the picture that is **different** in each row.

One Step Further
Find two of your favorite books.
What makes them different?

Everyday Success Preschool

68 Same and Different

Same

Directions: Look at the shapes in each row. Color the shape that is the **same** as the first shape in each row.

One Step Further
Draw two rhombuses and one square. Ask a friend to tell you which two are the same.

Everyday Success Preschool

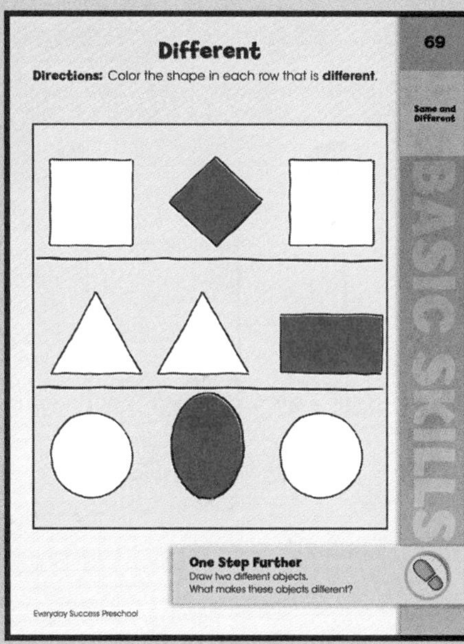

69 Same and Different

Different

Directions: Color the shape in each row that is **different**.

One Step Further
Draw two different objects.
What makes these objects different?

Everyday Success Preschool

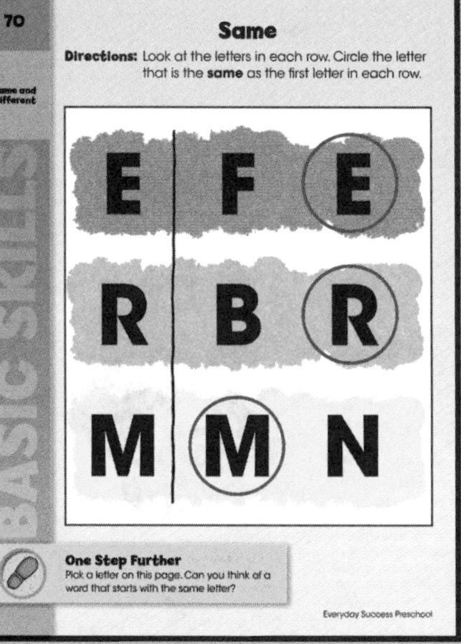

70 Same and Different

Same

Directions: Look at the letters in each row. Circle the letter that is the **same** as the first letter in each row.

E F E
R B R
M M N

One Step Further
Pick a letter on this page. Can you think of a word that starts with the same letter?

Everyday Success Preschool

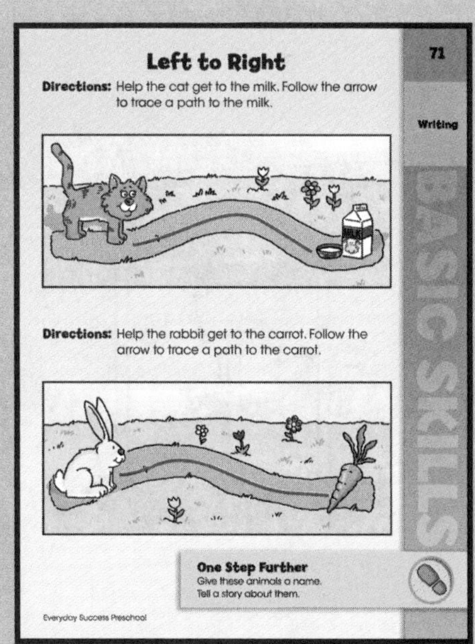

71 Writing

Left to Right

Directions: Help the cat get to the milk. Follow the arrow to trace a path to the milk.

Directions: Help the rabbit get to the carrot. Follow the arrow to trace a path to the carrot.

One Step Further
Give these animals a name.
Tell a story about them.

Everyday Success Preschool

72

Writing

BASIC SKILLS

Left to Right

Directions: Help the bear get to the honey. Follow the arrow to trace a path to the honey.

Directions: Help the cow get to the grass. Follow the arrow to trace a path to the grass.

One Step Further
What do you think the bear will do when he gets to the honey?

Everyday Success Preschool

73

Writing

BASIC SKILLS

Left to Right

Directions: Trace the lines from left to right to help each mother find her baby.

One Step Further
Look outside. Do any of these animals live near you?

Everyday Success Preschool

74

Writing

BASIC SKILLS

Top to Bottom

Directions: Help the children hold onto their balloons. Trace the balloon strings from top to bottom.

One Step Further
Tell a story about this picture.
Where do you think the kids are going?

Everyday Success Preschool

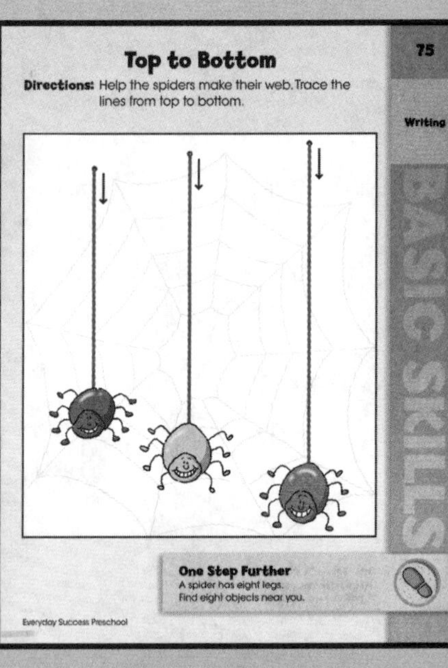

75

Writing

BASIC SKILLS

Top to Bottom

Directions: Help the spiders make their web. Trace the lines from top to bottom.

One Step Further
A spider has eight legs.
Find eight objects near you.

Everyday Success Preschool

76

Writing

BASIC SKILLS

Top to Bottom

Directions: Trace the lines from top to bottom to make stems on the flowers.

One Step Further
What is your favorite flower?
What do you like about it?

Everyday Success Preschool

77

Writing

BASIC SKILLS

Slanted Lines

Directions: Help the children slide down the hill. Trace the lines from top to bottom.

One Step Further
Pretend it's snowing outside.
Play your favorite indoor game.

Everyday Success Preschool

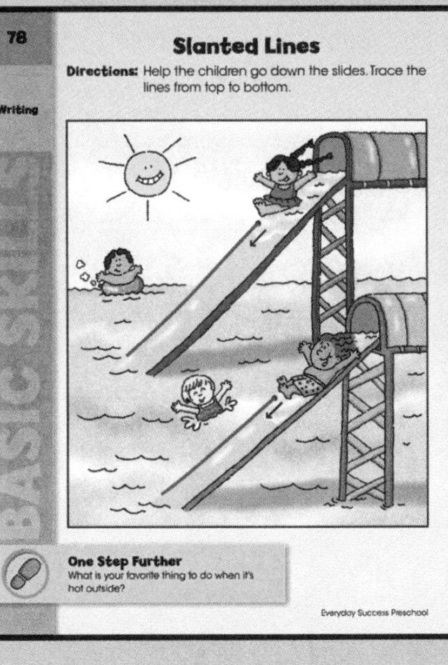

78

Writing

Slanted Lines

Directions: Help the children go down the slides. Trace the lines from top to bottom.

BASIC SKILLS

One Step Further
What is your favorite thing to do when it's hot outside?

Everyday Success Preschool

79

Writing

Curved Lines

Directions: Trace each ball's bounces from left to right.

Directions: Draw the ball's bounces from left to right.

BASIC SKILLS

One Step Further
Bounce from left to right four times. How far can you bounce?

Everyday Success Preschool

80

Writing

Forward Circles

Directions: Follow the arrows to trace the circles on each scoop of ice cream.

BASIC SKILLS

One Step Further
Ice cream is a yummy summer treat. What other treats do you like to eat?

Everyday Success Preschool

81

Writing

Backward Circles

Directions: Follow the arrows to trace the plates on the picnic table.

BASIC SKILLS

One Step Further
Pretend you and a friend are having a picnic. What will you bring with you?

Everyday Success Preschool

82

Writing

Top-to-bottom Lines

Directions: Start at the top. Follow the arrows to trace the dotted lines.

BASIC SKILLS

One Step Further
Toss a small object straight up. Watch the line it makes as it falls straight down.

Everyday Success Preschool

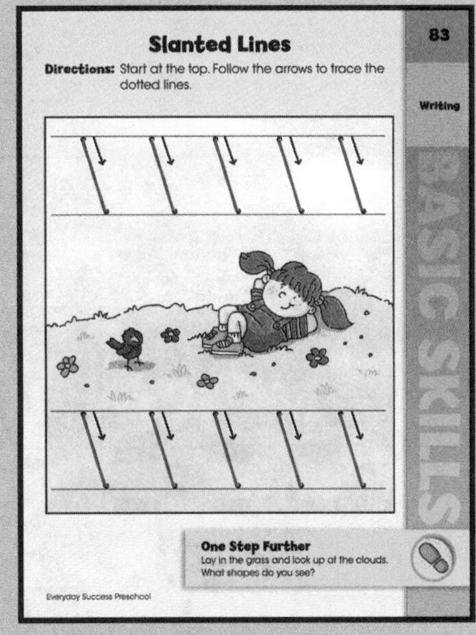

83

Writing

Slanted Lines

Directions: Start at the top. Follow the arrows to trace the dotted lines.

BASIC SKILLS

One Step Further
Lay in the grass and look up at the clouds. What shapes do you see?

Everyday Success Preschool

84

Writing

BASIC SKILLS

Curved Lines

Directions: Start at the dots on the left. Follow the arrows to trace the dotted lines.

One Step Further
Go outside and take one big hop as far as you can.

Everyday Success Preschool

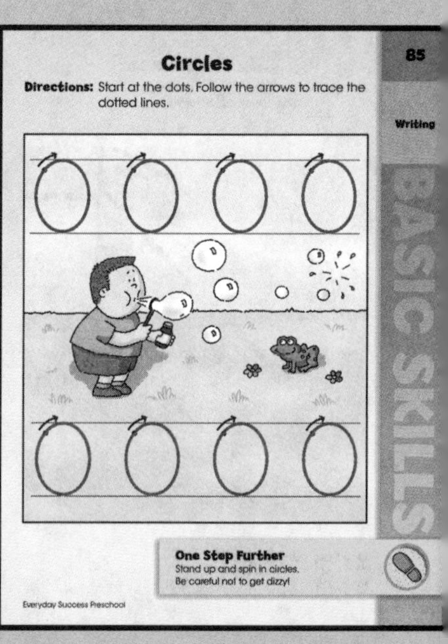
85

Writing

BASIC SKILLS

Circles

Directions: Start at the dots. Follow the arrows to trace the dotted lines.

One Step Further
Stand up and spin in circles. Be careful not to get dizzy!

Everyday Success Preschool

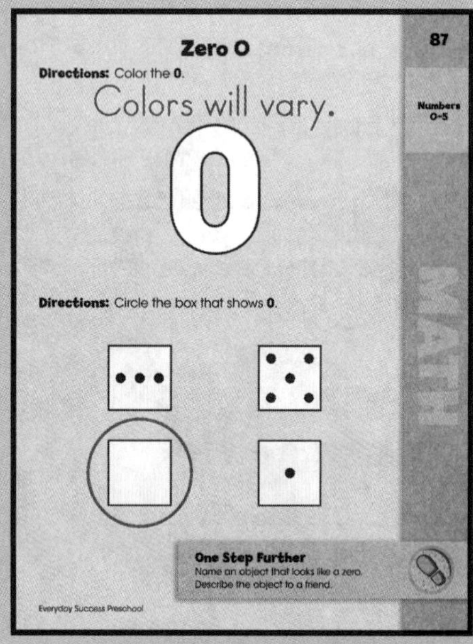
87

Numbers 0–5

MATH

Zero 0

Directions: Color the **0**.

Colors will vary.

0

Directions: Circle the box that shows **0**.

One Step Further
Name an object that looks like a zero. Describe the object to a friend.

Everyday Success Preschool

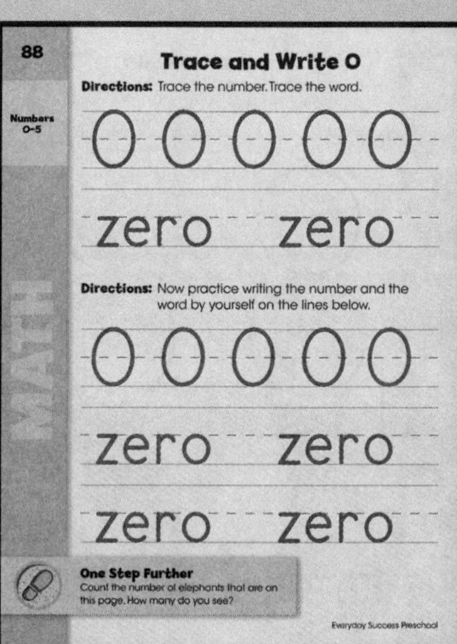
88

Numbers 0–5

MATH

Trace and Write 0

Directions: Trace the number. Trace the word.

0 0 0 0 0

zero zero

Directions: Now practice writing the number and the word by yourself on the lines below.

0 0 0 0 0

zero zero

zero zero

One Step Further
Count the number of elephants that are on this page. How many do you see?

Everyday Success Preschool

89

Numbers 0–5

MATH

Number 0

Directions: Color the fish with **0** spots orange.

One Step Further
Color the rest of the fish blue. How many of these fish are green?

Everyday Success Preschool

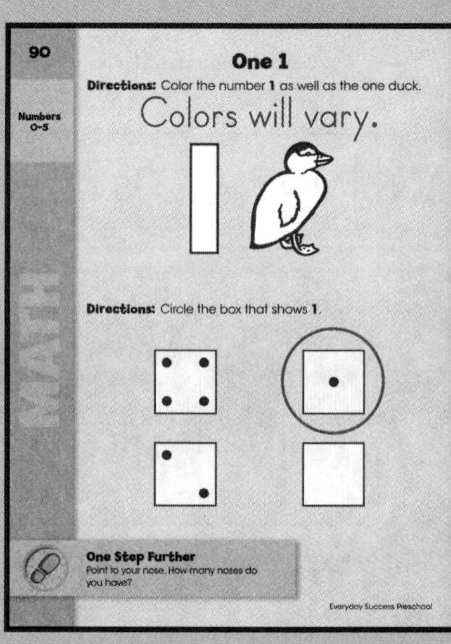
90

Numbers 0–5

MATH

One 1

Directions: Color the number **1** as well as the one duck.

Colors will vary.

Directions: Circle the box that shows **1**.

One Step Further
Point to your nose. How many noses do you have?

Everyday Success Preschool

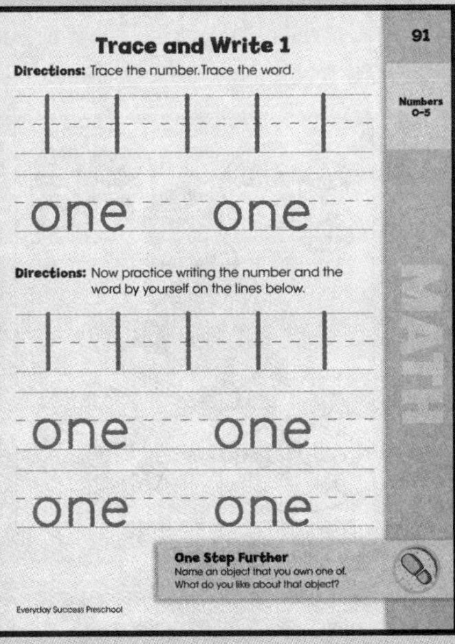

91

Numbers 0–5

MATH

Trace and Write 1

Directions: Trace the number. Trace the word.

1 1 1 1 1

one one

Directions: Now practice writing the number and the word by yourself on the lines below.

1 1 1 1 1

one one

one one

One Step Further
Name an object that you own one of. What do you like about that object?

Everyday Success Preschool

92

Numbers 0–5

MATH

Number 1

Directions: Color **1** glass of juice **purple**, **1** glass of juice orange, and **1** glass of juice **red**.

One Step Further
What is your favorite kind of juice? What color is it?

Everyday Success Preschool

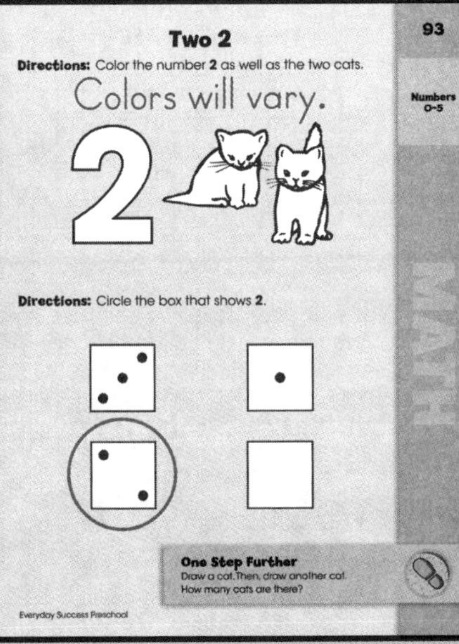

93

Numbers 0–5

MATH

Two 2

Directions: Color the number **2** as well as the two cats.

Colors will vary.

2

Directions: Circle the box that shows **2**.

One Step Further
Draw a cat. Then, draw another cat. How many cats are there?

Everyday Success Preschool

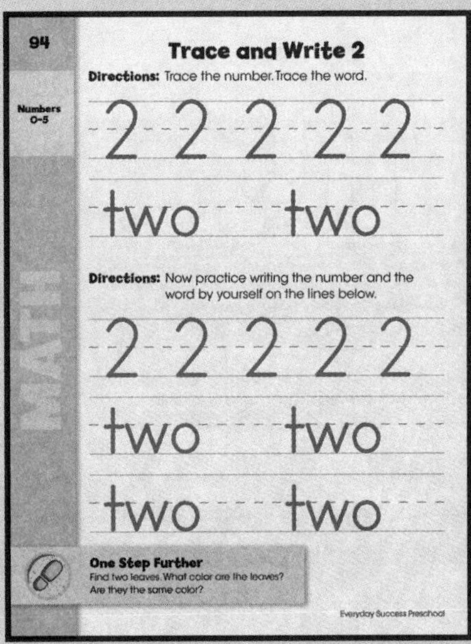

94

Numbers 0–5

MATH

Trace and Write 2

Directions: Trace the number. Trace the word.

2 2 2 2 2

two two

Directions: Now practice writing the number and the word by yourself on the lines below.

2 2 2 2 2

two two

two two

One Step Further
Find two leaves. What color are the leaves? Are they the same color?

Everyday Success Preschool

95

Numbers 0–5

MATH

Number 2

Directions: Color the spaces: 2 = **black**, two = **blue**, 1 = white, and ●● = orange.

One Step Further
After you finish coloring this picture, count the feet. How many do you see?

Everyday Success Preschool

96

Numbers 0–5

MATH

Three 3

Directions: Color the number **3** as well as the three dogs.

Colors will vary.

3

Directions: Circle the box that shows **3**.

One Step Further
Make three greeting cards. Give them to three friends.

Everyday Success Preschool

ANSWER KEY

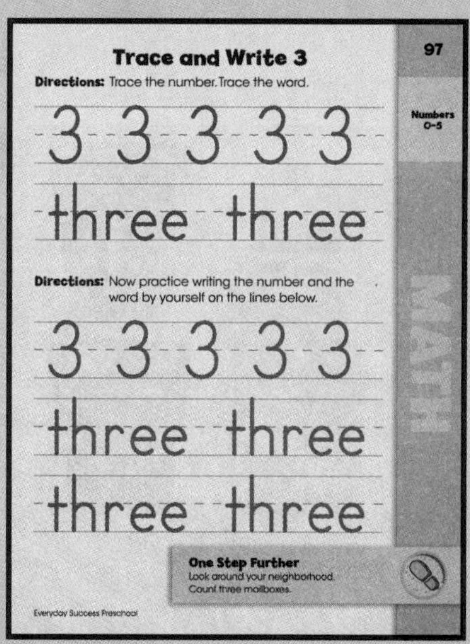
97

Numbers 0–5

MATH

Trace and Write 3

Directions: Trace the number. Trace the word.

3 3 3 3 3

three three

Directions: Now practice writing the number and the word by yourself on the lines below.

3 3 3 3 3

three three

three three

One Step Further
Look around your neighborhood. Count three mailboxes.

Everyday Success Preschool

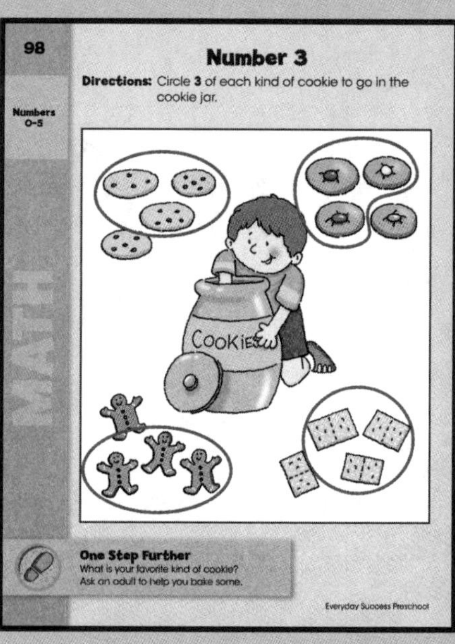
98

Numbers 0–5

MATH

Number 3

Directions: Circle **3** of each kind of cookie to go in the cookie jar.

One Step Further
What is your favorite kind of cookie? Ask an adult to help you bake some.

Everyday Success Preschool

99

Numbers 0–5

MATH

Four 4

Directions: Color the number **4** as well as the four animals.

Colors will vary.

Directions: Circle the boxes that show **4**.

One Step Further
Name four different animals. Which is your favorite? Why?

Everyday Success Preschool

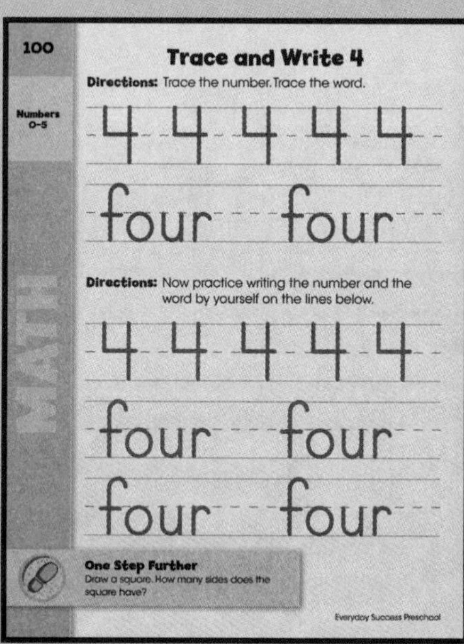
100

Numbers 0–5

MATH

Trace and Write 4

Directions: Trace the number. Trace the word.

4 4 4 4 4

four four

Directions: Now practice writing the number and the word by yourself on the lines below.

4 4 4 4 4

four four

four four

One Step Further
Draw a square. How many sides does the square have?

Everyday Success Preschool

101

Numbers 0–5

MATH

Number 4

Directions: Draw **4** flowers in the vase.

Pictures will vary.

One Step Further
Count the petals on the flowers you drew. How many are there?

Everyday Success Preschool

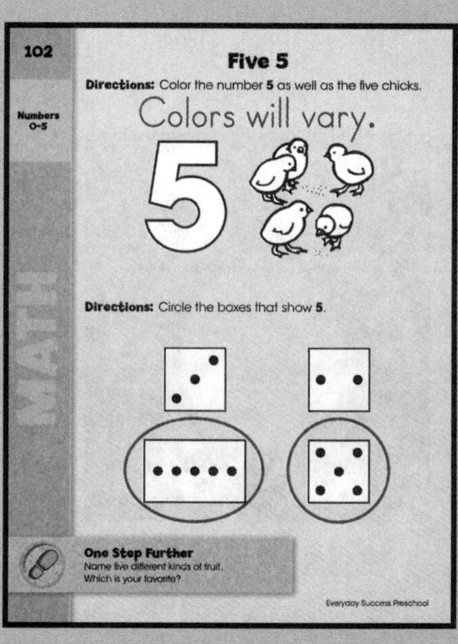
102

Numbers 0–5

MATH

Five 5

Directions: Color the number **5** as well as the five chicks.

Colors will vary.

Directions: Circle the boxes that show **5**.

One Step Further
Name five different kinds of fruit. Which is your favorite?

Everyday Success Preschool

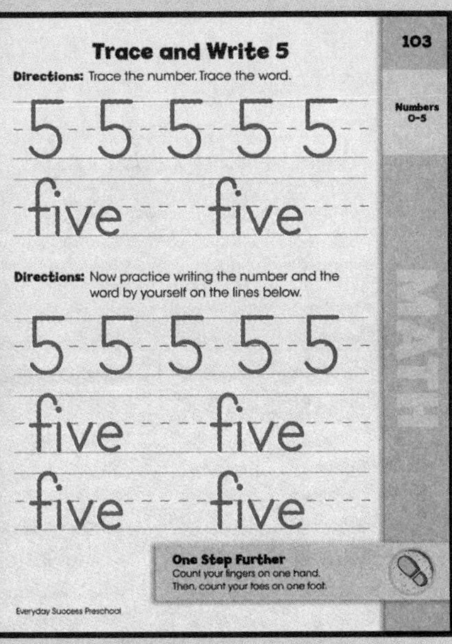

103

Numbers 0–5

Trace and Write 5

Directions: Trace the number. Trace the word.

5 5 5 5 5

five five

Directions: Now practice writing the number and the word by yourself on the lines below.

5 5 5 5 5

five five

five five

MATH

One Step Further
Count your fingers on one hand. Then, count your toes on one foot.

Everyday Success Preschool

104

Numbers 0–5

Number 5

Directions: Draw 5 ☆s on the ☁. Color the ☆s.

MATH

One Step Further
Draw a star. Count the points on the star. How many are there?

Everyday Success Preschool

105

Review

Numbers 0–5

Directions: Count the dots. Color the spaces: 1 = red, 2 = yellow, 3 = green, 4 = blue, and 5 = orange.

MATH

One Step Further
Pretend it's raining! Snuggle under a blanket and read a book.

Everyday Success Preschool

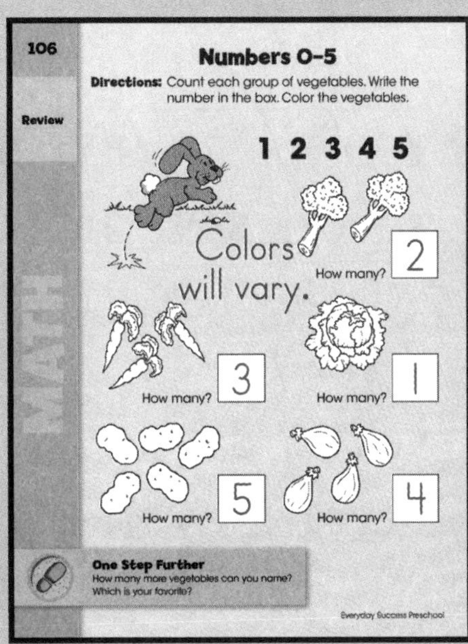

106

Review

Numbers 0–5

Directions: Count each group of vegetables. Write the number in the box. Color the vegetables.

1 2 3 4 5

Colors will vary.

How many? 2

How many? 3

How many? 1

How many? 5

How many? 4

MATH

One Step Further
How many more vegetables can you name? Which is your favorite?

Everyday Success Preschool

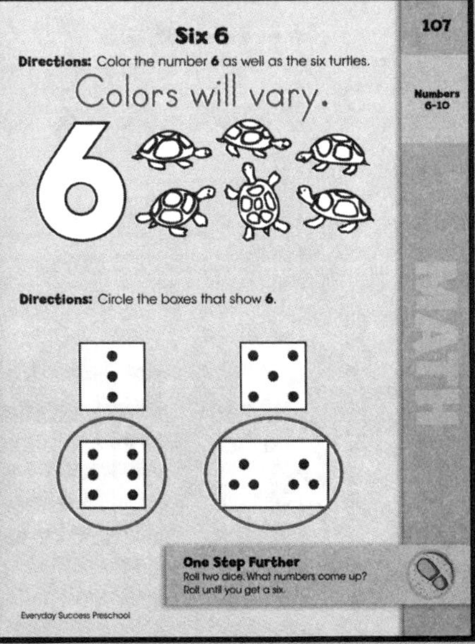

107

Numbers 6–10

Six 6

Directions: Color the number **6** as well as the six turtles.

Colors will vary.

6

Directions: Circle the boxes that show **6**.

MATH

One Step Further
Roll two dice. What numbers come up? Roll until you get a six.

Everyday Success Preschool

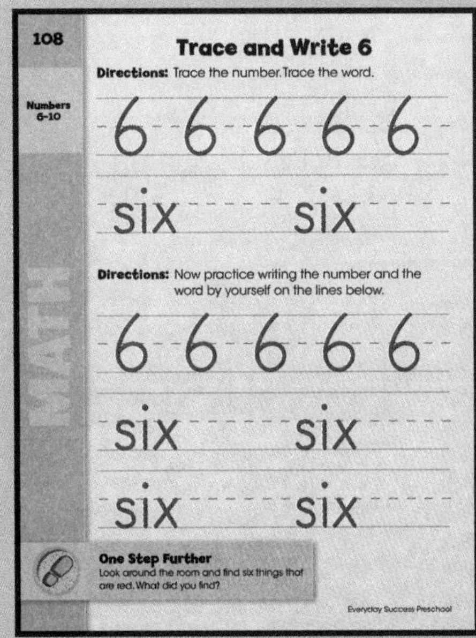

108

Numbers 6–10

Trace and Write 6

Directions: Trace the number. Trace the word.

6 6 6 6 6

six six

Directions: Now practice writing the number and the word by yourself on the lines below.

6 6 6 6 6

six six

six six

MATH

One Step Further
Look around the room and find six things that are red. What did you find?

Everyday Success Preschool

ANSWER KEY

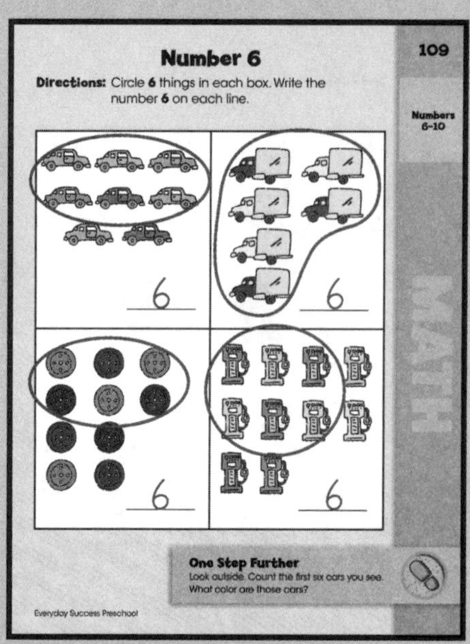
Number 6
109
Directions: Circle 6 things in each box. Write the number 6 on each line.
Numbers 6-10
6
6
6
6
MATH
One Step Further
Look outside. Count the first six cars you see. What color are those cars?
Everyday Success Preschool

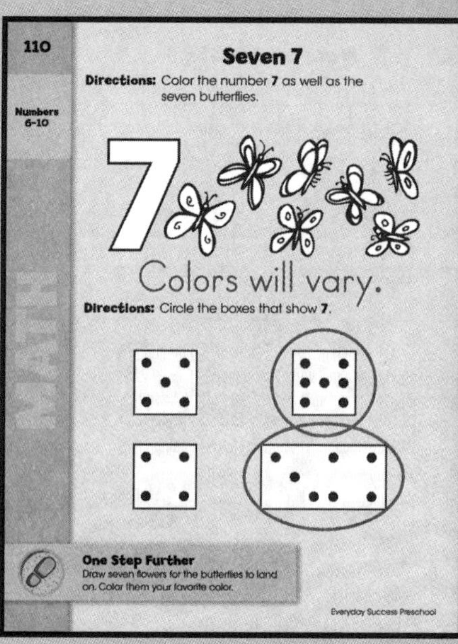
110
Seven 7
Directions: Color the number 7 as well as the seven butterflies.
Numbers 6-10
Colors will vary.
Directions: Circle the boxes that show 7.
MATH
One Step Further
Draw seven flowers for the butterflies to land on. Color them your favorite color.
Everyday Success Preschool

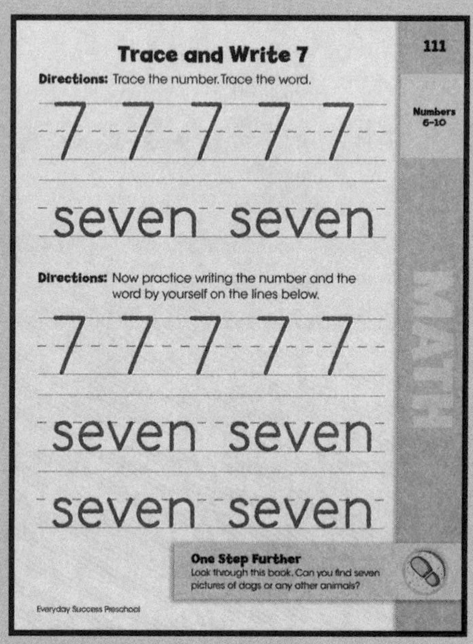
Trace and Write 7
111
Directions: Trace the number. Trace the word.
Numbers 6-10
7 7 7 7 7
seven seven
Directions: Now practice writing the number and the word by yourself on the lines below.
7 7 7 7 7
seven seven
seven seven
MATH
One Step Further
Look through this book. Can you find seven pictures of dogs or any other animals?
Everyday Success Preschool

112
Number 7
Directions: Circle 7 things on each shelf.
Numbers 6-10
MATH
One Step Further
What are seven things you might buy at a grocery store?
Everyday Success Preschool

Eight 8
113
Directions: Color the number 8 as well as the eight bees.
Colors will vary.
Numbers 6-10
Directions: Circle the boxes that show 8.
MATH
One Step Further
Name an animal that has eight legs. How many legs do you have?
Everyday Success Preschool

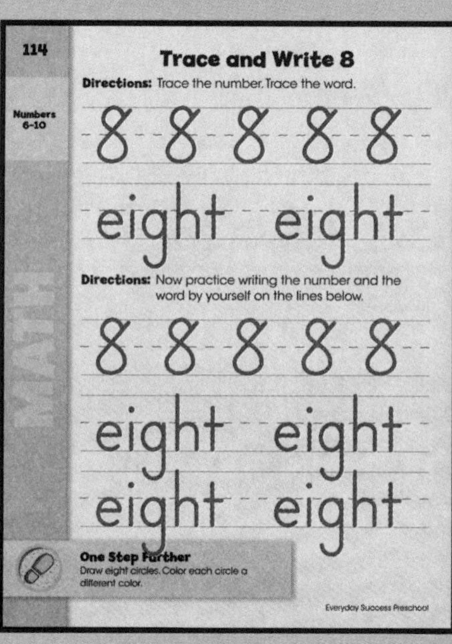
114
Trace and Write 8
Directions: Trace the number. Trace the word.
Numbers 6-10
8 8 8 8 8
eight eight
Directions: Now practice writing the number and the word by yourself on the lines below.
8 8 8 8 8
eight eight
eight eight
MATH
One Step Further
Draw eight circles. Color each circle a different color.
Everyday Success Preschool

115

Numbers 6-10

MATH

Number 8

Directions: Put these **8** shoes into pairs. Draw a line to match each shoe on the left with a shoe that is the same on the right.

One Step Further
Find your favorite pair of shoes. Put them on and walk eight steps.

Everyday Success Preschool

116

Numbers 6-10

MATH

Nine 9

Directions: Color the number **9** as well as the nine birds.

Colors will vary.

Directions: Circle the boxes that show **9**.

One Step Further
Name nine things you do every day. What is your favorite thing to do?

Everyday Success Preschool

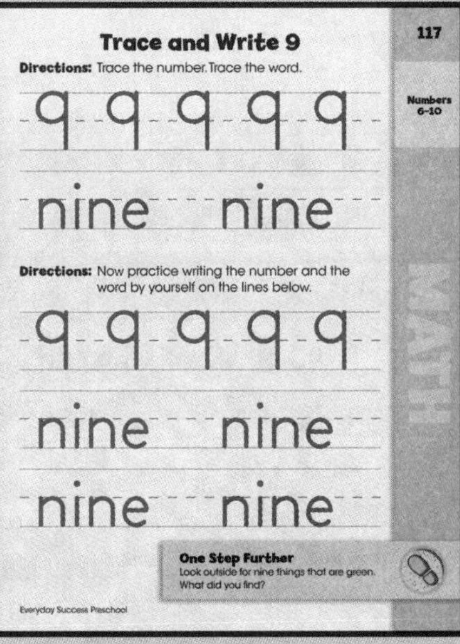
117

Numbers 6-10

MATH

Trace and Write 9

Directions: Trace the number. Trace the word.

9 9 9 9 9

nine nine

Directions: Now practice writing the number and the word by yourself on the lines below.

9 9 9 9 9

nine nine

nine nine

One Step Further
Look outside for nine things that are green. What did you find?

Everyday Success Preschool

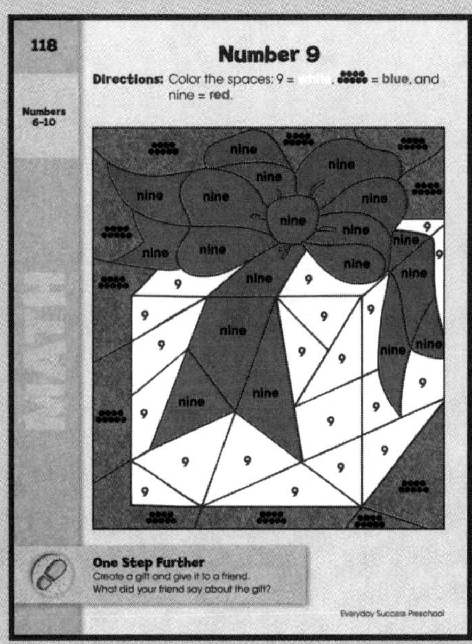
118

Numbers 6-10

MATH

Number 9

Directions: Color the spaces: 9 = white, ●●●●● = blue, and nine = red.

One Step Further
Create a gift and give it to a friend. What did your friend say about the gift?

Everyday Success Preschool

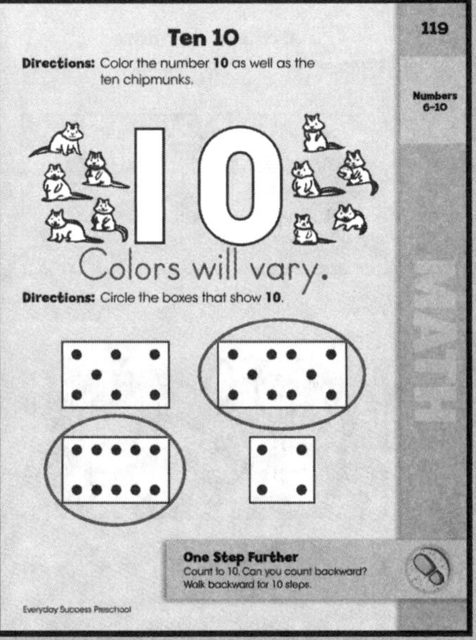
119

Numbers 6-10

MATH

Ten 10

Directions: Color the number **10** as well as the ten chipmunks.

Colors will vary.

Directions: Circle the boxes that show **10**.

One Step Further
Count to 10. Can you count backward? Walk backward for 10 steps.

Everyday Success Preschool

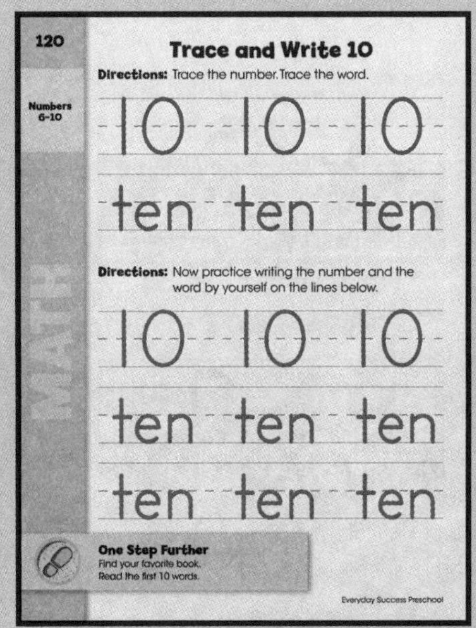
120

Numbers 6-10

MATH

Trace and Write 10

Directions: Trace the number. Trace the word.

10 10 10

ten ten ten

Directions: Now practice writing the number and the word by yourself on the lines below.

10 10 10

ten ten ten

ten ten ten

One Step Further
Find your favorite book. Read the first 10 words.

Everyday Success Preschool

ANSWER KEY

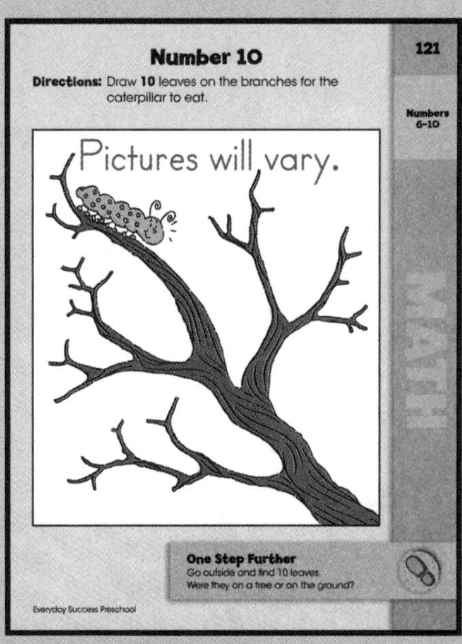

121

Numbers 6–10

Number 10

Directions: Draw **10** leaves on the branches for the caterpillar to eat.

One Step Further
Go outside and find 10 leaves. Were they on a tree or on the ground?

MATH

Everyday Success Preschool

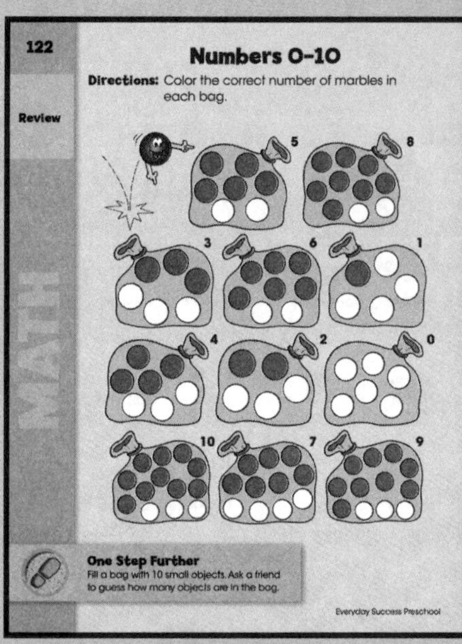

122

Review

Numbers 0–10

Directions: Color the correct number of marbles in each bag.

One Step Further
Fill a bag with 10 small objects. Ask a friend to guess how many objects are in the bag.

MATH

Everyday Success Preschool

123

Review

Numbers 0–10

Directions: Count each picture. Write the number on each line.

One Step Further
Find 10 plastic cups. Stack them in a pyramid as high as you can.

MATH

Everyday Success Preschool

124

Review

Numbers 0–10

Directions: Draw an **X** on the extra things in each row.

One Step Further
Choose an object on this page. Can you find it in your home?

MATH

Everyday Success Preschool

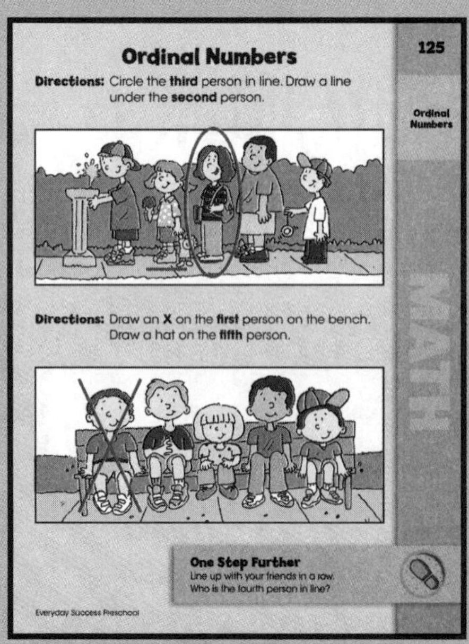

125

Ordinal Numbers

Ordinal Numbers

Directions: Circle the **third** person in line. Draw a line under the **second** person.

Directions: Draw an **X** on the **first** person on the bench. Draw a hat on the **fifth** person.

One Step Further
Line up with your friends in a row. Who is the fourth person in line?

MATH

Everyday Success Preschool

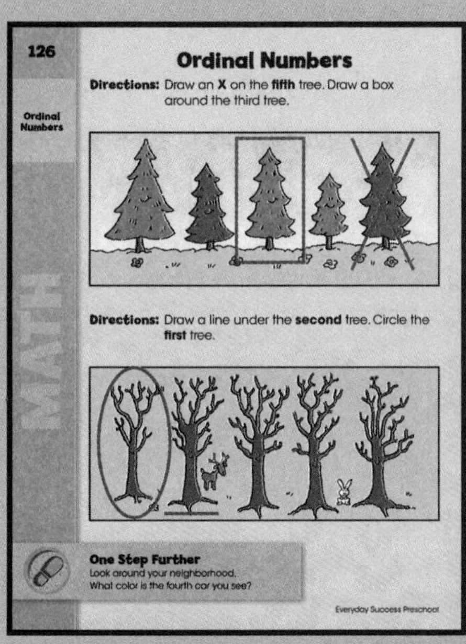

126

Ordinal Numbers

Ordinal Numbers

Directions: Draw an **X** on the **fifth** tree. Draw a box around the third tree.

Directions: Draw a line under the **second** tree. Circle the **first** tree.

One Step Further
Look around your neighborhood. What color is the fourth car you see?

MATH

Everyday Success Preschool

127

Ordinal Numbers

Ordinal Numbers

Directions: Circle the **second** box. Draw a **green** line under the **fifth** box.

Directions: Draw **red** dots on the **third** box. Draw a **blue** bow on the **fourth** box.

MATH

One Step Further
What do you think is inside the boxes? Tell a story about the picture.

Everyday Success Preschool

128

Ordinal Numbers

Ordinal Numbers

Directions: Look at the pictures. What happened **first**? What happened **second**? What happened **third**? Draw a line from the correct word to the picture.

first

second

third

MATH

One Step Further
What is the first thing you did today? What is the first thing you will do tomorrow?

Everyday Success Preschool

129

Ordinal Numbers

Ordinal Numbers

Directions: Write **1**, **2**, and **3** in the boxes to show what happens **first**, **second**, and **third**.

3 2 1

2 3 1

MATH

One Step Further
It's time for dinner! What is the first thing you do? What is the second?

Everyday Success Preschool

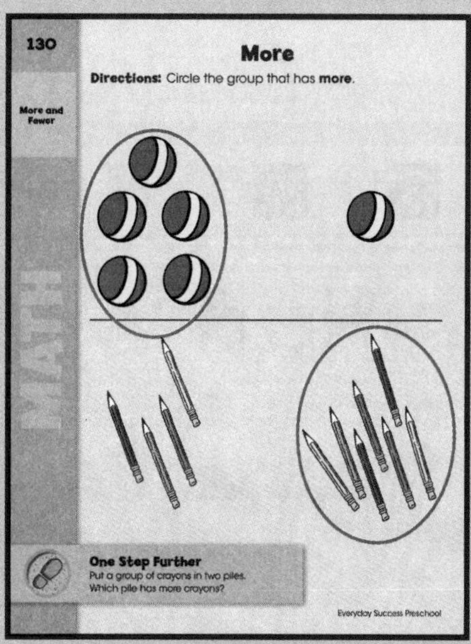

130

More and Fewer

More

Directions: Circle the group that has **more**.

MATH

One Step Further
Put a group of crayons in two piles. Which pile has more crayons?

Everyday Success Preschool

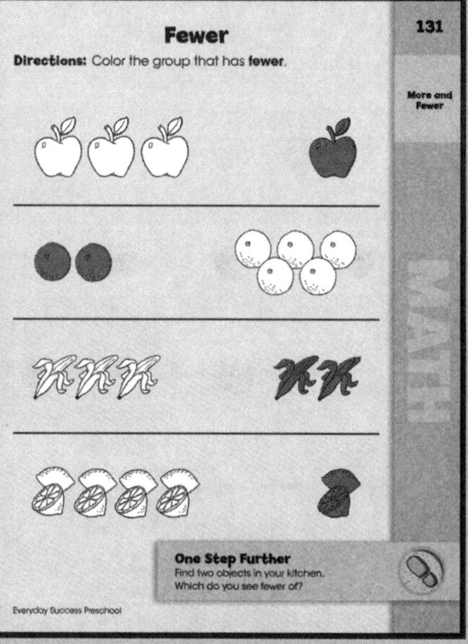

131

More and Fewer

Fewer

Directions: Color the group that has **fewer**.

MATH

One Step Further
Find two objects in your kitchen. Which do you see fewer of?

Everyday Success Preschool

132

More and Fewer

More

Directions: Count the blocks each child is playing with. Circle the child who has **more** blocks.

MATH

One Step Further
Count the blocks you own. Do you have more than the children on this page?

Everyday Success Preschool

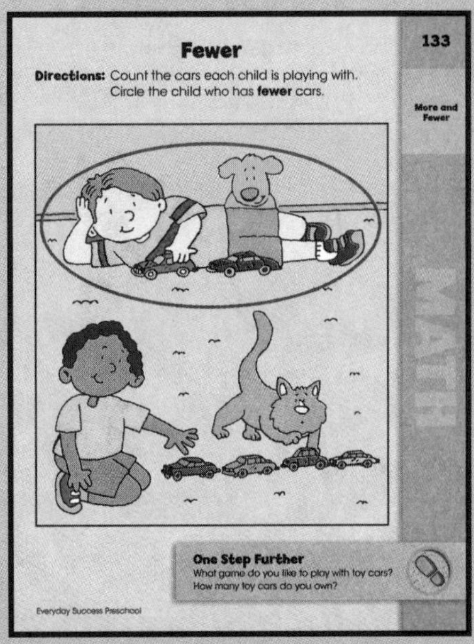

133
Fewer
Directions: Count the cars each child is playing with. Circle the child who has fewer cars.
More and Fewer
MATH
One Step Further
What game do you like to play with toy cars? How many toy cars do you own?
Everyday Success Preschool

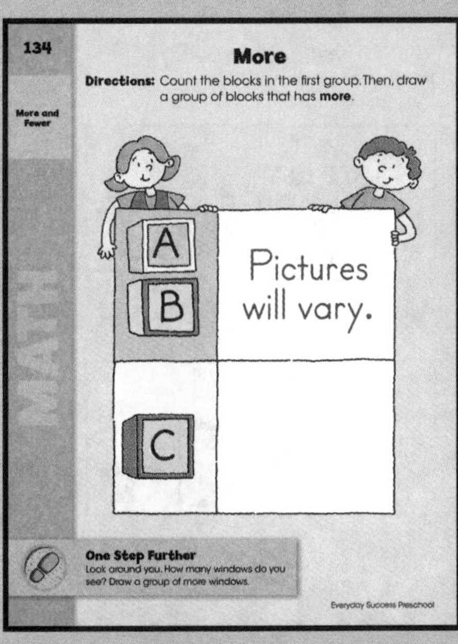

134
More
Directions: Count the blocks in the first group. Then, draw a group of blocks that has more.
More and Fewer
MATH
A
B
C
Pictures will vary.
One Step Further
Look around you. How many windows do you see? Draw a group of more windows.
Everyday Success Preschool

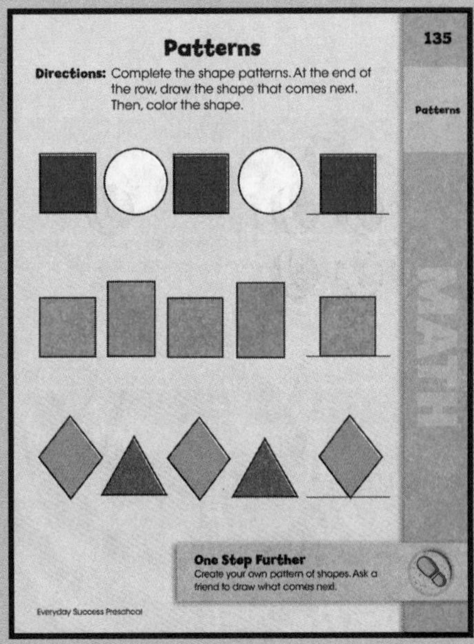

135
Patterns
Directions: Complete the shape patterns. At the end of the row, draw the shape that comes next. Then, color the shape.
Patterns
MATH
One Step Further
Create your own pattern of shapes. Ask a friend to draw what comes next.
Everyday Success Preschool

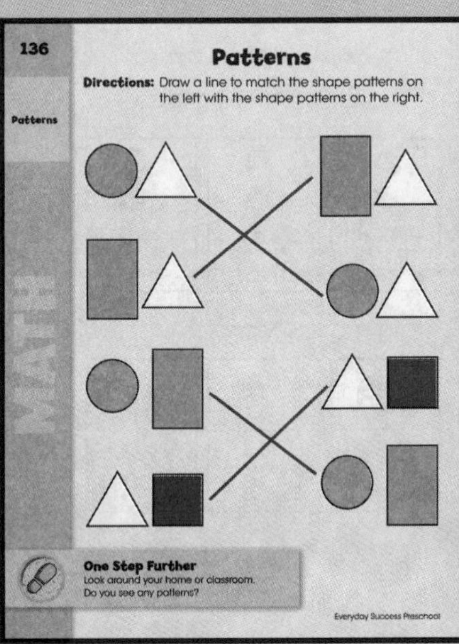

136
Patterns
Directions: Draw a line to match the shape patterns on the left with the shape patterns on the right.
Patterns
MATH
One Step Further
Look around your home or classroom. Do you see any patterns?
Everyday Success Preschool

137
Patterns
Directions: What comes next? Draw the picture that comes next in each row.
Patterns
MATH
One Step Further
Play a game of tic-tac-toe with a friend. What patterns do you see on the grid?
Everyday Success Preschool

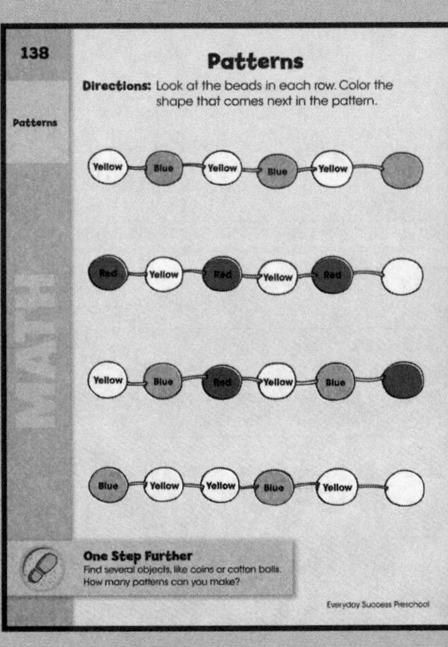

138
Patterns
Directions: Look at the beads in each row. Color the shape that comes next in the pattern.
Patterns
MATH
Yellow
Blue
Yellow
Blue
Yellow
Red
Yellow
Red
Yellow
Red
Yellow
Blue
Red
Yellow
Blue
Blue
Yellow
Yellow
Blue
Yellow
One Step Further
Find several objects, like coins or cotton balls. How many patterns can you make?
Everyday Success Preschool

ANSWER KEY

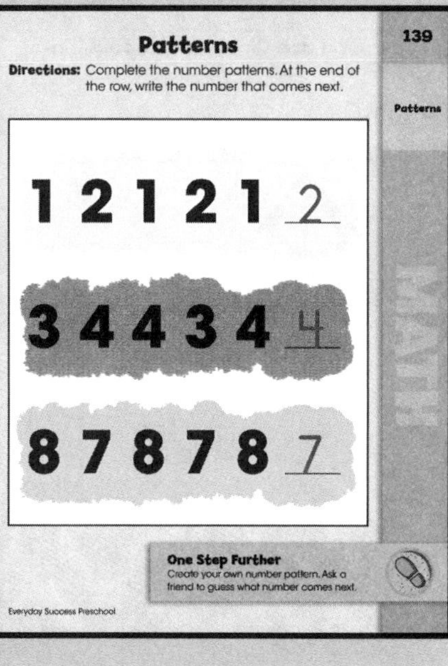
Patterns
139
Directions: Complete the number patterns. At the end of the row, write the number that comes next.
1 2 1 2 1 2
3 4 4 3 4 4
8 7 8 7 8 7
One Step Further
Create your own number pattern. Ask a friend to guess what number comes next.
Everyday Success Preschool

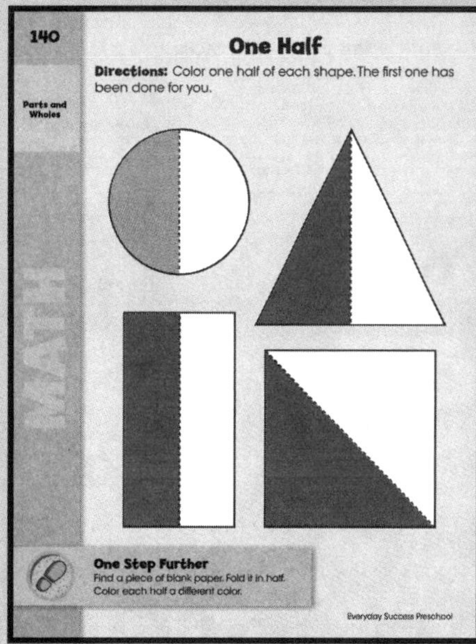
140
One Half
Directions: Color one half of each shape. The first one has been done for you.
One Step Further
Find a piece of blank paper. Fold it in half. Color each half a different color.
Everyday Success Preschool

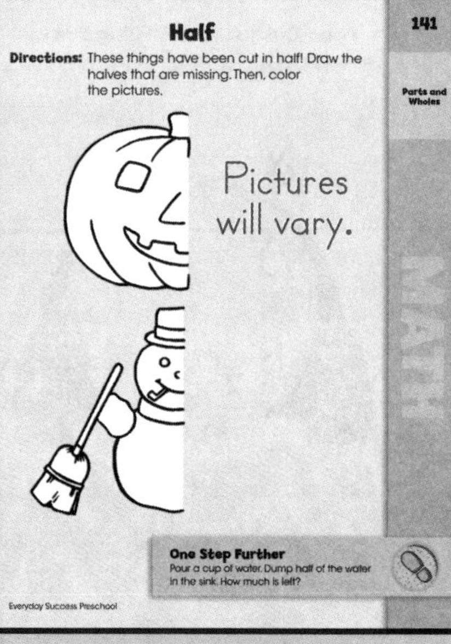
Half
141
Directions: These things have been cut in half! Draw the halves that are missing. Then, color the pictures.
Pictures will vary.
One Step Further
Pour a cup of water. Dump half of the water in the sink. How much is left?
Everyday Success Preschool

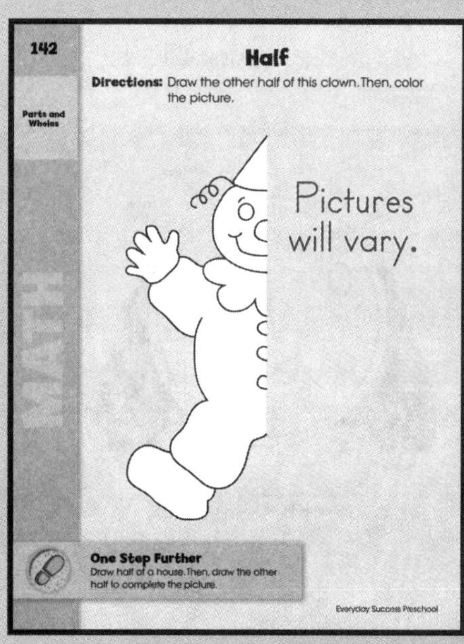
142
Half
Directions: Draw the other half of this clown. Then, color the picture.
Pictures will vary.
One Step Further
Draw half of a house. Then, draw the other half to complete the picture.
Everyday Success Preschool

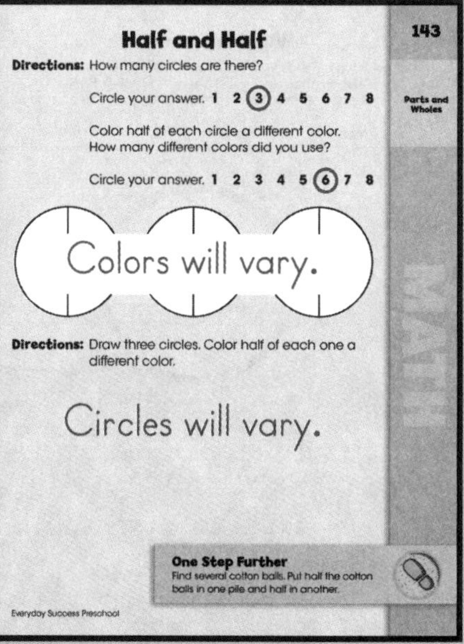
Half and Half
143
Directions: How many circles are there?
Circle your answer. 1 2 3 4 5 6 7 8
Color half of each circle a different color. How many different colors did you use?
Circle your answer. 1 2 3 4 5 6 7 8
Colors will vary.
Directions: Draw three circles. Color half of each one a different color.
Circles will vary.
One Step Further
Find several cotton balls. Put half the cotton balls in one pile and half in another.
Everyday Success Preschool

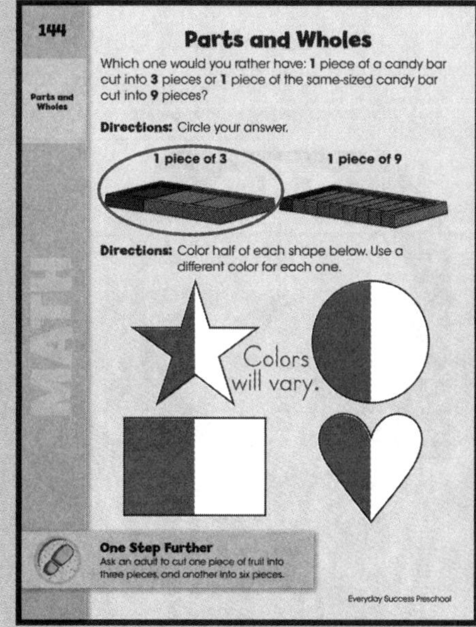
144
Parts and Wholes
Which one would you rather have: 1 piece of a candy bar cut into 3 pieces or 1 piece of the same-sized candy bar cut into 9 pieces?
Directions: Circle your answer.
1 piece of 3
1 piece of 9
Directions: Color half of each shape below. Use a different color for each one.
Colors will vary.
One Step Further
Ask an adult to cut one piece of fruit into three pieces, and another into six pieces.
Everyday Success Preschool

ANSWER KEY

145

Parts and Wholes

Parts and Wholes

Mom cut a pie into eight pieces. Her children ate half ($\frac{1}{2}$) of the pie for dessert. How many pieces were left?

Directions: Circle your answer.

0 1 2 3 (4) 5 6 7 8

Directions: Color only half of the circles in each row below. Use a different color for each one.

How many circles are **not** colored?

Directions: Circle your answer.

0 1 2 (3) 4 5 6 7 8

How many circles are **not** colored?

Directions: Circle your answer.

0 1 2 3 4 (5) 6 7 8

One Step Further
What is your favorite kind of pie? How many slices of pie do you eat at once?

MATH

Everyday Success Preschool

146

Face Clocks: Introduction

Clocks and Time

What is the best way to tell what time it is? Look at a clock. There are all kinds of clocks.

Directions: Circle the ones you have seen.

Answers will vary.

One Step Further
Look around you. How many types of clocks can you see right now?

MATH

Everyday Success Preschool

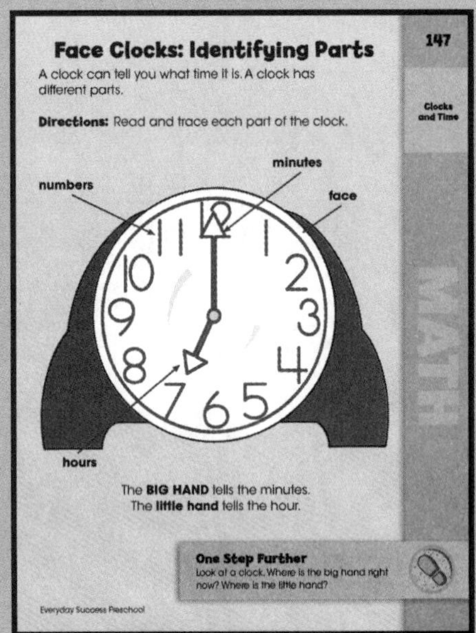

147

Face Clocks: Identifying Parts

Clocks and Time

A clock can tell you what time it is. A clock has different parts.

Directions: Read and trace each part of the clock.

The **BIG HAND** tells the minutes. The **little hand** tells the hour.

One Step Further
Look at a clock. Where is the big hand right now? Where is the little hand?

MATH

Everyday Success Preschool

148

Face Clocks: Identifying Parts

Clocks and Time

Directions: A clock has numbers. Trace the numbers on the clock.

One Step Further
What time does your clock say when you get up in the morning?

MATH

Everyday Success Preschool

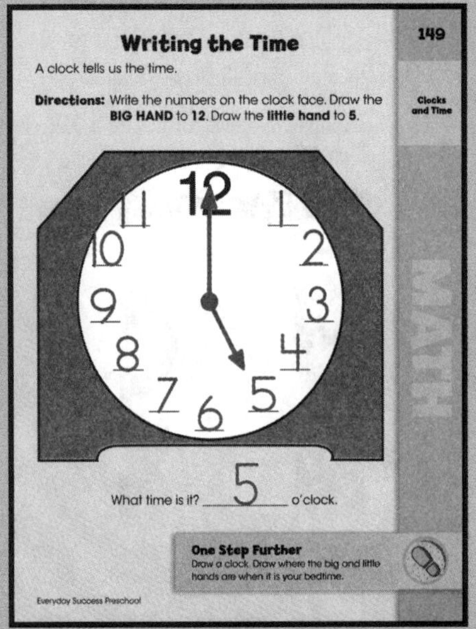

149

Writing the Time

Clocks and Time

A clock tells us the time.

Directions: Write the numbers on the clock face. Draw the **BIG HAND** to **12**. Draw the **little hand** to **5**.

What time is it? 5 o'clock.

One Step Further
Draw a clock. Draw where the big and little hands are when it is your bedtime.

MATH

Everyday Success Preschool

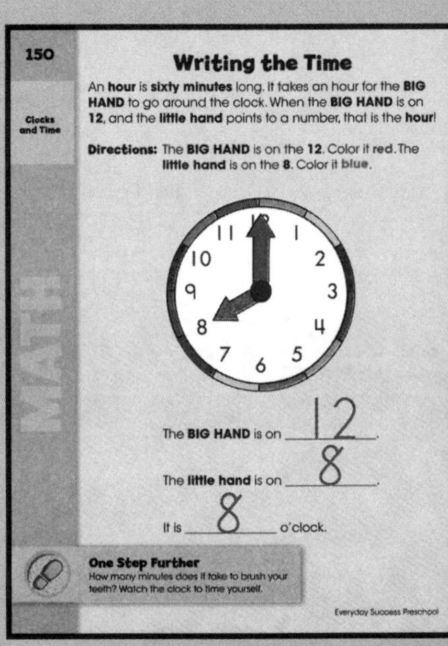

150

Writing the Time

Clocks and Time

An **hour** is **sixty minutes** long. It takes an hour for the **BIG HAND** to go around the clock. When the **BIG HAND** is on **12**, and the **little hand** points to a number, that is the **hour**!

Directions: The **BIG HAND** is on the **12**. Color it **red**. The **little hand** is on the **8**. Color it **blue**.

The **BIG HAND** is on 12.

The **little hand** is on 8.

It is 8 o'clock.

One Step Further
How many minutes does it take to brush your teeth? Watch the clock to time yourself.

MATH

Everyday Success Preschool

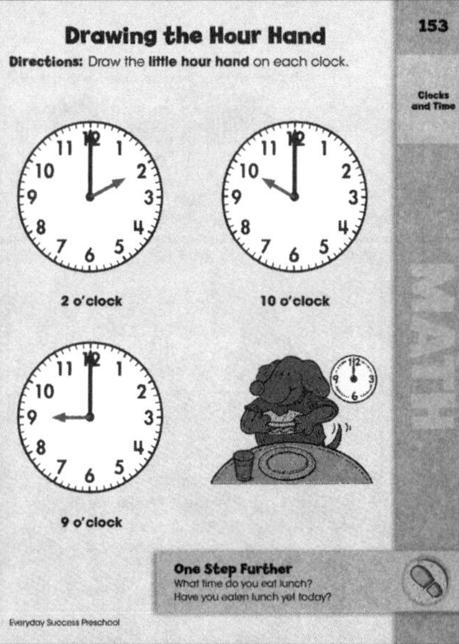

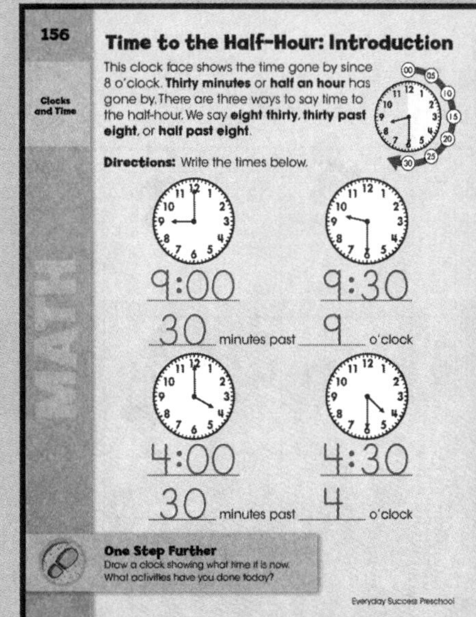

ANSWER KEY

ANSWER KEY

157 Clocks and Time MATH

Writing Time on the Half-Hour

Directions: Write the times below.

11:00 11:30

30 minutes past 11 o'clock

1:00 1:30

30 minutes past 1 o'clock

One Step Further
Look at the clock. Where will the big and little hands be 30 minutes from now?

Everyday Success Preschool

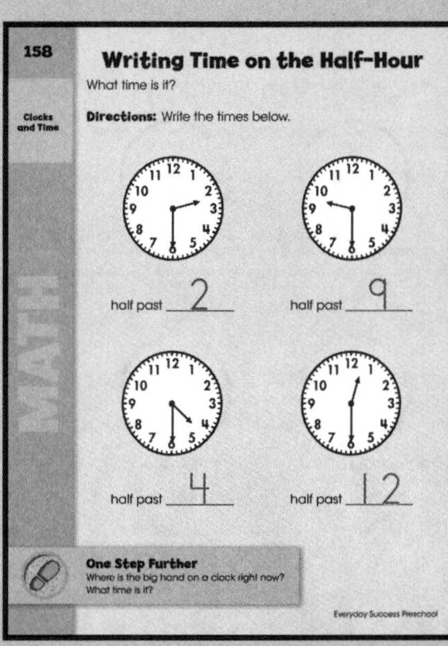

158 Clocks and Time MATH

Writing Time on the Half-Hour

What time is it?

Directions: Write the times below.

half past 2 half past 9

half past 4 half past 12

One Step Further
Where is the big hand on a clock right now? What time is it?

Everyday Success Preschool

159 Clocks and Time MATH

Writing Time on the Half-Hour

Who "nose" these times?

Directions: Write the time under each clock. Color the noses.

Colors will vary.

9:00 9:30 2:00 2:30

5:00 5:30 8:00 8:30

One Step Further
Where is the little hand on a clock right now? Touch your nose that number of times.

Everyday Success Preschool

160 Clocks and Time MATH

Favorite Time

Directions: Draw a special watch for yourself using some of these shapes. Show your favorite time of day.

Pictures will vary.

Answers will vary.

My favorite time of day is ________ o'clock.

One Step Further
Ask a friend about his or her favorite time of day. Draw a watch showing that time.

Everyday Success Preschool

161 Clocks and Time MATH

Important Hours

Directions: Write these important hours in your day.

Answers will vary.

________ o'clock
________ : 00
This is when I go to school.

________ o'clock
________ : 00
This is when I have dinner.

________ o'clock
________ : 00
This is when I watch my favorite TV program.

________ o'clock
________ : 00
This is when I would like to go to bed.

One Step Further
Ask a friend about his or her important hours. Are the answers the same as yours?

Everyday Success Preschool

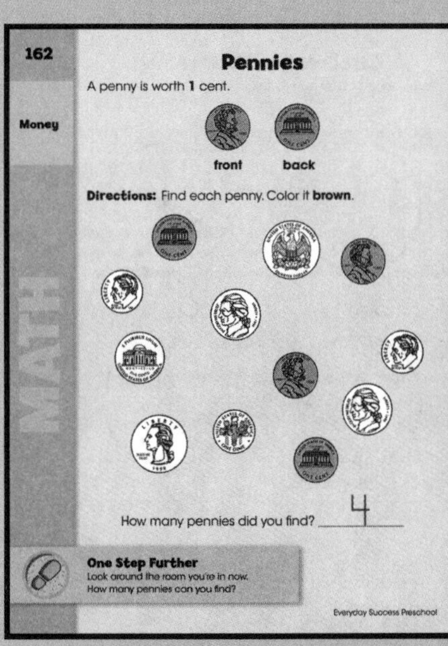

162 Money MATH

Pennies

A penny is worth **1** cent.

front back

Directions: Find each penny. Color it **brown**.

How many pennies did you find? 4

One Step Further
Look around the room you're in now. How many pennies can you find?

Everyday Success Preschool

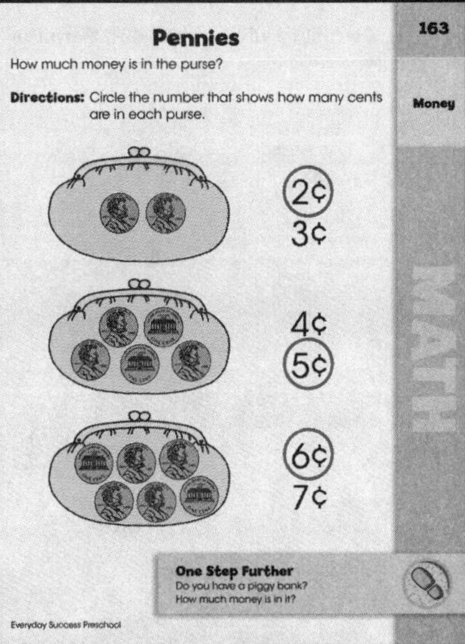

Pennies 163

How much money is in the purse?

Directions: Circle the number that shows how many cents are in each purse.

(2¢) 3¢

4¢ (5¢)

(6¢) 7¢

Money

MATH

One Step Further
Do you have a piggy bank?
How much money is in it?

Everyday Success Preschool

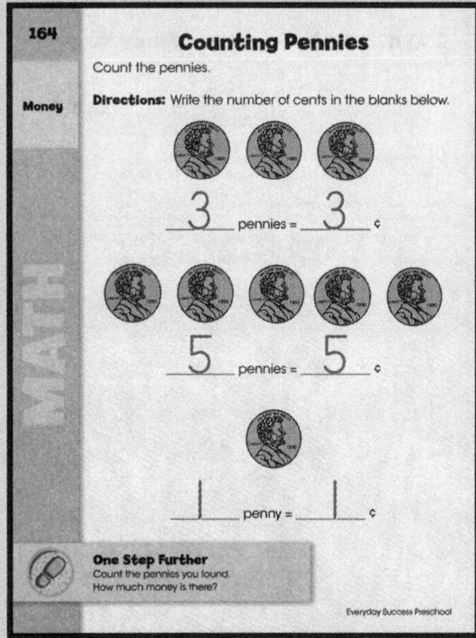

164 **Counting Pennies**

Count the pennies.

Directions: Write the number of cents in the blanks below.

3 pennies = 3 ¢

5 pennies = 5 ¢

1 penny = 1 ¢

Money

MATH

One Step Further
Count the pennies you found.
How much money is there?

Everyday Success Preschool

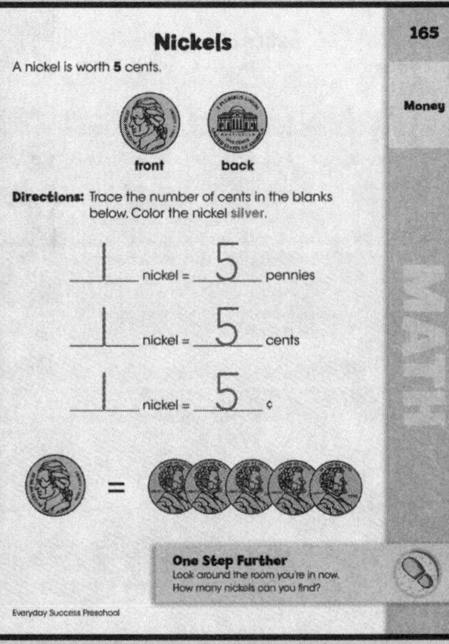

Nickels 165

A nickel is worth **5** cents.

front back

Directions: Trace the number of cents in the blanks below. Color the nickel silver.

1 nickel = 5 pennies

1 nickel = 5 cents

1 nickel = 5 ¢

=

Money

MATH

One Step Further
Look around the room you're in now.
How many nickels can you find?

Everyday Success Preschool

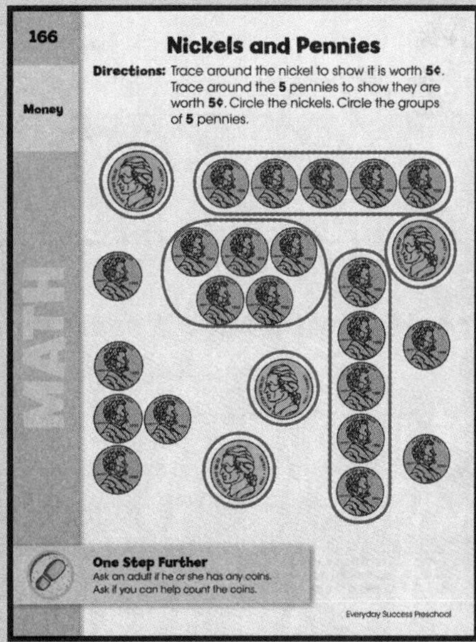

166 **Nickels and Pennies**

Directions: Trace around the nickel to show it is worth **5¢**. Trace around the **5** pennies to show they are worth **5¢**. Circle the nickels. Circle the groups of **5** pennies.

Money

MATH

One Step Further
Ask an adult if he or she has any coins.
Ask if you can help count the coins.

Everyday Success Preschool

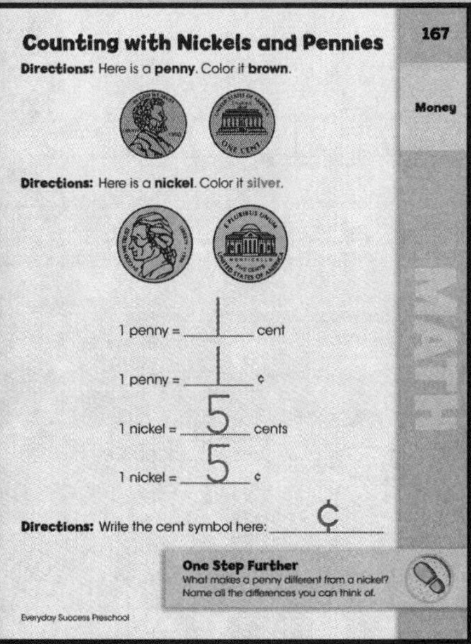

Counting with Nickels and Pennies 167

Directions: Here is a **penny**. Color it **brown**.

Directions: Here is a **nickel**. Color it silver.

1 penny = 1 cent

1 penny = 1 ¢

1 nickel = 5 cents

1 nickel = 5 ¢

Directions: Write the cent symbol here: ¢

Money

MATH

One Step Further
What makes a penny different from a nickel?
Name all the differences you can think of.

Everyday Success Preschool

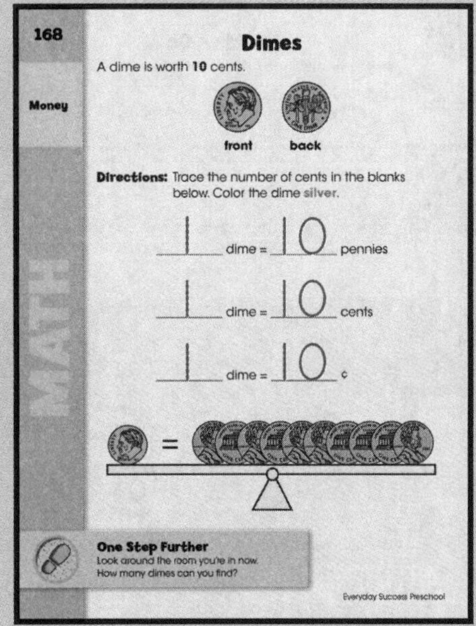

168 **Dimes**

A dime is worth **10** cents.

front back

Directions: Trace the number of cents in the blanks below. Color the dime silver.

1 dime = 10 pennies

1 dime = 10 cents

1 dime = 10 ¢

=

Money

MATH

One Step Further
Look around the room you're in now.
How many dimes can you find?

Everyday Success Preschool

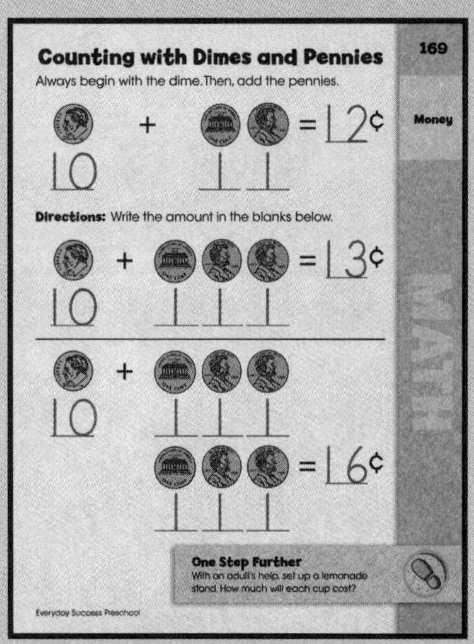

169

Money

MATH

Counting with Dimes and Pennies

Always begin with the dime. Then, add the pennies.

10 + 1 1 = 12¢

Directions: Write the amount in the blanks below.

10 + 1 1 1 = 13¢

10 + 1 1 1

1 1 1 = 16¢

One Step Further
With an adult's help, set up a lemonade stand. How much will each cup cost?

Everyday Success Preschool

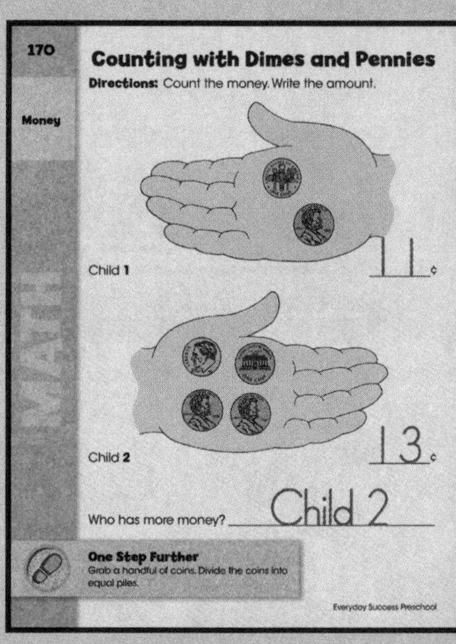

170

Money

MATH

Counting with Dimes and Pennies

Directions: Count the money. Write the amount.

Child 1 11¢

Child 2 13¢

Who has more money? Child 2

One Step Further
Grab a handful of coins. Divide the coins into equal piles.

Everyday Success Preschool

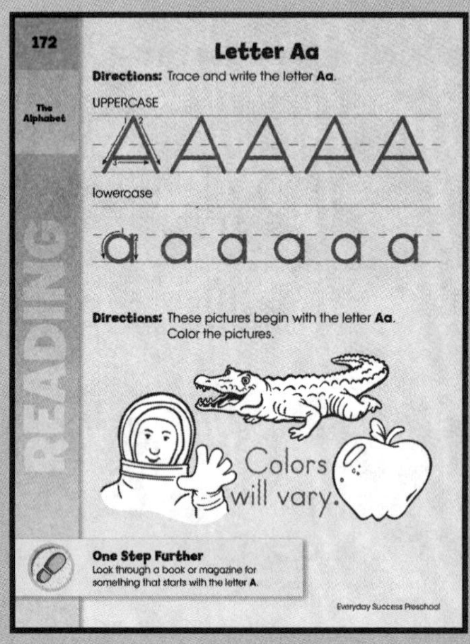

172

The Alphabet

READING

Letter Aa

Directions: Trace and write the letter **Aa**.

UPPERCASE

A A A A A

lowercase

a a a a a a

Directions: These pictures begin with the letter **Aa**. Color the pictures.

Colors will vary.

One Step Further
Look through a book or magazine for something that starts with the letter **A**.

Everyday Success Preschool

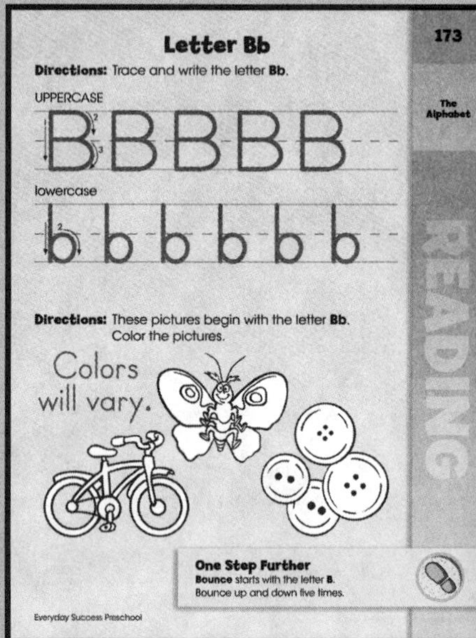

173

The Alphabet

READING

Letter Bb

Directions: Trace and write the letter **Bb**.

UPPERCASE

B B B B B

lowercase

b b b b b b

Directions: These pictures begin with the letter **Bb**. Color the pictures.

Colors will vary.

One Step Further
Bounce starts with the letter **B**. Bounce up and down five times.

Everyday Success Preschool

174

The Alphabet

READING

Letter Cc

Directions: Trace and write the letter **Cc**.

UPPERCASE

C C C C C C

lowercase

c c c c c c c

Directions: These pictures begin with the letter **Cc**. Color the pictures.

Colors will vary.

One Step Further
Clap starts with the letter **C**. Clap your hands 10 times.

Everyday Success Preschool

175

The Alphabet

READING

Letter Dd

Directions: Trace and write the letter **Dd**.

UPPERCASE

D D D D D

lowercase

d d d d d d

Directions: These pictures begin with the letter **Dd**. Color the pictures.

Colors will vary.

One Step Further
Name something else that starts with the letter **D**.

Everyday Success Preschool

176

The Alphabet

READING

Letter Ee

Directions: Trace and write the letter **Ee**.

UPPERCASE

E E E E E E

lowercase

e e e e e e e

Directions: These pictures begin with the letter **Ee**. Color the pictures. Colors will vary.

One Step Further
Elephant starts with the letter **E**. Name another animal that starts with the letter **E**.

Everyday Success Preschool

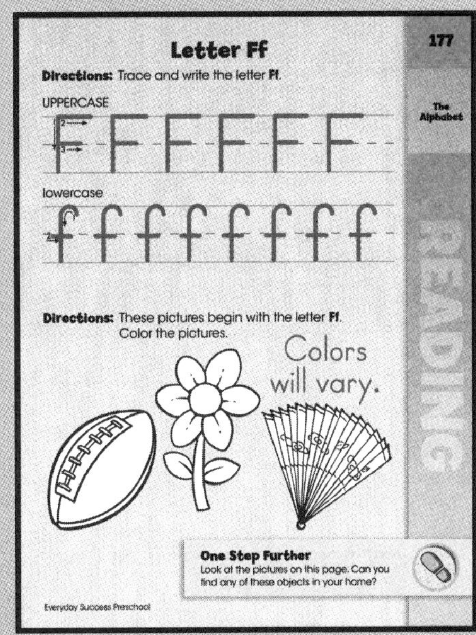

177

The Alphabet

READING

Letter Ff

Directions: Trace and write the letter **Ff**.

UPPERCASE

F F F F F F

lowercase

f f f f f f f f

Directions: These pictures begin with the letter **Ff**. Color the pictures. Colors will vary.

One Step Further
Look at the pictures on this page. Can you find any of these objects in your home?

Everyday Success Preschool

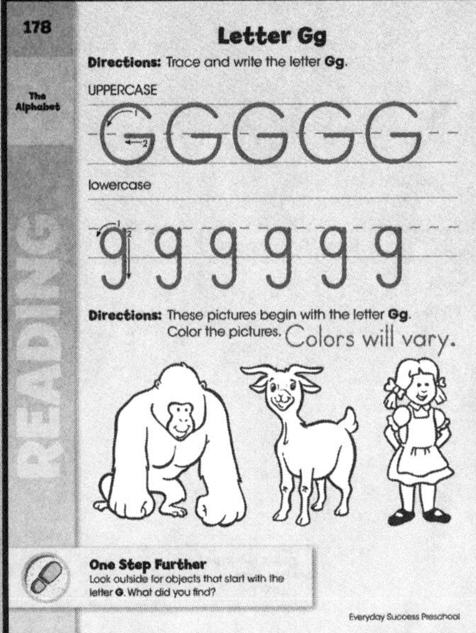

178

The Alphabet

READING

Letter Gg

Directions: Trace and write the letter **Gg**.

UPPERCASE

G G G G G

lowercase

g g g g g g

Directions: These pictures begin with the letter **Gg**. Color the pictures. Colors will vary.

One Step Further
Look outside for objects that start with the letter **G**. What did you find?

Everyday Success Preschool

179

The Alphabet

READING

Letter Hh

Directions: Trace and write the letter **Hh**.

UPPERCASE

H H H H H

lowercase

h h h h h h

Directions: These pictures begin with the letter **Hh**. Color the pictures. Colors will vary.

One Step Further
Hop starts with the letter **H**. Hop like a rabbit 10 times.

Everyday Success Preschool

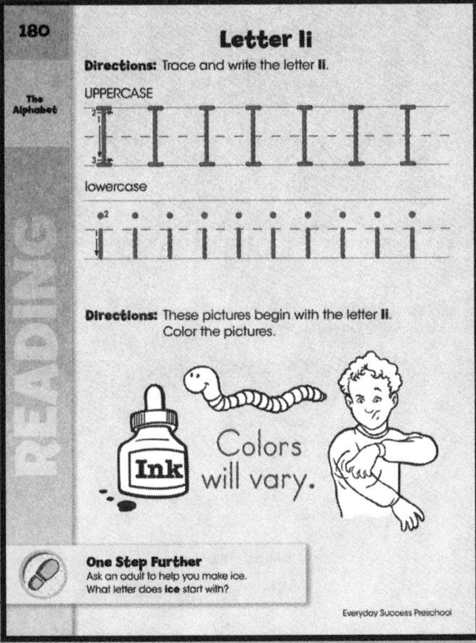

180

The Alphabet

READING

Letter Ii

Directions: Trace and write the letter **Ii**.

UPPERCASE

I I I I I I I

lowercase

i i i i i i i i i i

Directions: These pictures begin with the letter **Ii**. Color the pictures.

Colors will vary.

One Step Further
Ask an adult to help you make ice. What letter does **ice** start with?

Everyday Success Preschool

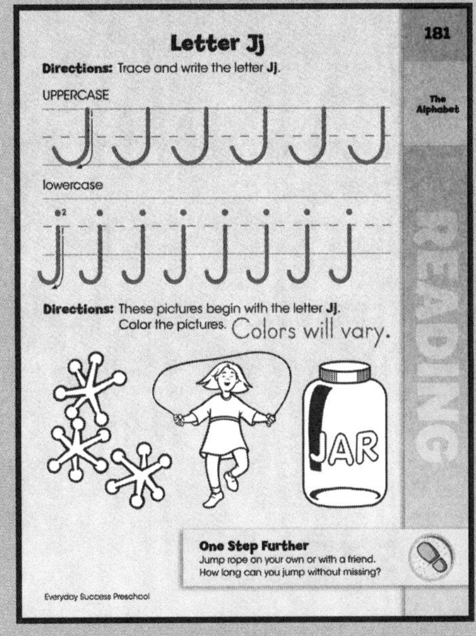

181

The Alphabet

READING

Letter Jj

Directions: Trace and write the letter **Jj**.

UPPERCASE

J J J J J J

lowercase

j j j j j j j j

Directions: These pictures begin with the letter **Jj**. Color the pictures. Colors will vary.

One Step Further
Jump rope on your own or with a friend. How long can you jump without missing?

Everyday Success Preschool

ANSWER KEY

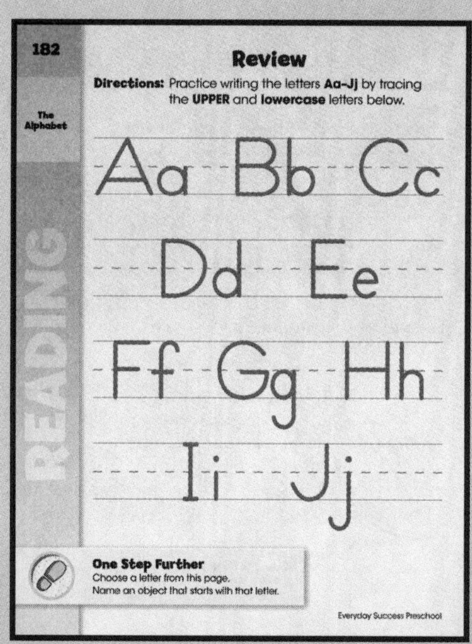
182

The Alphabet

READING

Review

Directions: Practice writing the letters **Aa–Jj** by tracing the **UPPER** and **lowercase** letters below.

Aa Bb Cc
Dd Ee
Ff Gg Hh
Ii Jj

One Step Further
Choose a letter from this page.
Name an object that starts with that letter.

Everyday Success Preschool

183

The Alphabet

READING

Letter Kk

Directions: Trace and write the letter **Kk**.

UPPERCASE

K K K K K

lowercase

k k k k k k k

Directions: These pictures begin with the letter **Kk**. Color the pictures.

Colors will vary.

One Step Further
With a friend, go outside and fly a kite.
What color is your kite?

Everyday Success Preschool

184

The Alphabet

READING

Letter Ll

Directions: Trace and write the letter **Ll**.

UPPERCASE

L L L L L L

lowercase

l l l l l l l l l l

Directions: These pictures begin with the letter **Ll**. Color the pictures.

Colors will vary.

One Step Further
Turn the lights off, and back on again.
How many lamps are in your home?

Everyday Success Preschool

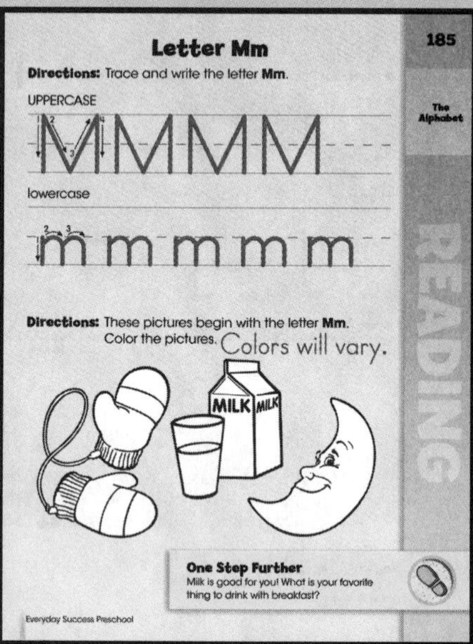
185

The Alphabet

READING

Letter Mm

Directions: Trace and write the letter **Mm**.

UPPERCASE

M M M M

lowercase

m m m m m

Directions: These pictures begin with the letter **Mm**. Color the pictures. Colors will vary.

One Step Further
Milk is good for you! What is your favorite thing to drink with breakfast?

Everyday Success Preschool

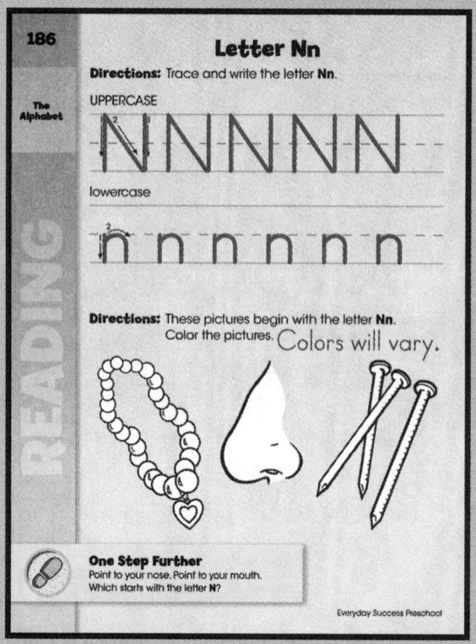
186

The Alphabet

READING

Letter Nn

Directions: Trace and write the letter **Nn**.

UPPERCASE

N N N N N

lowercase

n n n n n n

Directions: These pictures begin with the letter **Nn**. Color the pictures. Colors will vary.

One Step Further
Point to your nose. Point to your mouth.
Which starts with the letter **N**?

Everyday Success Preschool

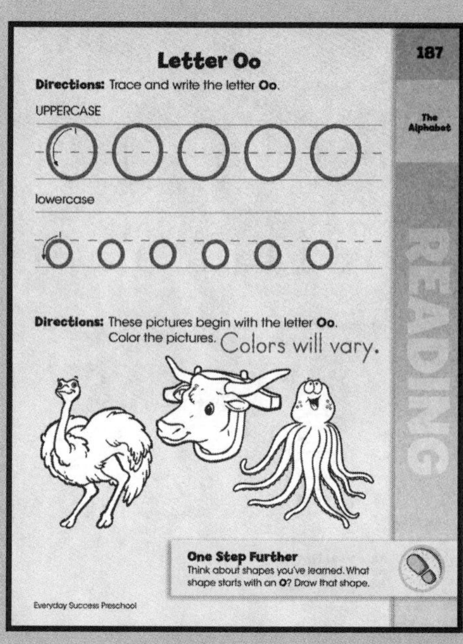
187

The Alphabet

READING

Letter Oo

Directions: Trace and write the letter **Oo**.

UPPERCASE

O O O O O O

lowercase

o o o o o o

Directions: These pictures begin with the letter **Oo**. Color the pictures. Colors will vary.

One Step Further
Think about shapes you've learned. What shape starts with an **O**? Draw that shape.

Everyday Success Preschool

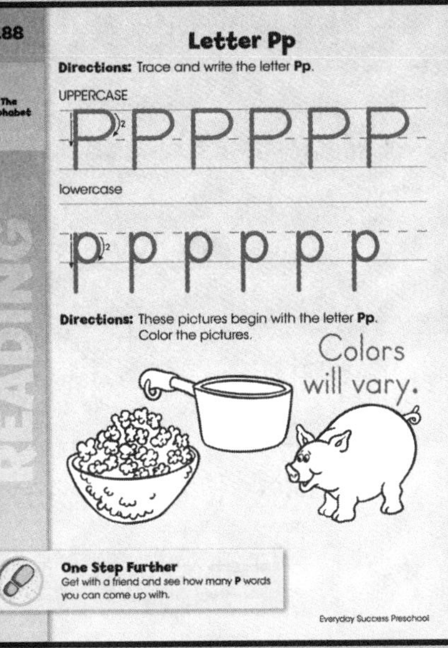
188 The Alphabet READING

Letter Pp

Directions: Trace and write the letter **Pp**.

UPPERCASE

P P P P P P

lowercase

p p p p p p

Directions: These pictures begin with the letter **Pp**. Color the pictures.

Colors will vary.

One Step Further
Get with a friend and see how many **P** words you can come up with.

Everyday Success Preschool

189 The Alphabet READING

Letter Qq

Directions: Trace and write the letter **Qq**.

UPPERCASE

Q Q Q Q Q

lowercase

q q q q q q q

Directions: These pictures begin with the letter **Qq**. Color the pictures. Colors will vary.

One Step Further
Look around your home. How many quarters can you find?

Everyday Success Preschool

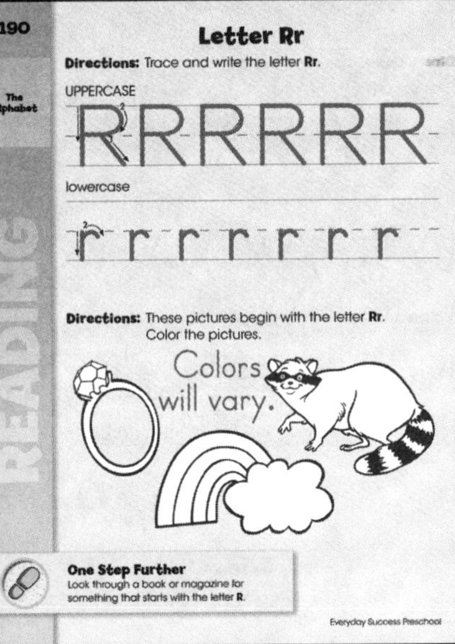
190 The Alphabet READING

Letter Rr

Directions: Trace and write the letter **Rr**.

UPPERCASE

R R R R R R

lowercase

r r r r r r r

Directions: These pictures begin with the letter **Rr**. Color the pictures.

Colors will vary.

One Step Further
Look through a book or magazine for something that starts with the letter **R**.

Everyday Success Preschool

191 The Alphabet READING

Letter Ss

Directions: Trace and write the letter **Ss**.

UPPERCASE

S S S S S S

lowercase

s s s s s s s s

Directions: These pictures begin with the letter **Ss**. Color the pictures. Colors will vary.

One Step Further
Look around the room. Can you find anything that starts with the letter **S**?

Everyday Success Preschool

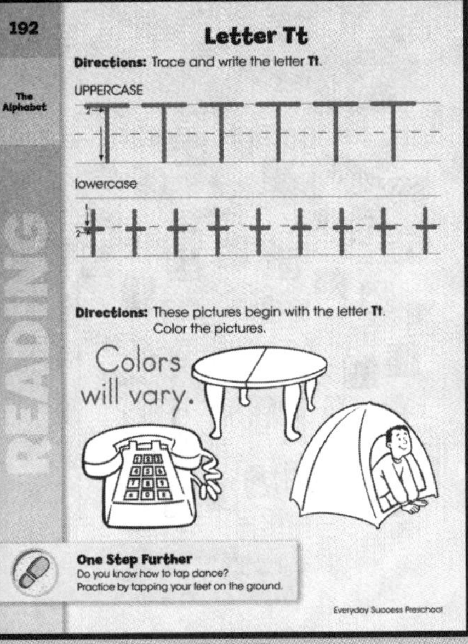
192 The Alphabet READING

Letter Tt

Directions: Trace and write the letter **Tt**.

UPPERCASE

T T T T T T

lowercase

t t t t t t t t t

Directions: These pictures begin with the letter **Tt**. Color the pictures.

Colors will vary.

One Step Further
Do you know how to tap dance? Practice by tapping your feet on the ground.

Everyday Success Preschool

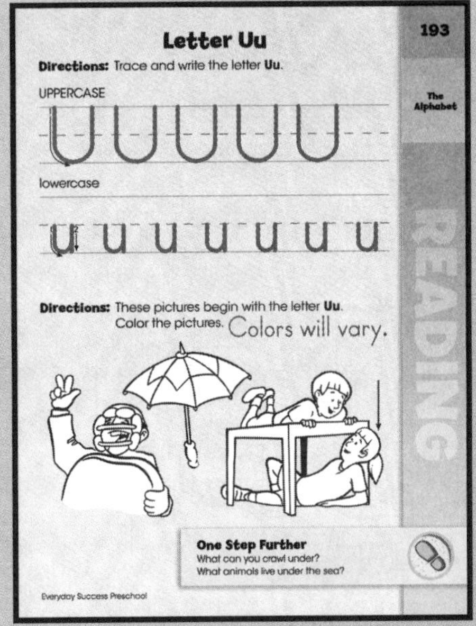
193 The Alphabet READING

Letter Uu

Directions: Trace and write the letter **Uu**.

UPPERCASE

U U U U U

lowercase

u u u u u u u

Directions: These pictures begin with the letter **Uu**. Color the pictures. Colors will vary.

One Step Further
What can you crawl under? What animals live under the sea?

Everyday Success Preschool

ANSWER KEY

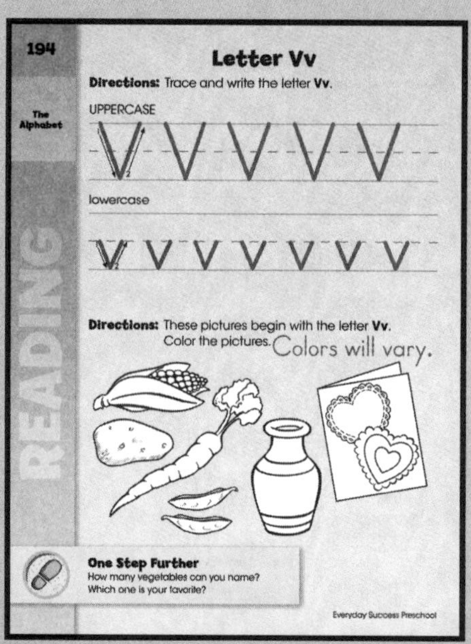
194 The Alphabet READING

Letter Vv

Directions: Trace and write the letter **Vv**.

UPPERCASE

lowercase

Directions: These pictures begin with the letter **Vv**. Color the pictures. Colors will vary.

One Step Further
How many vegetables can you name?
Which one is your favorite?

Everyday Success Preschool

195 The Alphabet READING

Letter Ww

Directions: Trace and write the letter **Ww**.

UPPERCASE

lowercase

Directions: These pictures begin with the letter **Ww**. Color the pictures. Colors will vary.

One Step Further
Go to the sink and run some water.
What letter does **water** start with?

Everyday Success Preschool

196 The Alphabet READING

Letter Xx

Directions: Trace and write the letter **Xx**.

UPPERCASE

lowercase

Directions: These pictures contain the letter **Xx**. Color the pictures.

Colors will vary.

One Step Further
Create a treasure map, where **X** marks the spot of the hidden treasure.

Everyday Success Preschool

197 The Alphabet READING

Letter Yy

Directions: Trace and write the letter **Yy**.

UPPERCASE

lowercase

Directions: These pictures begin with the letter **Yy**. Color the pictures.

Colors will vary.

One Step Further
What color is the sun?
Draw a picture of the sun and color it.

Everyday Success Preschool

198 The Alphabet READING

Letter Zz

Directions: Trace and write the letter **Zz**.

UPPERCASE

lowercase

Directions: These pictures begin with the letter **Zz**. Color the pictures.

Colors will vary.

One Step Further
Name your favorite zoo animal.
What letter does that animal start with?

Everyday Success Preschool

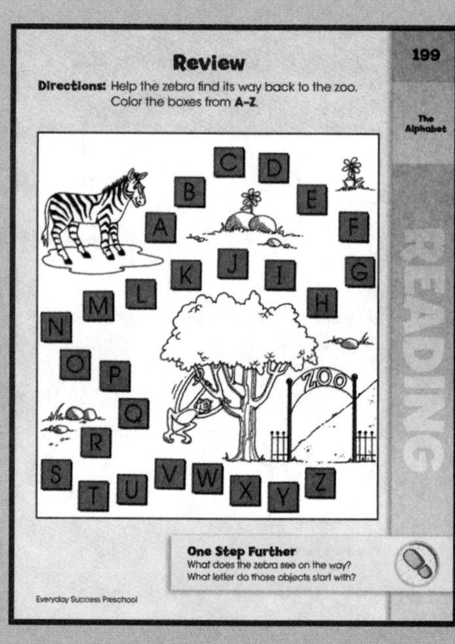
199 The Alphabet READING

Review

Directions: Help the zebra find its way back to the zoo. Color the boxes from **A–Z**.

One Step Further
What does the zebra see on the way?
What letter do those objects start with?

Everyday Success Preschool

200

Letter Recognition

READING

Letter Aa

Directions: Circle the **A** or **a** in these words:

apple alligator angel
Amy ant Andy

The letter **Aa** can have more than one sound.

Directions: Color the pictures that start with the sound of **Aa**.

One Step Further
Do you have a friend whose name starts with the letter **A**? What is it?

Everyday Success Preschool

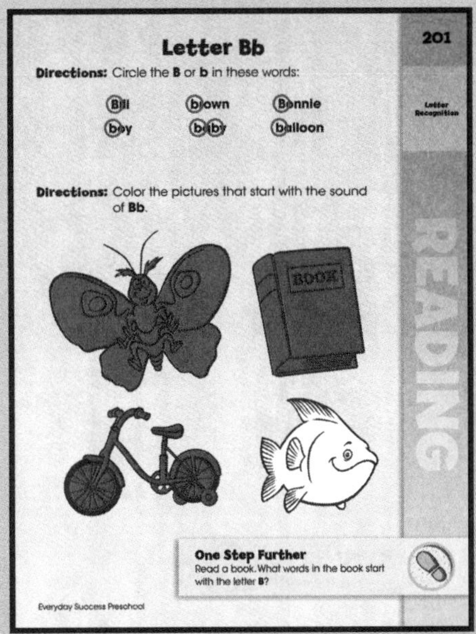
201

Letter Recognition

READING

Letter Bb

Directions: Circle the **B** or **b** in these words:

Bill blown Bonnie
boy baby balloon

Directions: Color the pictures that start with the sound of **Bb**.

One Step Further
Read a book. What words in the book start with the letter **B**?

Everyday Success Preschool

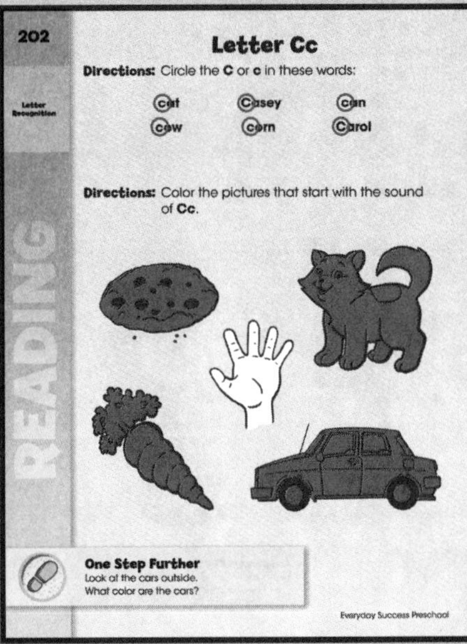
202

Letter Recognition

READING

Letter Cc

Directions: Circle the **C** or **c** in these words:

cat Casey can
cow corn Carol

Directions: Color the pictures that start with the sound of **Cc**.

One Step Further
Look at the cars outside.
What color are the cars?

Everyday Success Preschool

203

Letter Recognition

READING

Letter Dd

Directions: Circle the **D** or **d** in these words:

doll Darcy desk
door David dog

Directions: Color the pictures that start with the sound of **Dd**.

One Step Further
Dog starts with the letter **D**. Name another animal that starts with the letter **D**.

Everyday Success Preschool

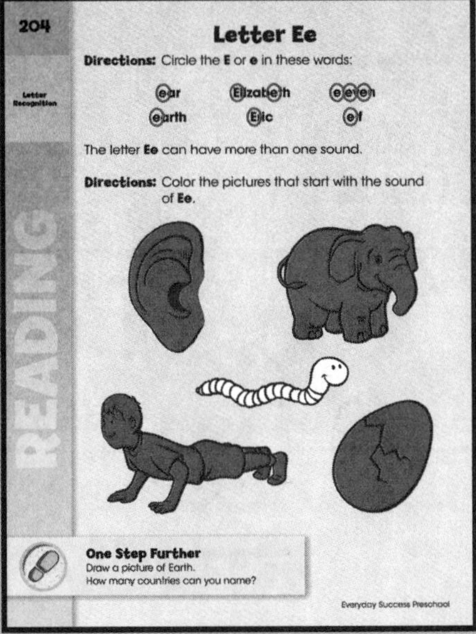
204

Letter Recognition

READING

Letter Ee

Directions: Circle the **E** or **e** in these words:

ear Elizabeth eleven
earth Eric elf

The letter **Ee** can have more than one sound.

Directions: Color the pictures that start with the sound of **Ee**.

One Step Further
Draw a picture of Earth.
How many countries can you name?

Everyday Success Preschool

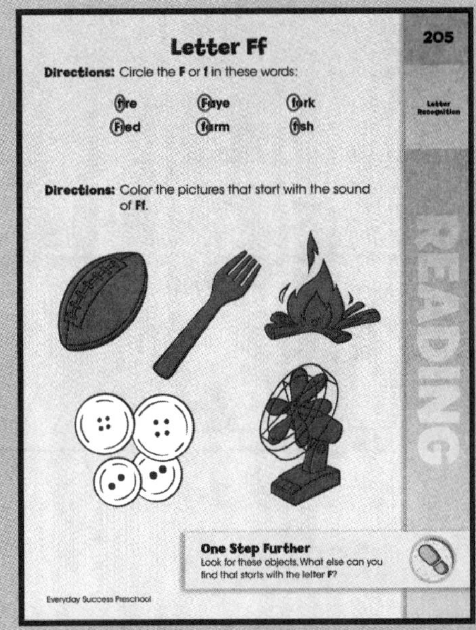
205

Letter Recognition

READING

Letter Ff

Directions: Circle the **F** or **f** in these words:

fire Faye fork
Fred farm fish

Directions: Color the pictures that start with the sound of **Ff**.

One Step Further
Look for these objects. What else can you find that starts with the letter **F**?

Everyday Success Preschool

ANSWER KEY

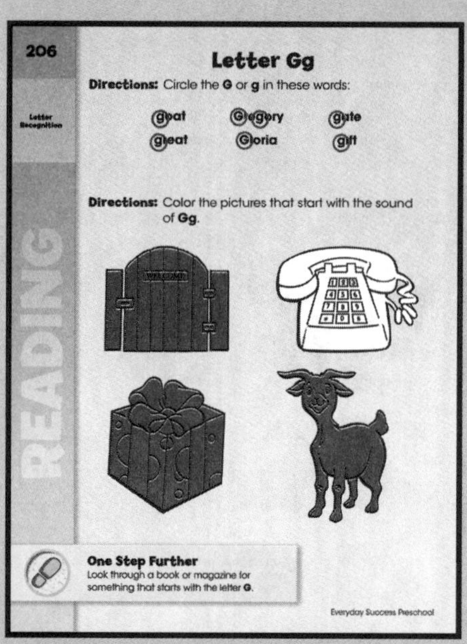

206

Letter Recognition

Letter Gg

Directions: Circle the **G** or **g** in these words:

goat Gregory gate
great Gloria gift

Directions: Color the pictures that start with the sound of **Gg**.

READING

One Step Further
Look through a book or magazine for something that starts with the letter **G**.

Everyday Success Preschool

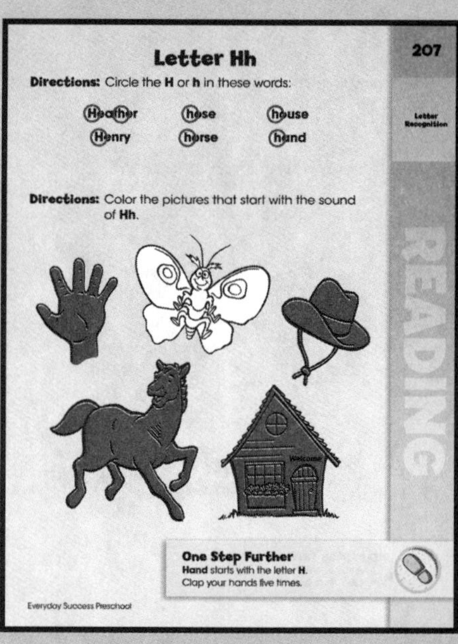

207

Letter Recognition

Letter Hh

Directions: Circle the **H** or **h** in these words:

Heather hose house
Henry horse hand

Directions: Color the pictures that start with the sound of **Hh**.

READING

One Step Further
Hand starts with the letter **H**.
Clap your hands five times.

Everyday Success Preschool

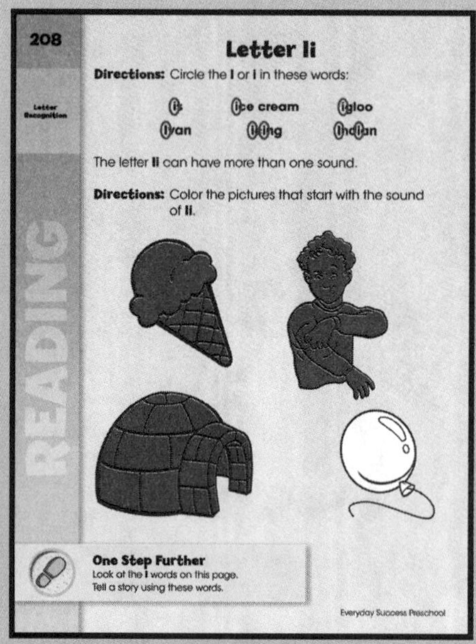

208

Letter Recognition

Letter Ii

Directions: Circle the **I** or **i** in these words:

it ice cream igloo
Ivan icing Indian

The letter **Ii** can have more than one sound.

Directions: Color the pictures that start with the sound of **Ii**.

READING

One Step Further
Look at the **I** words on this page.
Tell a story using these words.

Everyday Success Preschool

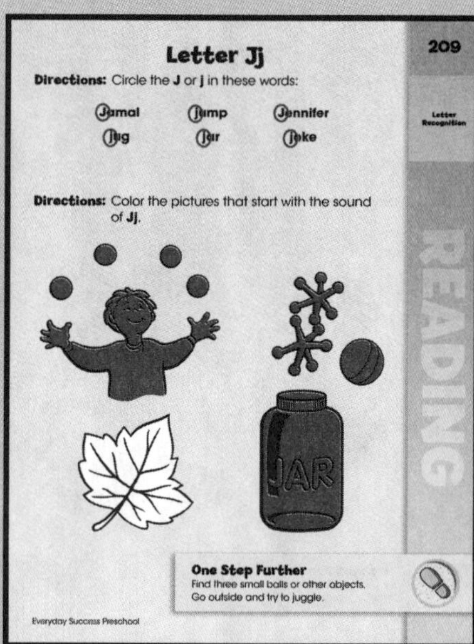

209

Letter Recognition

Letter Jj

Directions: Circle the **J** or **j** in these words:

Jamal jump Jennifer
jug jar joke

Directions: Color the pictures that start with the sound of **Jj**.

READING

One Step Further
Find three small balls or other objects.
Go outside and try to juggle.

Everyday Success Preschool

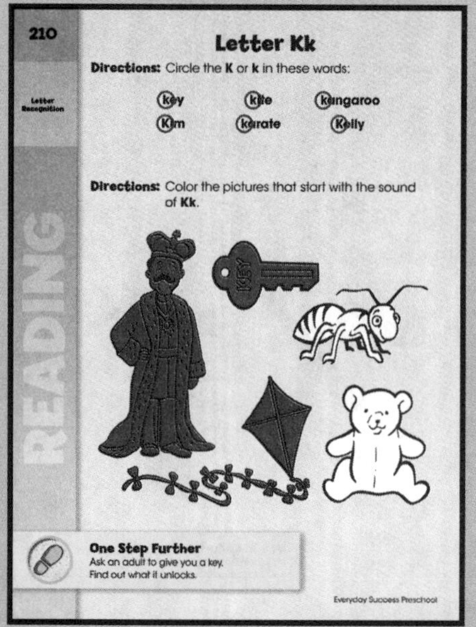

210

Letter Recognition

Letter Kk

Directions: Circle the **K** or **k** in these words:

key kite kangaroo
Kim karate Kelly

Directions: Color the pictures that start with the sound of **Kk**.

READING

One Step Further
Ask an adult to give you a key.
Find out what it unlocks.

Everyday Success Preschool

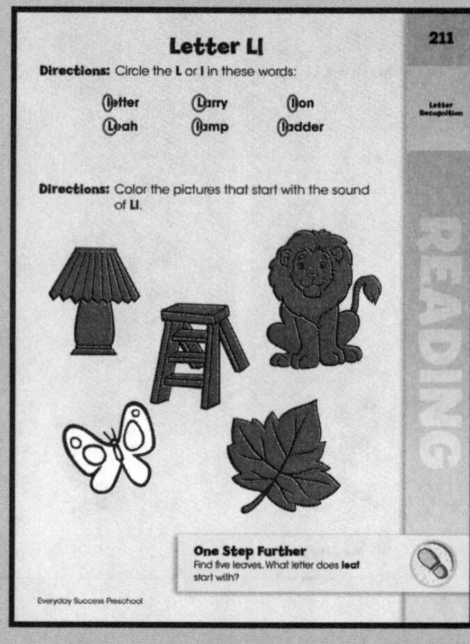

211

Letter Recognition

Letter Ll

Directions: Circle the **L** or **l** in these words:

letter Larry lion
Leah lamp ladder

Directions: Color the pictures that start with the sound of **Ll**.

READING

One Step Further
Find five leaves. What letter does **leaf** start with?

Everyday Success Preschool

212

Letter Mm

Directions: Circle the **M** or **m** in these words:

man monkey Maria
mask make Martin

Directions: Color the pictures that start with the sound of **Mm**.

One Step Further
With an adult's help, create a mask to wear. Put on a show wearing the mask.

Everyday Success Preschool

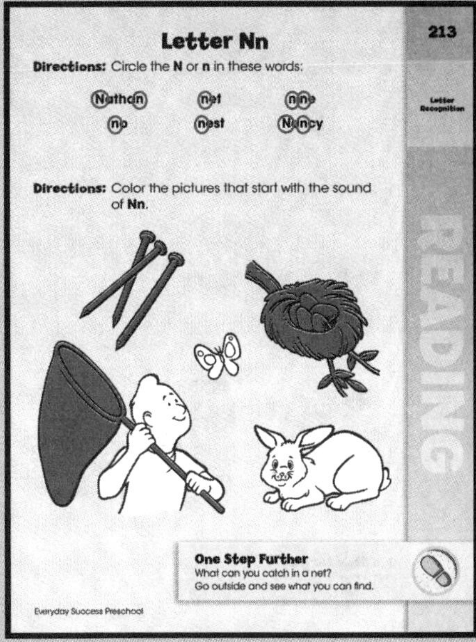

213

Letter Nn

Directions: Circle the **N** or **n** in these words:

Nathan net nine
no nest Nancy

Directions: Color the pictures that start with the sound of **Nn**.

One Step Further
What can you catch in a net? Go outside and see what you can find.

Everyday Success Preschool

214

Letter Oo

Directions: Circle the **O** or **o** in these words:

Olivia owl octopus
once only Owen

The letter **Oo** can have more than one sound.

Directions: Color the pictures that start with the sound of **Oo**.

One Step Further
Walk around your home. Name things that you can open.

Everyday Success Preschool

215

Letter Pp

Directions: Circle the **P** or **p** in these words:

pencil Paul pig
party penny Patty

Directions: Color the pictures that start with the sound of **Pp**.

One Step Further
Look at the **P** words on this page. Tell a story using these words.

Everyday Success Preschool

216

Letter Qq

Directions: Circle the **Q** or **q** in these words:

Quincy quarter quilt
quit quake quiet

Directions: Color the pictures that start with the sound of **Qq**.

One Step Further
What can you buy with a quarter? What can you buy with four quarters?

Everyday Success Preschool

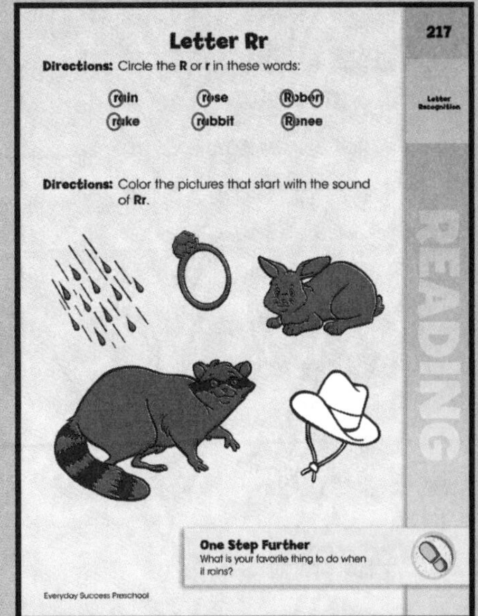

217

Letter Rr

Directions: Circle the **R** or **r** in these words:

rain rose Robert
rake rabbit Renee

Directions: Color the pictures that start with the sound of **Rr**.

One Step Further
What is your favorite thing to do when it rains?

Everyday Success Preschool

ANSWER KEY

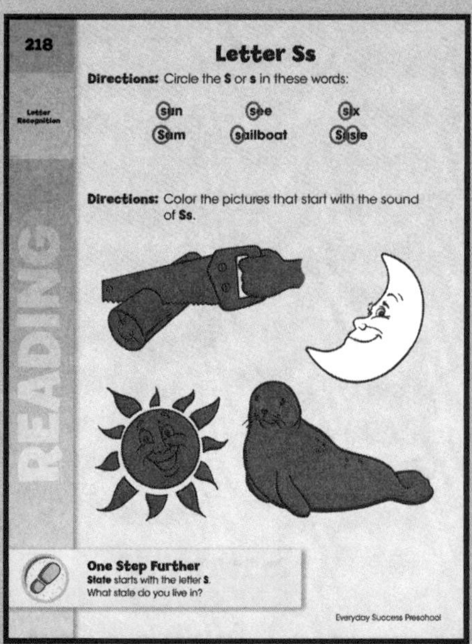
218

Letter Recognition

READING

Letter Ss

Directions: Circle the **S** or **s** in these words:

sun see six
Sam sailboat Susie

Directions: Color the pictures that start with the sound of **Ss**.

One Step Further
State starts with the letter **S**.
What state do you live in?

Everyday Success Preschool

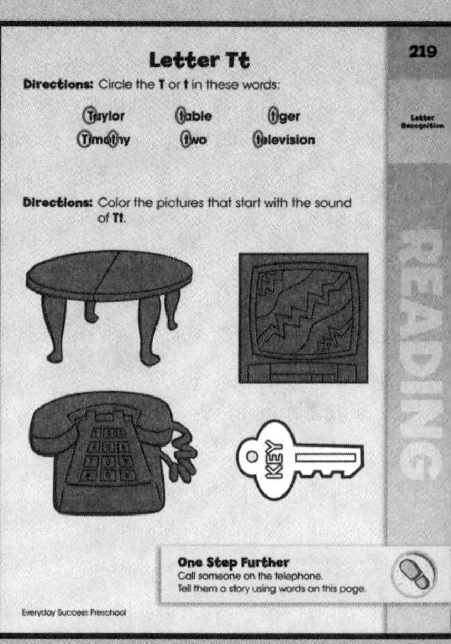
219

Letter Recognition

READING

Letter Tt

Directions: Circle the **T** or **t** in these words:

Taylor table tiger
Timothy two television

Directions: Color the pictures that start with the sound of **Tt**.

One Step Further
Call someone on the telephone.
Tell them a story using words on this page.

Everyday Success Preschool

220

Letter Recognition

READING

Letter Uu

Directions: Circle the **U** or **u** in these words:

under unicorn unless
umbrella up use

The letter **Uu** can have more than one sound.

Directions: Color the pictures that start with the sound of **Uu**.

One Step Further
Look up. What do you see? Look under your bed. What do you see there?

Everyday Success Preschool

221

Letter Recognition

READING

Letter Vv

Directions: Circle the **V** or **v** in these words:

Valerie violin vest
Victor valentine van

Directions: Color the pictures that start with the sound of **Vv**.

One Step Further
Make a valentine to give to a friend.
Decorate it using your favorite colors.

Everyday Success Preschool

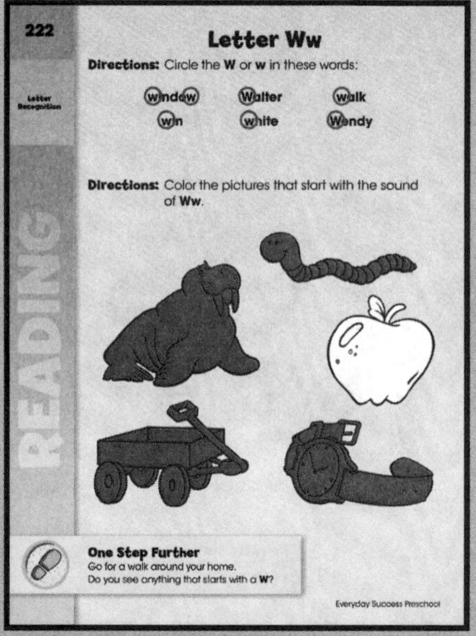
222

Letter Recognition

READING

Letter Ww

Directions: Circle the **W** or **w** in these words:

window Walter walk
win white Wendy

Directions: Color the pictures that start with the sound of **Ww**.

One Step Further
Go for a walk around your home.
Do you see anything that starts with a **W**?

Everyday Success Preschool

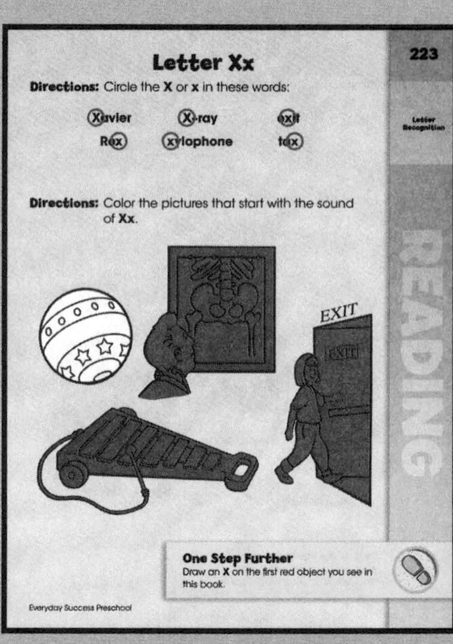
223

Letter Recognition

READING

Letter Xx

Directions: Circle the **X** or **x** in these words:

Xavier X-ray exit
Rex xylophone tax

Directions: Color the pictures that start with the sound of **Xx**.

One Step Further
Draw an **X** on the first red object you see in this book.

Everyday Success Preschool

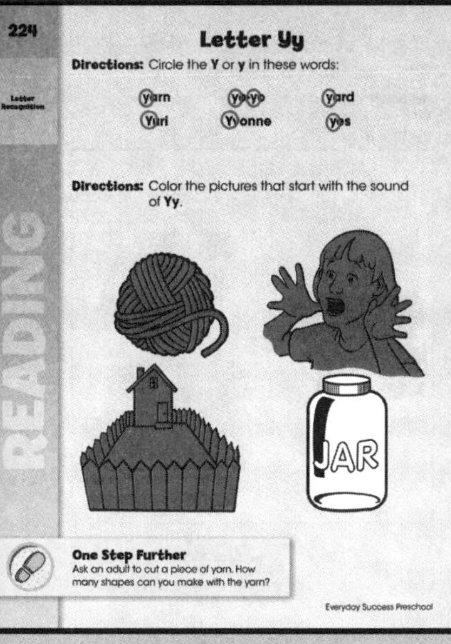

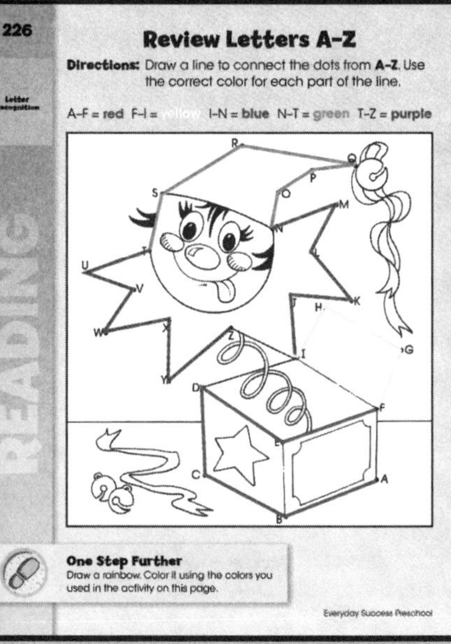

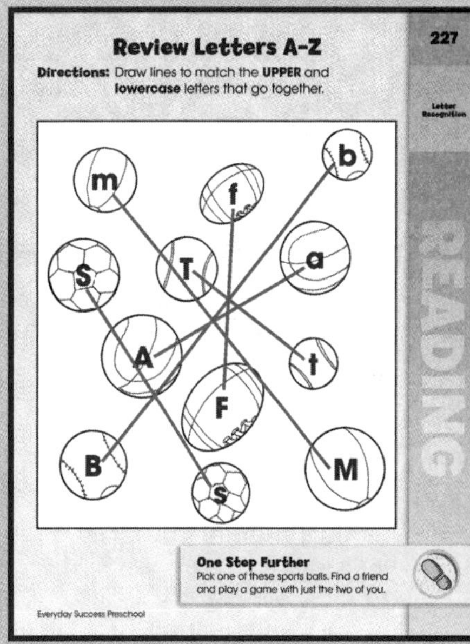

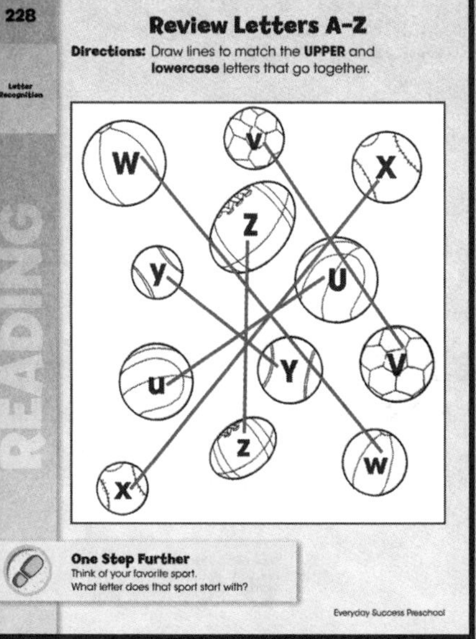

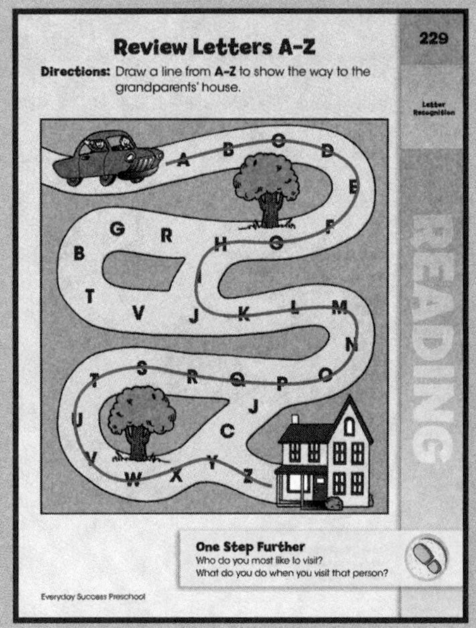

ANSWER KEY

230

Letter Recognition

Review Letters A-Z

Directions: Draw a line from **A-Z** to show the way to Penguin's house.

READING

One Step Further
Draw a picture of you doing your favorite activity. Mail it to someone special.

Everyday Success Preschool

231

Reading Comprehension

Color These Cows

Directions: Color the cows using the clues below.

The **brown** cow is hiding.
The **black-and-pink** spotted cow is eating.
The **blue** cow is fat!

READING

One Step Further
Pretend you are on a farm.
What are some fun things you would do?

Everyday Success Preschool

232

Reading Comprehension

Stop Making Sense!

Directions: Look at the picture. A lot of silly things are happening! Circle all of the things that do **not** make sense.

READING

One Step Further
Make up a story about a picnic.
Tell it to a friend.

Everyday Success Preschool

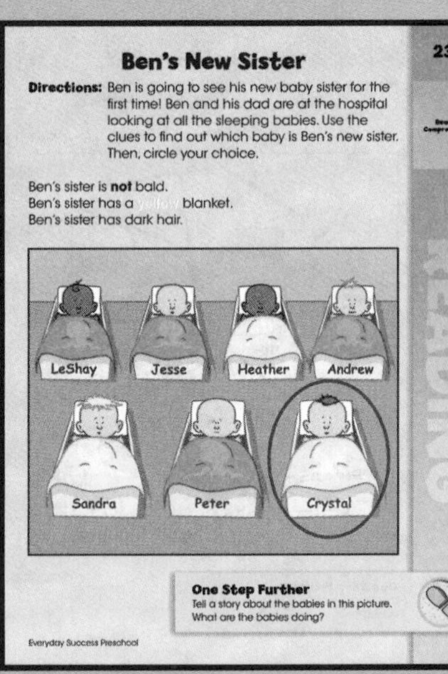

233

Reading Comprehension

Ben's New Sister

Directions: Ben is going to see his new baby sister for the first time! Ben and his dad are at the hospital looking at all the sleeping babies. Use the clues to find out which baby is Ben's new sister. Then, circle your choice.

Ben's sister is **not** bald.
Ben's sister has a yellow blanket.
Ben's sister has dark hair.

READING

One Step Further
Tell a story about the babies in this picture.
What are the babies doing?

Everyday Success Preschool

234

Reading Comprehension

Tim's Turtle

Directions: Help Tim pick out a turtle at the pet shop.

Tim does **not** want a turtle with circles on its back.
Tim does **not** want a green turtle.
Tim does **not** want a turtle with triangles on its back.

Circle the turtle that Tim should pick.

READING

One Step Further
Which turtle would you pick?
What would you name it?

Everyday Success Preschool

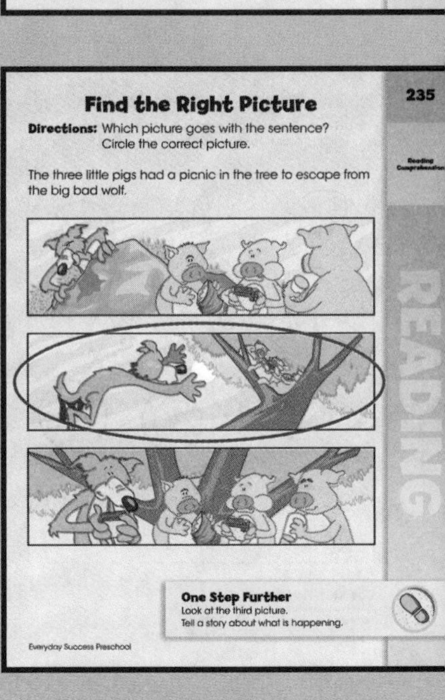

235

Reading Comprehension

Find the Right Picture

Directions: Which picture goes with the sentence?
Circle the correct picture.

The three little pigs had a picnic in the tree to escape from the big bad wolf.

READING

One Step Further
Look at the third picture.
Tell a story about what is happening.

Everyday Success Preschool

236
Find the Right Picture
Directions: Which picture goes with the sentence? Circle the correct picture.
Marilyn and Mindy went on a Ferris wheel ride with their parents.
One Step Further
What is your favorite ride at the fair?
What else do you like about the fair?
Everyday Success Preschool

237
Find the Right Picture
Directions: Which picture goes with the sentence? Circle the correct picture.
Raju and her mom spent Saturday alone. They painted pictures together.
One Step Further
Paint a picture with a friend.
What did you paint?
Everyday Success Preschool

238
Which Picture is Missing?
Directions: Look at the pictures below. There is a picture missing.
Directions: Circle the missing picture.
One Step Further
Think about your bath time.
What do you do first?
Everyday Success Preschool

239
Which Picture is Missing?
Directions: Look at the pictures below. There is a picture missing.
Directions: Circle the missing picture.
One Step Further
Tell a story about getting a haircut.
Do you like getting your hair cut?
Everyday Success Preschool

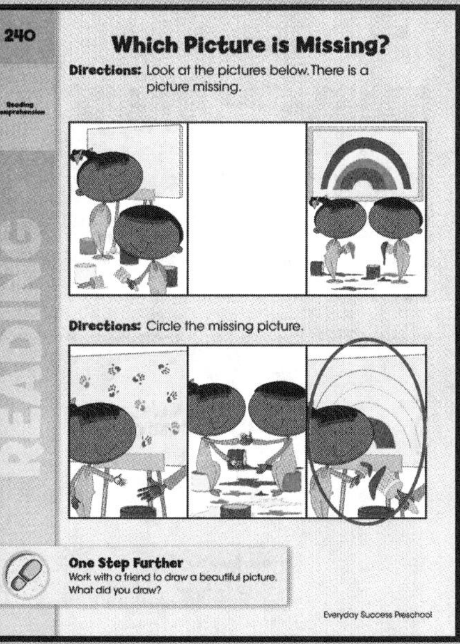
240
Which Picture is Missing?
Directions: Look at the pictures below. There is a picture missing.
Directions: Circle the missing picture.
One Step Further
Work with a friend to draw a beautiful picture.
What did you draw?
Everyday Success Preschool

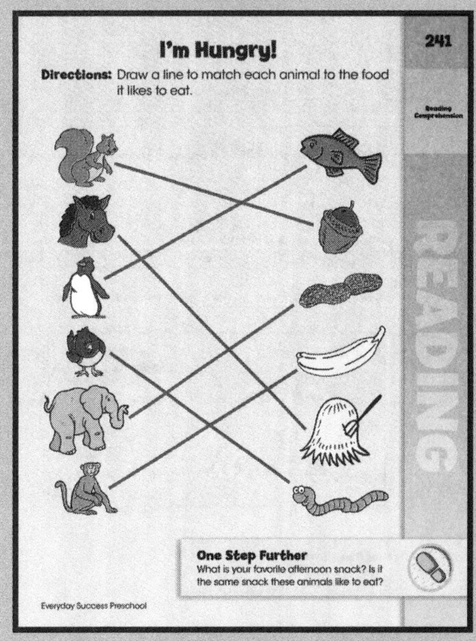
241
I'm Hungry!
Directions: Draw a line to match each animal to the food it likes to eat.
One Step Further
What is your favorite afternoon snack? Is it the same snack these animals like to eat?
Everyday Success Preschool

ANSWER KEY

242
Not in the Nest
Directions: A mother robin wants to build a nest for her new babies. Draw an X on the things they will not need. Then, draw a picture of some other things she might need.
Pictures will vary.
One Step Further
Look up in some trees around your neighborhood. Do you see any nests?
Everyday Success Preschool

243
Puppy Needs
Directions: Marcy and her dad want to build a doghouse for their new puppy. Draw an X on the things they will not need. Then, draw a picture of some other things they might need.
Pictures will vary.
One Step Further
What other things do puppies need, besides a doghouse? Draw them.
Everyday Success Preschool

244
Super Ice-Cream Sundaes!
Directions: Janet and her mom want to make ice-cream sundaes. Draw an X on the things they will not need. Then, draw a picture of some other things they might need.
Pictures will vary.
One Step Further
Look around your kitchen. What items can you find for an ice-cream sundae?
Everyday Success Preschool

245
What's Missing?
Directions: Look at the pictures below. They start to tell a story. The last box is empty.
Directions: Which of these pictures helps finish the story? Circle it.
One Step Further
Help an adult bake a pie. What should you do first?
Everyday Success Preschool

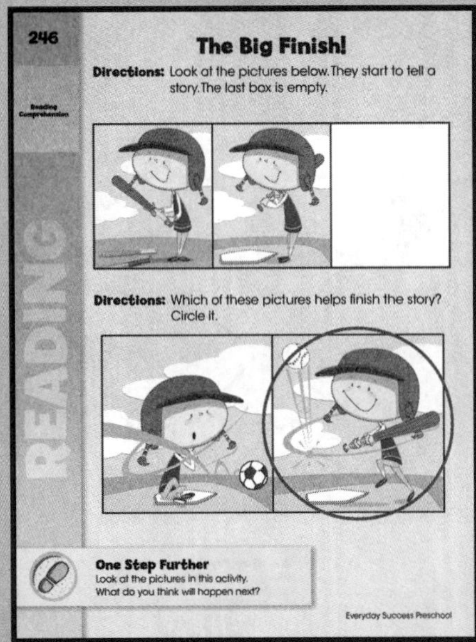
246
The Big Finish!
Directions: Look at the pictures below. They start to tell a story. The last box is empty.
Directions: Which of these pictures helps finish the story? Circle it.
One Step Further
Look at the pictures in this activity. What do you think will happen next?
Everyday Success Preschool

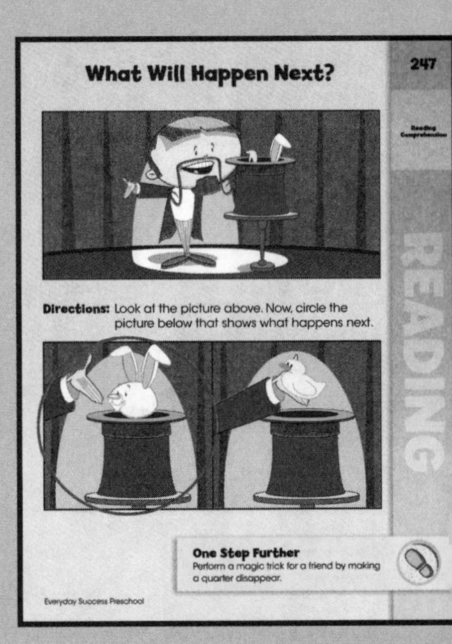
247
What Will Happen Next?
Directions: Look at the picture above. Now, circle the picture below that shows what happens next.
One Step Further
Perform a magic trick for a friend by making a quarter disappear.
Everyday Success Preschool